DATE DUE

The Limits of Order

The Limits
of Order

Lief H. Carter
The University of Georgia

Lexington Books
D.C. Heath and Company
Lexington, Massachusetts
Toronto   London

Library of Congress Cataloging in Publication Data

Carter, Lief H
  The limits of order.

  1. Criminal justice, Administration of—California—Case studies.
2. Public prosecutors—California—Case studies. I. Title
KFC1102.C37   345'.794'05   74-19182
ISBN 0-669-96644-4

Copyright © 1974 by D.C. Heath and Company

Published simultaneously in Canada.

Printed in the United States of America.

International Standard Book Number: 0-669-96644-4

Library of Congress Catalog Card Number: 74-19182

For my parents—Cynthia and Bob

Contents

List of Figures

Preface

This book is something of a hybrid. It has grown from intellectual roots separated by the unavoidable division of academic labor, among them organization theory, social psychology, and jurisprudence. The fruits of what follows (to keep the metaphor straight) will hopefully nourish each of these disciplines, but academic compartmentalization does not best serve our collective efforts to inform those who must make difficult policy choices. Thus, this case study of the operation of a prosecuting attorney's office in California seeks less to inform separate disciplines than to combine some diverse points of view in a way that may improve our ability to prescribe sensible reforms for the enterprise of doing justice. Principally, I want to suggest that criminal justice research has tended to neglect some useful principles of organization theory that may bear critically on the direction that reform should take. Legal educators have yet to incorporate fully social science concepts such as those this book utilizes, and it is hoped that they particularly will benefit from what follows.

This book also seeks to fill a gap in the criminal justice literature by providing a social science analysis of the daily activities of a prosecutor's office. I have therefore directed this work at a fairly wide audience, one that would include most social science undergraduates as well as law students and other graduate students in criminal justice, public law, and public administration. This selection of audience has required some simplifications in the discussion of organization theory, a simplification that I hope organization theory specialists will tolerate. However, organization theorists will, I hope, find in the work some heuristically useful descriptions that confirm many of the predictive hypotheses the late James D. Thompson formulated in *Organizations in Action*.

Acknowledgements

Thanks must go first to the lawyers and judges whose cooperation and candor made this research possible. They remain anonymous because I routinely promised anonymity; very few in fact seemed to care about it. William K. Muir and Robert P. Biller of the University of California, Berkeley, provided the usual combination of specific suggestions, criticisms, and sanctions that overcome personal trepidation and produce completed dissertations, but I am more grateful for their insistence that I deal directly with moral questions and that I avoid hiding behind safe academic formulae. Many of those associated with Berkeley's Center for the Study of Law and Society, led by Philip Selznick, contributed, often without knowing it, to my own learning and growth. Frank Thompson, Jay Starling, Bruce Buchanan, and William Zinn have also made very helpful suggestions at critical points in the argument. I am, of course, solely responsible for the uses to which I have put all suggestions. My wife, Nancy, in addition to making valuable suggestions, has endured the uncertainties and demands of research and writing with a fine blend of cheerfulness and pressure to get it done. To her goes abundant love as well as thanks.

The Limits of Order

Lawyers learn not to take law seriously.

David Riesman

The law can in theory be a cold hard fact, but in practice it has to be bendable, and if it weren't, I don't think many of us would stay in the office. Who would care to prosecute the law as the law?

Arthur Pollack, deputy district attorney
in Vario County, California

1

Order, Learning, and the Assessment of Criminal Justice

Introduction

How "just" is our system of criminal justice? In what ways and in what circumstances do the decisions of prosecutors, defense attorneys, and judges achieve or defeat justice? How shall we, concerned with the quality of criminal justice in the United States, evaluate the kind of justice we expect of this enterprise? What standards should we use to recommend changes in the administration of criminal justice?

The following chapters describe and assess the variety of ways and circumstances in which prosecuting attorneys disposed of criminal cases in "Vario County," California, in 1970.[1] I observed many case dispositions, among them these three. How shall we assess the adequacy of these dispositions?

1. Two prosecutors at separate times handled very similar cases of suspects arrested for drunk driving. Both suspects held jobs requiring valid driver's licenses, and both would lose their licenses upon conviction for drunk driving. Both suspects, in their mid-forties, supported families. The district attorney's office had had for some time a "strict policy" against reducing charges in drunk driving cases. One prosecutor permitted the suspect to plead guilty to reckless driving, thus saving his job. The other prosecutor insisted on a plea to drunk driving.

2. An inexperienced new deputy in the public defender's office entered a plea of guilty to the charge of burglary placed against a client with a history of mental disorders. The deputy's superior, Bob Stern, upon reviewing the disposition, called the prosecuting attorney who handled the case and asked whether the prosecutor would agree to a withdrawal of the plea to test the defense of insanity. The prosecutor agreed, and explained to me:

We really did Bob a favor on that case. . . . The case was a ripe N.G.I. [not guilty by reason of insanity]. Not that he was, necessarily, but the case had N.G.I. written all over it. Bob is a nice guy, without necessarily giving anything away, and we can talk to him. But if somebody like Joe Ryan over there had called me, I probably would have said, "Tough luck!"

3. An officer in a local police department brought a Xerox copy of a document to the district attorney himself in which his police chief had given written approval for the local Little League to hold a "Little Las Vegas Night" to raise money for new uniforms. California law prohibits any gambling in which "the house" takes a percentage of the monies wagered, and

1

California law also makes it a felony for any public official to sanction such gambling activities. The district attorney knew that the officer presenting the evidence was dissatisfied with the performance of his boss. The district attorney did not prosecute the chief.

These examples suggest familiar criticisms of criminal justice administration that derive from the normative desire for regularity and order in the application of criminal laws. We believe that varying individual preferences and changing interpersonal relationships should not independently influence the disposition of cases, that legal and administrative rules should be applied evenly and uniformly, and that a man's political or social position should not protect him from well-founded prosecution or subject him to questionable prosecution. In short, we tend to assume that criminal justice should somehow be "organized," should articulate and follow sensible rules and procedures. We value this kind of order because we literally cannot survive unless we can make accurate predictions about the consequences of most actions we take and because rules, precedents, and standards prevent arbitrary acts of judgment that offend our "sense of injustice."[2]

Set against this concept of justice, each of the prosecutors in these examples could have acted unjustly. But did they? The following pages present arguments that they did not, or, more precisely, that when we assess the performance of the criminal justice system, we should not limit ourselves to using only the criteria of order and regularity. We shall see that in evaluating the decisions of those who do justice, the concept of justice fails to provide useful assessment criteria. It fails because the concept of justice itself embodies two mutually incompatible standards: order and learning. The incompatibility arises because the objective of ordered application of law, unquestionably desirable in itself, presents a pragmatic tactical question: What administrative apparatus can achieve it? The conventional administrative apparatus for making behavior uniform—bureaucracy—imposes costs of its own. Specifically, bureaucratic controls can interfere with the alternative conception of justice as learning. This alternative conception requires that those who do justice maintain the capacity to learn new information about the cases they handle, about social preferences concerning crime, and about the consequences of punishment. I have designated these three kinds of learning "adaptation," and we shall examine how administrative efforts to achieve rule-consistency and uniform case treatment, which I have designated "order," can inhibit adaptation. In short, the task of assessment directs us down the path of administrative and organizational theory.

These pages thus challenge the premise that those who do justice *should*, as a practical administrative matter, seek primarily to treat similar cases similarly. These pages also challenge the assumption that we could in fact create an administrative system that achieves ordered or controlled case dispositions, even if we decided to try. Organization theory also provides a bases for challenging the assumption that those who do justice *can* treat similar cases similarly. We shall investigate the possibility that those systems that *are* highly rule-ordered normally operate with "technologies" and in "environments" that provide a high degree of certainty. Perhaps, if the techniques of doing justice were clear and those with whom criminal justice administrators deal behaved predictably, we could create uniform systems of case dispositions. But we shall see that prosecutors, as do other participants in the criminal justice system, operate with "technologies" and in "environments" that pose for them high degrees of uncertainty. We shall explore the concepts of technology and environment more fully shortly. For the moment, uncertainty means that prosecutors possess no accepted body of knowledge that explains: (1) precisely why they punish, (2) when a given punishment is or is not appropriate, (3) how the facts of a case may change as it moves from filing to disposition, and (4) how police, judges, defense attorneys, and the public will react to decisions they make.

The following pages describe the nature of organizational problem solving that emerged from these two principal conditions, from the ambiguous and uncertain technology for dealing with crime and from an unpredictable working environment. The problem solving pattern that emerged was highly flexible and idiosyncratic. We shall pay special attention to the reasons why administrative attempts to make prosecutorial decisions more orderly and regular, why attempts to control or regulate the ways prosecutors behaved, failed. This book argues that, on balance, we should prefer that such control efforts fail, that criminal justice reform should instead seek primarily to develop men and organizations that change, innovate, and learn in a sustained rather than haphazard fashion.

My argument, of course, presumes that, for the citizen, criminal justice is adequately predictable: those who do not engage in proscribed behavior can safely assume they will avoid prosecution, and those who are prosecuted can predict the maximum sanction. The argument also presupposes that most actors do not use their position for personal gain.

Research Setting and Format

The following chapters are based on a year spent observing a prosecuting attorney's office in a California county, which I have designated "Vario County." Vario County, with a population of about 600,000, contains a heterogeneous mixture of communities: rapidly growing upper- and middle-class suburbs, several old, small rural towns, and two moderately industrialized urban areas. The larger of these, the city of Condenado (75,000 population), faces many problems typical of decaying inner cities: a high proportion of the population is poor, undereducated, and nonwhite; the tax base is declining; and the crime rate significantly exceeds the rest of the county. The district attorney maintains a branch office in Condenado which serves this city and several more affluent communities in the southern end of the county. The prosecutor's main office is in Centerville, the county seat, twenty miles to the north; the bulk of the cases arising in the main office originate in the county's affluent suburbs and older semirural communities.

The district attorney, Robert Nolan, age forty-six, was raised in Boston and came to California with his family in the 1950s to enter a law school in the area. He worked for three years as a deputy prosecutor in the county following graduation and moved from there to the county's public defender office when it was established in 1966. He practiced privately in the county from 1967 until the Board of Supervisors appointed him district attorney in August of 1969. At the begining of that year the previous D.A. moved to the California senate, and the supervisors appointed Nolan as a compromise candidate after a prolonged period in which several prominent private attorneys rejected the job and the Board of Supervisors rejected three experienced deputy district attorneys, each of whom wanted the job badly. The residual animosities among these three created a considerable headache for the new D.A. after he assumed office. Nolan ran successfully for reelection in June of 1970, midway through my year observing the office, against the head of the county's legal aid service, a Negro and former deputy prosecutor.

The D.A. was quite receptive to my request in December of 1969 to spend the bulk of the following year observing his office's internal operations. Possessing a law degree and having served briefly with a law firm, I no doubt seemed capable of understanding and empathizing with his problems and not motivated to exploit them. I also suspect that not only his receptivity but also the rather remarkable degree of cooperation and candor that most men I contacted gave me derived from a genuine curiosity on the part of most lawyers to find out something about their profession and from their own doubts about the effectiveness and efficiency of the system of justice in which they played a part. Several men, including Robert Nolan, reported, "We don't really know what the hell we're doing around here." And a private attorney speculated that there was something "clean" about academic life and that most lawyers yearned to reestablish ties with their own substantial academic backgrounds.

I began my observations in early January 1970. I had access to nearly all phases of office operation and most office files. I was not allowed access to the padlocked files of the investigative unit, and I intruded only when a prosecutor invited me into the sensitive dealings the D.A. himself had with various outsiders in his private office. I observed citizens presenting their often heated plaints to the prosecutor, usually one of the least experienced, at the "complaint desk." I observed the frequent and usually amicable haggling between the police and the prosecutors concerning the filing of charges derived from police work. I spent brief periods with prosecutors as they worked with police in police stations. I sat in on numerous "bargaining sessions" with defense attorneys, both formally in judicial chambers and informally in corridors and in prosecutor's offices. I traced several major cases from initiation to disposition. I joined the infrequent training sessions, staff meetings, and sessions in which senior deputies determined the offers to make on felonies in advance of pretrial negotiations with defense attorneys. I attended farewell luncheons (during the year, nearly a third of the office staff resigned), "happy hours" after work, and many bull sessions both during and outside office hours. Whenever possible I inquired about reasons and strategies by which men arrived at their decisions. I took notes of these observations at the time, extended them on tape at home the same evening, and later had these taped notes transcribed.

I supplemented these observations in three ways. The first was through a review of office files containing such things as the completed forms on which deputies explained why they reduced or dismissed certain cases and the files assessing the office's performance statistically. Second, I distributed to pro-secutors an eight-page questionnaire that sought socioeconomic data, some general attitudinal data concerning law and penology, and responses assess-ing their feelings about some policies and practices in the office. In addition to gathering information, the questionnaire was designed to lead into a follow-up semistructured and tape-recorded interview lasting from 1½ to 3½ hours. Of the thirty-six prosecutors, thirty agreed to an interview, although several of these refused to complete the questionnaire, usually objecting, with some insight, that questionnaires were "too simplistic to reveal anything meaningful."[4]

Finally, I sent out 125 shorter questionnaires to defense attorneys, both private and public defenders, and judges. Of these, eighty were returned, and these yielded about thirty more semistructured interviews. The sample of 125 included all municipal and superior court judges in the county, fifteen of twenty-three of whom responded, and all public defenders, fifteen of eighteen of whom responded; the remainder were sent to private attorneys in the county. I chose those private attorneys whom I had encountered in my own observations. (These questionnaires were sent out after nine months observing the district attorney's office.) I also submitted a list of all practicing attorneys in the county (over three hundred names compiled by a clerk in the county courthouse) to two of the prosecutors with more than ten years' experience in the district attorney's office and asked them to choose those attorneys whom they felt had enough contact with the office to be able to comment intelligently on its operations. I checked these choices against the lists posted daily of attorneys appearing in criminal matters and added a few more private attorneys to the sample from this source. Of eighty-four attorneys so contacted, fifty responded. I had informal conversations with police and probation officers, but I did not systematically interview or question them.

During the year several events made this setting particularly fruitful for a case study of legal administration. I have already mentioned the election campaign, and I shall trace the impact of his candidacy on the district attorney's performance as an organizational leader, and the impact the campaign had on the office itself. In addition, most attorneys agreed that during the year several judges perceived an increase in the public's demand for punitive penal policies and, together with some prosecutors, adjusted their behavior accordingly. The research attempted to clarify just what these public demands constituted, how they were expressed, and how men with different personal philosophies reacted to these demands differently, as well as the extent to which actual policy changes resulted. Finally, following his election, Robert Nolan attempted to change some aspects of office operations. He chose a strategy involving impersonal directives and shifts in personnel that in the short term failed and tended to isolate the district attorney from his office and from friends outside on whom he had earlier relied for advice and support. We shall examine the confluence of circumstances and attitudes that contributed to this result.

I have patterned the research reported here on models (*The Forest Ranger* and *Justice Without Trial* are good examples) that draw on descriptive data, on field observations, and on open-ended interviews to support the plausibility of an essentially heuristic framework.[5] My objectives were quasi-anthropological in this sense: I sought to describe and to understand criminal prosecution in terms of the means/ends calculations of the prosecutors themselves and in terms of their personal values and the perceptions they had of each other and of others with whom they worked.[6]

An essentially qualitative study is of course prone to warping by the investigator's own biases. My biases, or more precisely those questions that interested me when I undertook this study, no doubt influenced what I searched for, my perceptions of it when I thought I found it, and how I reported it. And of course the prosecutors' perceptions of me may have conditioned their behavior toward me. I tried to minimize these dangers by probing into as many different aspects of the prosecutor's operations as the prosecutors themselves permitted, and in dealing with prosecutors I tried to be as noncommittal as possible concerning my objectives. When prosecutors frequently asked what I was up to, I usually replied that I was interested in learning about the practical problems they faced and how they tried to solve them. However, since I also sought to develop trustful and, hence, candid communications with prosecutors, when pressed by them, I chose in most cases to elaborate on my goals and thoughts. Most prosecutors did accept me; I became known as "the shrink" to several prosecutors in the branch office and have found that contacts with prosecutors since the end of my study have remained warm and open. I believe the research benefited more from the candor of their remarks to me than it lost from any preconditioning tendency my candor with them may have had.

Like Solnick's Westville, we are dealing here with a system plagued by no obvious or unusual difficulties. The county is not swamped by its criminal case load. The criminal calendar is kept up to date. Although the jail in the county seat used for preconviction and other temporary detentions is miserably overcrowded and dangerous, the county's rehabilitation facility, known as "the farm," appears, except for the absence of conjugal visiting, to be a fine model of a penal facility: no walls, adequate food, work furlough programs, and work detail for inmates. In 1970 it was clean and not fully occupied, and its management appeared progressive enough for one of my students to conduct open-ended interviews with inmates without any apparent show of alarm by prison management. The county supports a well-staffed and well-paid probation office and a highly regarded and aggressive public defender's office, about which later chapters will say more. In short, criminal justice in Vario County did not display the worst pathologies of criminal justice in major urban centers. Rather, it suggests what we can reasonably expect from these systems if we could eliminate the worst of these pathologies.

Four kinds of factors help explain why Vario County's prosecuting attorneys failed to develop common or ordered procedures for disposing of criminal cases (Figure 1-1). The first, which chapter 3 will examine, concerns the nature of the prosecutors themselves, who they are, why they became prosecutors, and what they expected to gain from the job. The second and third reasons, explored in chapter 4, revolve around the degree to which in doing their jobs prosecutors needed to cope with informational unpredictability imposed by a working environment over which prosecutors had little control and by a political environment the demands of which were difficult to reconcile with what many prosecutors believed were sensible ways of disposing of criminal cases. The fourth reason deals with the nature of the technology of prosecution itself, the implications of which chapter 5 will develop. Throughout we shall see that attempts to impose organizational order either failed or, to the extent they succeeded, tended to impair the quality of case dispositions because they blocked adaptation.

Before turning our attention to these matters in chapter 3, however, we must do two things. The remainder of this chapter amplifies the concepts presented in the introduction: the tradeoff between order and learning and the organization theory framework incorporated in later chapters. We shall then briefly review some trends in the literature on prosecution and criminal justice generally and explore the linkages between this literature and the theoretical model used here. Chapter 2 describes the formal structure and operational characteristics of the Vario County office.

8

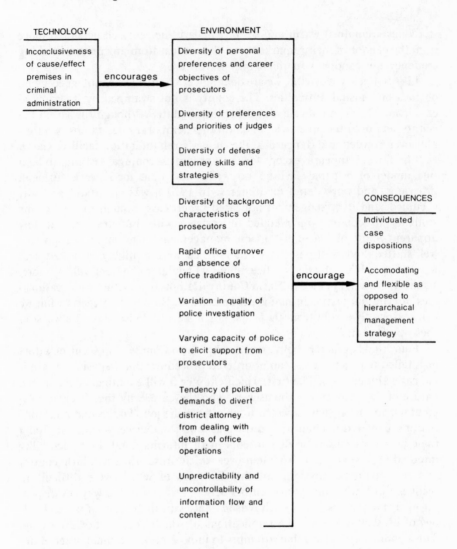

Figure 1-1. Theoretical Summary

The Problem of Assessment: The Antinomy Between
Order and Learning

Let us return, for a moment, to the intuitive "sense of injustice." When we assess the performance of a legal system we fear that adjudicators may abuse their position for personal gain, or may decide cases on whim or personal preferences, or may subvert social policy by substituting their own judgment for the collective will. More abstractly, if we believe that the dignified impartiality of the legal system reinforces common societal loyalties and values and thus reduces conflict, we may agree with Cardozo: "One of the most fundamental social interests is that law shall be uniform and impartial. There must be nothing in its action that savors of prejudice or favor or even arbitrary whim or fitfulness. Therefore in the main there shall be adherence to precedent."[7] We believe that rules and precedents provide for an impartiality that enhances social peace.[8]

If, however, we put ourselves in the position of the judged, we shall also be concerned that those who make judgments about us—a parent, a police officer who stops us on the street, a prosecutor, or a probation officer, as well as a judge—learn enough about us to treat us not as a member of a category but as an individual. I suspect we have all at times experienced injustice because someone judged us on the basis of inadequate information. A parent may discipline an innocent child for breaking a window because the culpable child succeeds in shifting the blame. Or a superior may deny a promotion to a subordinate for failing to complete an assignment because he has not learned that the subordinate had no control over the conditions that prevented him from performing. These are two examples of the importance of learning in doing justice: information may exculpate and exonerate. Since most criminal cases are settled without trial, the prosecutor often acts as adjudicator. We expect a prosecutor to be able to learn that conditions prevented the defendant from doing other than what he did. We also expect the prosecutor to learn and act upon four other kinds of information: information that mitigates the seriousness of the act (Did the victim start the fight?), information that assesses the consequences of punishment (Should a youthful first offender be imprisoned?), information that measures the administrative likelihood of success at trial (Did the police violate constitutional standards in obtaining important evidence?), and information that measures the importance of prosecuting one case rather than another (Do office resources permit trying a minor case? What are the public expectations concerning the seriousness of crimes?).

But are the order model and the learning (or adaptation) model of justice necessarily inconsistent? Both the tension between law and equity, recognized philosophically and historically in the development of common law, and the tension between bureaucratic (or hierarchical and rule-bound) and non-bureaucratic (collegial and flexible) forms of organization described in the literature on organization theory suggest that they are.

The Legal and Equitable Perspectives

The philosophical recognition of the antinomy between law and equity begins, of course, with Aristotle, who argued that, given natural and just law, which will be found within the framework of "that constitution which is by nature best," ". . . justice can exist only between men whose relations are regulated by law."[9] Yet Aristotle also acknowledged, in Friedrich's words, that

[equity] is the corrective for the generality of laws which do not take care of the individual case, a generality which is grounded in law's very nature. Aristotle tried to elucidate this thought by a rather interesting comparison. He says equity is like the Lydian kind of measure which was made of lead and which therefore could be adjusted to the contours of a line that was not straight. But he points out that such a measuring rod is of no use if it is too soft, and likewise *epieikeia* loses all value if it is employed without rhyme, reason, or limitation.[10]

As Aristotle himself put it:

It is equitable to pardon human weaknesses and to look not to the law but to the legislator . . . , not to the acts themselves but to the moral purpose, not to the part but to the whole, not to what a man is now but to what he has been always or generally, to remember good rather than ill treatment and benefits received rather than those conferred, to bear injury with patience, to be willing to appeal to the judgment of reason rather than to violence, to prefer arbitration to the law court, for the arbitrator keeps equity in view, whereas the judge looks only to the law.[11]

In this passage Aristotle suggests adjudicators ought not simply to apply a rule but should seek to fit the policy or reason for the rule to the facts of the case, thus achieving case dispositions that "appeal to the judgment of reason." If the intent of the legislator is to bind men to one another, then the act of mercy and pardon of universal weakness may do so. If the legislator seeks to deter a man from future misconduct, what that man has been always sensibly tells something about the likelihood that he will do harm again.

The Anglo-American legal tradition legitimates the balance between law and equity, recognizes the need for correcting the inability of general laws to "take care of the individual case." King James I, in his decree in 1616 sanctioning the continuation of equity jurisdiction in England to overcome the rigidities of the common law, stated:

We . . . do will and command that our Chancellor, or Keeper of the Great Seal for the time being, shall not hereafter desist to give unto our Subjects, upon their several Complaints now or hereafter to be made, such Relief in Equity (notwithstanding any Procedures at the Common Law against them) as shall stand with the *Merit and Justice of their Cause.*[12]

As the examples at the beginning of the chapter suggest, particularly the examples of Bob Stern and of the felonious police chief, prosecutors, although with varying results, look to the moral purposes rather than to acts themselves, to the man as "he has been always or generally," rather than to what he is at the moment. These equitable notions, which prosecutors themselves often only dimly recognize, help shape their decisions.

The Inadequacies of Bureaucratic Decision Making

When prosecutors adopt an equitable style of case disposition, they avoid the inadequacies of bureaucratic decision making. Would it be wise for men who manage a prosecutor's office to seek by rule making to eliminate all potential for arbitrary dispositions of cases handled by subordinates? Both the English common law system and Weberian bureaucracy are built upon adherence to written rules and formalized procedures, and both have been criticized for their inability to learn facts of specific cases and to adapt to changing circumstances. Crozier, for example, suggests that learning and adaptation are not common to rule-oriented organizations, and he suggests executives in such contexts cannot both learn and innovate and simultaneously conform to rules.

Let us analyze the case of an executive faced with the problem of making a decision which can hurt or further the feelings and interests of some of his subordinate units without being able to ascertain the value of their conflicting arguments. He is most likely to try to find some impersonal rules, or at least some precedent, on which to rely. His decision will probably be inadequate; but given his special predicament, it will be the best solution in the long run.

Our division head might make better decisions if he tried to establish for himself some special channel of information, or if he were ready to trust one or several of his subordinates. But if he did either, he would probably have to combat accusations of favoritism and to face the possibility of a serious deterioration of the climate, whatever the soundness of the end result. . . . Routine remains the safest way for him, whatever his own feelings. One may wonder more about the (very infrequent) innovating decisions than about the reiteration of routinized behavior.[13]

Similarly, Daniel Katz and Robert L. Kahn have written:

The ritualistic bureaucracy becomes inefficient partly because the prescribed behavior of role requirements is virtually the only form of behavior which remains. Clerks react to cases which cross their desks on the basis of the rules provided for their disposition.

Cases occur, however, which are too complex or too difficult to handle within the existing rules. Instead of making the extra effort to meet such problems, the bureaucratized clerk, who is not sticking his neck out, pushes the atypical cases to one side of his desk for his supervisor to look at in the weekly checkup. In turn, the supervisor may accumulate his own set of exceptional cases to be pushed into a drawer for future consideration with the head of the department. Memoranda are exchanged, precedents are invoked, and an already overspecified book of rules is enlarged yet again. The organization moves in a costly and inefficient way.[14]

And Warren Bennis has described the tendency of rule-oriented bureaucracies to repress personal growth, to encourage conformity, and to prevent the anticipation of consequences of action.[15] The following section explores further the reasons why prosecutorial learning is desirable.

Assessing Prosecutorial Behavior

As with most human activity, we can evaluate the quality of prosecutorial decisions on several levels. The narrowest level employs purely legal criteria. It enquires only whether the prosecutor complies with those rules made specifically to limit the behavior of prosecutors. On this level, the task of evaluation is not difficult, for prosecutors have operated in the United States with legally almost unlimited discretion. Many jurisdictions prohibit only prosecutions motivated by the prosecutor's personal malice toward the suspect and make no attempt to require the prosecutor to press charges even in the most serious of cases. The judicial branch has sporadically created a few limitations on prosecutorial discretion, which deal principally with the introduction of false or misleading testimony at trial.[16]

While this narrow level has the virtue of specificity (and sometimes not even that: proof to sustain an allegation of malicious prosecution is extremely difficult to obtain), it fails as an evaluative standard because it bears little relation to the functions of prosecution. This legalistic standard does not help us assess the prosecutor's deployment of his limited resources and the extent to which his choices plausibly further legitimate objectives of prosecution.

Let us therefore attempt to assess on the basis of his functions, his objectives. We ask prosecutors to cope with a social problem, crime. In theory we punish to increase social stability and individual security in one of four ways.[17] We may believe that punishment increases social stability because it decreases the frequency with which people believe they must personally seek retribution because officials will not and "take the law into their own hands." We may punish to reinforce the credibility of social prohibitions, thus discouraging others from violating social norms—general deterrence. We may punish to coerce, or physically prevent, the offender from offending again—specific deterrence. And we may use the machinery of punishment to provide the offender with skills and values that will reward him for legitimate rather than proscribed behavior.

From this functional perspective we can derive evaluative standards that go beyond the legal obligations of prosecutors. Given their limited resources, we would expect prosecutors to choose whether and in what manner to prosecute cases according to the following standards:

1. Regarding the statutory law itself, the greater the plausibility that the proscribed behavior is indeed harmful, and the greater the plausibility that the sanctions prescribed by law will reduce such harm in the future, then the greater the justification for prosecution. Prosecution for violation of rules that demand impossible behavior, or of rules the compliance with which requires violation of other rules, or of rules that presume relationships and consequences that the bulk of available knowledge demonstrates to be false would, under this standard, be undesirable.[18]

2. Regarding the facts of the case itself, the greater the likelihood that the suspect's alleged behavior has done demonstrable harm, the greater the justification for prosecution. Thus, choosing cases to prosecute exclusively on the basis of administrative efficiency would be undesirable.

3. The greater the probability that the suspect in fact committed the alleged acts, the greater the justification for prosecution. To prosecute a suspect whose guilt is doubtful in order to satisfy public pressure would thus presumably be undesirable.

4. The greater the probability that, upon a finding of guilt, the suspect will be treated in a manner that will promote the objectives of criminal justice, the greater the justification for prosecution. By this standard prosecutors should not prosecute for a crime someone whose mental condition makes him incapable of responding to any of the conventional sentencing options.

Does this functional approach provide a useful measure of the adequacy of prosecutorial behavior? Without considerable modification, no. It does not, first, because each of the theories that proposes desirable consequences of punishment is for many categories of behavior under serious attack. John Griffiths summarizes what we call the technology of criminal prosecution this way:

I am thoroughly convinced that the traditional jurisprudence of criminal law has reached essential sterility. This is particularly true of the most basic level of all. . . . No one is presently capable of giving an adequate, intelligible and coherent account of why it is useful and right to punish men and, *a fortiori*, no one can explain which men ought to be punished in which circumstances.[19]

While Griffiths may overstate, the premise that many forms of behavior produce direct or remote harm has been questioned, in particular, gambling, prostitution, and marijuana use. And in many categories of crime where harm exists, incarceration or fines increasingly appear unable to deter or rehabilitate, and may do the reverse. If we must concede the changing character of knowledge about the dangerousness of acts and about the consequences of punishment, we cannot assess prosecutorial behavior by standards that presume knowledge of cause and effect or an ability to compare one harm with another.

Furthermore, the functional approach assumes that the prosecutor can take as given the facts of specific cases, the degree of harm, the strength of the evidence, the character of the suspect. Yet, as Jerome Frank has bluntly put it, "facts are guesses."[20] We are, he asserts, fooling ourselves by the pretense of impartiality:

Under our existing system, when litigation breaks out, the presence of the "unruly," the "constant inconstancy," in trial-court "fact-finding," causes . . . uncertainty. Only in appearance, not in reality, can men now usually rely with assurance on . . . precise legal rules.[21]

Because a police report or a witness can mislead, the prosecutor's "facts" are guesses. He can do little more than guess at the degree of harm the suspect has done or speculate about the strength of evidence in court. And his guesses about the general harmfulness of behavior proscribed by statute and his speculations about the inherent contradiction in penal theory between social retribution and individual rehabilitation—to take the extremes—will be even less informed than his guesses about the facts of a specific case.

Given that prosecutors work with an ambiguous technology in an unpredictable environment, attempts at functional assessment must focus primarily on those factors that encourage or prevent learning and acting upon new criminological knowledge, and on those characteristics of their daily work that influence the prosecutors' capacity to adjust to new facts of cases and to empathize with unique individual circumstances. Assessment should, in other words, focus on whether the ways prosecutors make decisions encourage substantive rather than formal rationality, encourage what Mannheim defines as behavior "which reveals intelligent insight into the inter-relations of events in a given situation."[22] The next sections review more precisely what the concepts of technology and environment mean, and why they are, in the prosecutor's case, uncertain.

The Concept of Organizational Technology

The concept of organizational "technology" derives from James Thompson, and Thompson's analysis bears repeating here. How men act, according to Thompson, depends upon the outcomes they hope to achieve and upon their beliefs about cause/effect relationships that may produce the desired outcome.[23] "Given," says Thompson, "a desire, the state of man's knowledge at any point in time dictates the kinds of variables required and the manner of their manipulation to bring that desire to fruition." Thus, Thompson designates the combination of "desired outcomes" and "beliefs about cause/effect relationships" an organization's "technology, or *technical rationality*."[24]

This definition leads Thompson to two positions. First, he suggests it is useful to assess organizational performance in terms of the degree to which standards of desirability are either *crystallized* or *ambiguous* and in terms of the degree to which men believe that their knowledge of cause/effect relationships is either *complete* or *incomplete*. Second, he derives basic organizational types from this analysis. Thompson suggests that we may roughly scale the degree to which organization members follow routinized or rule-ordered patterns of behavior in terms of the degree to which (1) standards of desirability are crystallized or ambiguous and (2) cause/effect beliefs are complete or incomplete. To illustrate, the technology of automobile production involves throughout the process relatively crystallized standards of desirability. At the top of the organization, it is clearly desirable that the organization make a profit adequate to satisfy the stockholders and to finance projected expansion. At the level of manufacture, it is a relatively unambiguous desire that smoothly running cars come off the assembly line most of the time. Cause/effect relationships are, furthermore, relatively complete. The employees of General Motors can specify in advance, without great difficulty, what actions should be taken and in what order with a high degree of probability that if the men on the line do what they are told, a completed car will come off the line. While compliance is not perfect in an automobile assembly plant, most workers most of the time are doing what their organization has told them to do. But this may not be so in a prosecutor's office.

Prosecuting attorneys in most jurisdictions must answer certain basic questions in order to get their job done: Should I file a complaint on the basis of an arrest report? Should I refuse any action on the basis of a police report? Should I seek further information before filing a complaint, either by asking the police to clarify certain points or by investigating myself? Should I call the suspect to appear in my office for an informal "warning" in the hopes that the warning will be sufficient to deter the suspect from further misbehavior? If I file a complaint (or seek an indictment from the grand jury) what charges should I propose? Should I file all charges conceivably justified by the police report, or should I file only charges on which I reasonably expect a conviction and which I think the gravity of the crime warrants? If I enter negotiations with a defense attorney, how much should I be willing to concede? What position should I take regarding sentencing, in the event of a plea or conviction at trial? Under what circumstances should I dismiss a case rather than take it to trial? How should I present the case at trial?

In some jurisdictions, some of these questions get automatic answers. The police may file complaints directly with the court. The judge may negotiate directly with the defense attorney, reducing the prosecutor to a passive role. Most prosecutors must answer most of these questions, however, but they do not, even within one office, necessarily answer the questions in the same way. In Vario County, where California law makes prosecutors responsible for answering all the above questions, some preferred to "overfile," while others did not. Some considered a sex offender dangerous and "worth putting away," and hence conceded little, while others hoped to spare the victim, especially if a child, the further anguish of reliving a difficult experience in a public trial, and hence conceded more and in some instances dismissed outright. These are judgmental decisions, and we must not allow our preference for justice as order to disguise the fact that the technology of criminal administration resembles technologies—those of psychiatry and college teaching are good examples—in which "judgmental" decisions are more frequent than programmed ones.

Prosecutors do not employ crystallized standards of desirability. While in the abstract nearly all the subjects of this study agreed that crime is a serious social problem for which solutions should be attempted, they did not necessarily believe that their decisions should bear any relationship to the goal of crime reduction. The protection of the rights of the accused is itself a competing standard the validity of which most prosecutors recognized. Furthermore, reducing crime is not the same thing as reducing social cost. Trials of minor offenders cost money. Incarceration of an habitual but petty offender may put a family of six on welfare.

Cause/effect beliefs are often ambiguous and incomplete. Incarceration will prevent a man from committing crimes while incarcerated, but whether incarceration will deter or rehabilitate or encourage the defendant to commit more crimes on his release is a prediction few prosecutors feel qualified to make, except on the basis of "educated guesses" derived from the facts of specific cases. Because prosecutors can make only crude and imperfect predictions about the consequences of any alternative action on the suspect, on the rate of crime in general, on their own reputations or success, and because, to the extent they can make them, these predictions derive from case-specific information, it is not surprising that we find little standardization. Unlike the production-line company or the bank, the prosecutor's success does not depend on the development of either widely shared standards of desirability or widely shared cause/effect premises. Because assessment is linked to specific cases, the technology of which is unclear, superiors may have little stake in strictly enforcing rules of operation. Furthermore, superiors may disagree rather fundamentally among themselves concerning both standards of desirability and how to achieve them. In Vario County some attempted to persuade their subordinates to adhere to their vision of "correct" procedures, while other superiors promoted inconsistent policies, and still other superiors deferred to the subordinate's "responsibility" to "use his own judgment."

One further illustration of the meaning of the term "uncertain technology" may be in order. Surely one of the most difficult prosecutorial decisions conceivable concerns the decision whether to prosecute Richard M. Nixon following his resignation of the presidency of the United States. (This is written within seventy-two hours of his resignation.) The case illustrates the uncertain technology of prosecution, because we have no body of generally accepted theory that answers four critical questions:

1. Is the punishment of "humiliation," imposed socially, politically, and psychologically but not legally, an appropriate alternative to criminal sanctions, one sufficient to deter or to serve other objectives of criminal justice?

2. Should the prosecutorial decision insure that Mr. Nixon receives the same treatment as others prosecuted for Watergate offenses? If so, by what criteria shall we determine equality? By the degree of suffering? By sentence formally imposed?

3. Is it appropriate to resolve such a question by applying, if it exists, a prevailing public judgment to the question?

4. Must the public record eventually reveal all details of Mr. Nixon's transgressions, or will legitimate public interests be served by granting swift amnesty?

While we may form strong and logically defensible opinions about these issues, the fact remains that no body of general or of professional theory or data exists to provide convincing and widely accepted answers.

The technology of criminal prosecution thus resembles Thompson's "intensive technology" type, in which operators of the technology draw upon a variety of techniques to achieve some change in a specific object, "but the selection, combination, and order of application are determined by feedback from the object itself."[25] The prosecutor behaves on the basis of information concerning the case and the suspect. How strong is the evidence in the case? How persuasive will the witnesses be? What is the suspect's prior record? What are the chances of an acquittal at trial? How effective is the defense attorney before a jury?

In organizations operating under intensive technologies, attempts to control behavior through statements of formal organizational rules and policies frequently fail because such rules are often too broad and/or inflexible to provide guides to action that have any demonstrable or consistent payoff. In this research setting, prosecutors with a variety of inconsistent personal belief systems who disagreed with the relatively few formal office policies frequently succeeded in ignoring them because superiors themselves had little knowledge with which to defend some policies and refute others.

The Concept of Organizational Environment

James Thompson also nicely describes the concept of environment. Organizations in varying degrees must, to survive, deal with people and events outside their formal boundaries. No organization is a completely closed system. They must initially, of course, recruit from outside, and therefore, they must often take as given the training and values members bring to the organization from outside. They also depend on information generated elsewhere—market research or decisions of competitors in the case of many businesses, for example. And they depend on the flow of materials, perhaps sheet steel, perhaps welfare cases, from other individuals and organizations they cannot fully control.

Just as the nature of its technology affects the way an organization does its work, Thompson suggests that different environments produce different organizational patterns. Thompson argues that organizations dealing with *homogeneous* environments (environments that contain people and institutions with similar interests and needs) and with *stable* environments (environments that make predictable demands on the organization) will develop structures and procedures that differ considerably from organizations dealing with *heterogeneous* and/or *shifting* environments.

Confronted with a heterogeneous environment (one that makes competing and inconsistent demands on the organization) and a shifting environment (where these demands and pressures change), organizations, Thompson argues, will adopt flexible and decentralized operations that do not rely heavily on rules.[26] The Vario County office behaved as Thompson predicts it would. Later chapters will describe in detail the heterogeneous and shifting character of the prosecutor's environment and its consequences in Vario County. A short summary of these findings follows.

The Impact of Prosecutors' Backgrounds and Aspirations

Most prosecutors made no career commitment to the office; they had relatively little motive for identifying strongly with the success of the office (itself difficult to define and measure) or with the electoral success of the district attorney.[27] The tentativeness of many "policy" decisions of office superiors reflected in part a desire to satisfy the motives of many young men who had chosen the job as a vehicle for gaining personal legal experience; a mutual respect for professional autonomy reinforced this tentativeness. In short, the extent to which prosecutors behaved as autonomous, self-regulating units may reflect the fact that men with professional training (in this study, often gained at some of California's well-reputed law schools) and a sense of personal competence may less willingly conform to formally expressed rules. Although prosecutors must to a degree coordinate among themselves the preparation of any one case, they were not here regularly assessed according to the extent to which their disposition of a given case conformed to any general office standard of uniformity for case dispositions.

The Role of Uncertainty

A second source of prosecutorial autonomy resulted from the fragmented way in which prosecutors learned the facts of cases. To get their work done, prosecutors must rely on the calculations and perceptions of others—police, defense attorneys, judges, and sometimes probation officers—whose values and interests and understanding of facts vary among themselves and from case to case. Because prosecutors learn from fragmented and competing sources, their sense of what is true remains tentative, and this continuous factual tentativeness and uncertainty (they are rarely sure that they know the entire story) further reduces the possible payoffs to the organization of any attempts to control prosecutorial behavior by rules. A rule, for example, that "all prosecutors shall dismiss cases when there is substantial evidence of innocence" would have little or no impact on daily behavior, because the evidence of innocence is so frequently ambiguous and dependent on qualitative estimates of the reliability of the police or defense attorneys who provide the evidence.

Furthermore, factual uncertainty also complicates the prosecutor's task of determining whether his actions will violate the legal rights of the accused. For example, the defendant who may appear to an outsider to have been "blackmailed" out of a chance to raise a legitimate defense, because the prosecutor has offered a lower criminal charge and/or sentence in return for a guilty plea, may appear to the prosecutor to be making a rational calculation of the cost of pleading as opposed to the risk of a conviction at trial. The prosecutor who willingly reduces a charge on a potentially weak case, but refuses to dismiss it outright, is not, from his perspective, levering a plea out of a legally innocent man but rather discounting the possibility that the "weakness" is only apparent, not real. The potential "weakness" may be only the product of the defendant's lie to his attorney or an honest inadequacy in the police officer's report that he will clarify on the witness stand. Since neither prosecuting nor defense attorney can ever *know* the result of a future trial, compromises that appear to prevent the suspect from exercising a legal right—here, to a public trial—may seem rational and beneficial to all concerned.

In organizations facing uncertain environments, rule-ordered behavior is less common than the kind of strategic guessing that Wildavsky finds in the budgetary process:

> Strategic moves take place in a rapidly changing environment in which no one is quite certain how things will turn out and new goals constantly emerge in response to experience. In this context of uncertainty, choice among existing strategies must be based on intuition and hunch, on an "educated guess," as well as on firm knowledge.[28]

We shall find parallels between the strategies of those who administer criminal justice and Wildavsky's description of the strategies that prove effective in budgetary advocacy:

> To be considered aboveboard, a fair and square shooter, a frank man is highly desirable. . . . Everyone agrees that the most important requirement of confidence, at least in a negative sense, is to be aboveboard. As [Congressman] Rooney once said, "There's only two things that get me mad. One is hare-brained schemes; the other is when they don't play it straight." A lie, an attempt to blatantly cover up some misdeed, a tricky move of any kind, can lead to an irreparable loss of confidence.[29]

Because the relationships across organizational boundaries do not provide automatically the solutions or answers to the questions the prosecutor asks (because relationships always carry the potential for misinformation and outright deceit), police, prosecutors, and defense attorneys may seek to reduce this inherent uncertainty by developing reciprocal bonds among themselves. By reciprocal bonds I am not referring to a pattern of mutual exchange akin to a sense of debt owed in return for a favor given. Rather, these bonds seem to emerge from frequent interpersonal contacts and the general match of personal preferences and interests, for example in fishing or in beer drinking after work. These ties are built on candor, honesty, and "being realistic," qualities that may reduce uncertainty for both members of the interacting pair. Indeed, instead of depending on exchange of favors— "I'll let you plead X to a reduced charge if you plead Y to the given charge" in the case where a defense attorney represents two clients—the reciprocal bond may facilitate the opposite, the capacity to deny the requests of another or to concede the justness of his position, because each member trusts the other's judgment and can afford to insist or concede without becoming further obligated or threatened. The significance of reciprocal bonds, which might be suppressed by aggressive management efforts to impose organizational uniformity, of course introduces another element of variation in organizational output, but such a bond is often a prerequisite for a prosecutor to learn and act upon unexpected (and usually mitigating) information about the suspect and the crime. While it may seem paradoxical, the bond of reciprocity, which is sometimes thought to be the converse of adversariness, can produce the same kinds of results the adversary model presumes: the sensitization of the decider to the truth of facts beyond his direct experience and the legitimacy of norms beyond his personal values.

The Impact of Local Politics on Office Leadership

In the jurisdiction I observed, political uncertainties further decreased the degree to which prosecutors developed a shared sense of organizational purpose. The district attorney himself lacked both political experience and a well-established political organization in his jurisdiction that could transfer its experience to him. Without this knowledge of the community and its preferences, he found it difficult to assess the consequences, and hence the risks, of any major innovative action. Lacking such knowledge, he tended to assume the risks would be high. He reacted to what he perceived to be a generally conservative and unenlightened public attitude toward crime, not by trying to define that attitude and incorporate it in office policy, but rather by preserving for himself the resources to cope with newspaper or other forms of public criticism. Handling these external demands prevented him from becoming regularly involved in office operations. (As one prosecutor put it, "Maybe because he's in an elected position, it's hard for us to suggest something to him. We feel it's out of our hands.") The district attorney did not, therefore, provide the kind of leadership that might have encouraged a more coherent and widely shared perspective of organizational goals.

Criminal Prosecution and Social Science

We do not possess an extensive body of literature on criminal prosecution, and some of the better materials, such as Eisenstein's study of United States attorneys, have not been published.[30] Taken together, the literature to date supports the following descriptions of the prosecutorial process. Bear in mind, however, that what follows contains general statements only. District attorneys' offices throughout the United States vary greatly. Their size, the political culture in which they operate, the legal definition of their responsibilities (some offices handle only felonies, while the police prosecute minor cases directly), their work load, and their method of staffing (from civil-service appointment to those based on political "connections") all vary. These factors may greatly influence the kinds of decisions prosecutors make. This study does not (and could not) prove that certain dynamics dominate all prosecutorial activity. It seeks only to suggest a framework for analyzing criminal justice that may, in some but not all circumstances, help orient future research and policy analysis.

1. Although he administers law, few laws explicitly constrain the decisions a prosecutor makes. Neither he nor his office is liable to be sued (or, of course, prosecuted!) for declining to prosecute those who are guilty or for prosecuting, absent a showing of personal malice, those against whom the evidence may be ambiguous. In this sense, prosecutors have considerable

legal "discretion." They may lose a case by ignoring a point of law, but whether they care about losing is often a situational or personal calculation, not a general constraint on their discretion. The general language of most penal statutes allows the prosecutor to choose from among a number of alternative charges for a given act, and no law prohibits prosecutors from altering these charges or recommending a sentence to the judge in exchange for a plea of guilty.[31]

2. But the absence of legal controls on prosecutorial decisions does not mean that no controls exist. Informal norms of fairness generated by reciprocal relationships with defense attorneys and judges, and the sense of objectivity instilled by legal training itself, can create real limits on prosecutorial discretion.[32]

3. The norms and relationships that minimize the extent to which prosecutors misuse their discretion do not, however, produce uniform case handling, and most observers find considerable disagreement among prosecutors concerning the cause/effect premises that guide their judgment. Most observers believe that prosecutors will proceed with prosecution only when they believe that the defendant is "morally guilty" of a legally proscribed act. But the strength of the evidence and the legal relevance and admissibility necessary to create the belief in moral guilt vary depending on the prosecutor's commitment to a crime-fighting or due process definition of his role.[3]

4. In terms of frequencies of case dispositions, prosecutors do *not* prosecute considerably more often where they are virtually certain the suspect committed a crime than they prosecute those whose connections to the crime are ambiguous. Limited resources, reluctant witnesses, concern for the welfare of the suspect, the availability of alternative methods of case dispositions—all push the prosecutor toward leniency. As a general rule, prosecutors do not vindictively pursue convictions simply because a crime has been committed.[34]

5. Prosecutors learn the facts of cases and determine how to dispose of cases primarily from people outside their office, from police, defense attorneys, and judges.[35]

6. A large majority of criminal cases in nearly all jurisdictions of any size are disposed of not by formal trial but by plea of guilty, brief informal judicial hearing, or dismissal. When judges routinely dispose of cases through informal hearing, direct plea bargaining between prosecuting and defense attorneys is less extensive, but where plea bargaining occurs, four studies focusing directly on this process collectively tend to confirm the following observations:[36]

a. Although the process of negotiating settlement of a criminal case does not resemble a barter model, in which things of roughly equal value are haggled over and exchanged, neither are negotiations a ritual in which each side knows the other's moves in advance or a charade designed to induce a plea from a defendant without granting meaningful concession to the defendant. The defendant thus may gain a significant reduction in charges and/or sentence.

b. Successful negotiations are dominated by a spirit of reasonableness and cooperation rather than adversariness. Alschuler quotes a Boston prosecutor: "When I sit down with a defense attorney who knows how to be reasonable, we judge the whole man. Neither of us cares what evidence would be admissable and what would not, or which one of us would win at trial. We simply try to do the fair thing with each case" (p. 54).

c. Attorneys frequently sacrifice evidentiary defenses that appear to have a respectable chance of success at trial. Alschuler believes that in some instances (the reduction of a charge of rape to a simple battery, for example) the defense attorney may abandon the defense of a case in which his chances of prevailing may be quite high, because he cannot afford the risk of losing if the original charge goes to trial. Most attorneys, Alschuler points out, can remember handling or hearing about seemingly airtight defenses that broke down at the last minute and sent the client to prison (p. 62).

d. Defense attorneys are generally reluctant to press all but the most obvious constitutional issues. Alschuler quotes an Oakland attorney:

I never use the Constitution. I bargain a case on the theory that it's a "cheap burglary" or a "cheap purse-snatching" or a "cheap whatever." Sure, I could suddenly start to negotiate by saying, "Ha, ha! You goofed. You should have given the defendant a warning." And I'd do fine in that case, but my other clients would pay for this isolated success. The next time the district attorney had his foot on my throat, he'd push too (pp. 79-80).

Each of the authors reporting on plea bargaining indicates that negotiations are dominated by the presumption that the defendant has in fact, if not in law, committed an illegal act and that the defendant may legitimately receive some punishment, despite the possibility that a jury would acquit him. If this negation of the presumption of innocence calls for policy reform, however, we may doubt whether anything short of a mandatory jury trial for all offenders would bring about the required changes, and given the decision in *Brady* and demands on limited county budgets for other meritorious causes—educational improvement, for example—such reform seems highly unlikely.

7. The backgrounds of prosecutors do not appear to differ from those of the bar in general.[37]

8. Although general political conditions, such as work load, crime rates, and nature of judicial appointment, vary among jurisdictions and do influence general patterns of prosecutorial behavior, most specific case decisions and dispositions are buffered from direct political influence.[38]

The existing literature on prosecutors tends to fall into either of two broad approaches to the assessment of criminal justice institutions. The first approach, embodied in the work of some sociologists and lawyers writing critically of criminal administration in the middle and late 1960s, adopts implicitly the rule-compliance definition of justice and also finds order in the patterns of deviations by legal administrators from what the authors take to be given legal standards.

This approach, which may be called the "system pathology" approach, stresses that those who administer norms of conduct must simultaneously adjust to the requirements of getting work done, of promoting themselves within the system, and of protecting themselves from criticism, and that these obligations prevent them from complying with legal norms. For example, Abraham Blumberg asserts that practical bureaucratic pressures prevent the achievement of due process ideals:

[T]here is an almost irreconcilable conflict: intense pressures to process large numbers of cases, on the one hand, and the stringent ideological and legal requirements of "due process of law," on the other. The dilemma is frequently resolved through bureaucratically ordained short cuts, deviations, and outright rule violations. . . . Because they fear criticism on ethical as well as legal grounds, all the significant participants in the court's social structure are bound into an organized system of complicity. Patterned, covert, informal breaches, and evasions of "due process" are accepted as routine—they are institutionalized—but are nevertheless denied to exist.[39]

The system pathology approach has tended to postulate that criminal justice administration, wherever located, operates systematically to violate unambiguous rules of law. Often the supporting data has been gathered impressionistically from a few major urban areas. Furthermore, this approach implies that reform must seek principally to increase rule-compliance. From the perspective of organization theory, however, this approach substantially overestimates the capacity of most human organizations to impose ordered forms of behavior upon their members. Organizations involve constantly shifting mixes of unrelated or only dimly related problems, fears, friendships, and hostilities that may vary over time and among the organization members. Few, if any, organizations, formal or informal, consist of a single set of identically perceived policies, goal hierarchies, or methods of controlling discretion and executing policies in daily operations.

The second "open system" approach, which characterizes this study of prosecutorial performance, has been used by political scientists who studied criminal justice and published their findings in the late 1960s. This approach, best typified by the work of James Q. Wilson[40] and those associated with him, contrasts with the system pathology approach in several respects.[41] The propensity of sociologists to choose the closed system approach while political scientists choose the open system approach confirms the conventional wisdom distinguishing the two disciplines: The sociologists seek pluralism but find elites, while political scientists search for elites but find pluralism.

While the system pathology approach tends to focus on the impact of what it believes to be essentially stable features of bureaucracy upon legal administration, the open system approach stresses the degree to which differences in political and social settings and among the preferences of individual administrators and actors create considerable variation in the output of organizations that bear legally identical labels. The pathological approach tends to assume that most legal norms are unequivocal (and hence that observers can easily spot deviations), while the open system approach stresses the indeterminacy of many legal norms and the impact of the absence of any consistent technology for managing the problem of crime or for guiding the decisions of legal administrators. Wilson, for example, finds large areas of police behavior, areas he calls "citizen-invoked order maintenance," in which the output of police is largely determined by the circumstances of the case and is beyond organizational control. While the pathological approach would suggest that output is an essentially predictable product of stable or homeostatic characteristics of the job and the organization (selection procedures, work loads, and reward systems), the open approach stresses the importance of personal and situational variation and the impact of changing external constraints and pressures on output.

Levin's findings, incidentally, fit the law/equity antinomy noted above. Levin argues that the machine style of politics in Pittsburgh brings into its judiciary men from backgrounds that help them understand and empathize with the plight of the accused. He finds judges in Pittsburgh impose sentences significantly lower in length than those imposed by Minneapolis judges (whose election the Bar Association heavily influences) in identical crime categories. Through interviews and observations Levin also concluded that Pittsburgh judges more frequently ignored due process directives than did the Minneapolis judges. The distinction between open system and pathological explanations, then, lies not in the absence or presence of specific behavioral patterns but in the open system's attribution of these patterns to diverse, changing, and complex environmental settings in contrast to the pathological approach's tendency to attribute patterns to "the system" of criminal administration itself.

The open system approach follows familiar developments in the fields of organization and decision theory, developments that emphasize the tenuousness of organizational order. We know, for example, that organizational goals and purposes usually conflict, that goal priorities are constantly renegotiated, that the statement of a goal does not guarantee that the organization can measure its attainment, that information evaluating performance is often unavailable, that attempts at organizational control must cope with the potential of communication systems for distortion and with the fact of individual members' diverse motives and rewards. And theory suggests that in conditions of uncertainty it may be rational for organizations to eschew attempts at internal ordering and to adopt consciously a flexible and adaptive posture toward new information and new demands in which standards of performance are constantly renegotiated.[42]

2

The District Attorney's Office and Its Work

This chapter traces the progress of an actual case through the Vario County district attorney's office. I began to follow the case at the "pre-pre-trial conference" about a year after the case was filed, so of necessity I recreated some of the details of the case history before 1970 by drawing on my observations of the handling of other cases in their early stages. The chapter describes the constants of the basic office structure and routines and introduces some of the variables on which a case disposition depends. The chapter serves two purposes: to illustrate with an extended example the theories just outlined, and to describe the social and legal setting and formal structure of the Vario County district attorney's office. Herbet Kaufman concluded *The Forest Ranger* with a goal that this and subsequent chapters attempt to achieve and with a caveat that I hope I and the reader do not forget: "It would be gratifying just to be able to portray an organization accurately, to capture the drama, the excitement, the spirit of administration. Even this limited goal is elusive. For the portrait, no matter how vivid, is at best a pale reflection of reality."

Jennings's Case

On a typically overcast Monday morning in late January 1969, Sergeant Hawk of the Condenado Police Department's patrol division delivered roughly a dozen files to the Vario County district attorney's branch office in Condenado. The files contained the crime and arrest reports of felony and misdemeanor arrests his division had made over the weekend. The Condenado district attorney's office occupies about a quarter of the second floor of the U-shaped municipal courthouse building that also houses Condenado's three municipal court judges and their clerks, portions of the county's welfare offices, and a variety of other administrative offices. Sergeant Hawk and officers from the five other police departments in the southern part of the county make the trip almost daily to the courthouse with the reports of arrests their divisions have made since their last visit. Hawk does not bring in reports on all arrests, for his department itself weeds out some cases in which the suspect has offered information in exchange for his release without prosecution, cases that contain obvious evidentiary weaknesses, cases that seem too minor to bother with (such as an arrest to cool off a family fight), or cases that involve a patent defect in search, arrest, or interrogation procedure.

In Condenado, a young deputy district attorney, Richard Schwartz, assisted the department in weeding out its own weak cases, but his frequent visits to the police station—he usually went from his home to the station each morning, where he reviewed the results of the previous night's activities and made himself available to any officers who needed advice before going to his own office—was exceptional for Vario County. Schwartz undertook the job himself without any urging from his superiors. He generated close and generally cooperative relationships between Condenado's police officers and the D.A.'s office, a relationship that the office lacks with several other police departments in the county. But his superiors, sensing that his success derived from his personal skills, did not instruct other deputies to follow his lead. Most deputies visited police departments only when the investigation of complicated and usually very serious cases, such as homicides, required it.

Sergeant Hawk deposited the bulk of the files—misdemeanor arrests—without comment on the cluttered desk of the complaint deputy, who added these files to the misdemeanor reports other officers from other departments had left with him earlier in the morning, and headed with the remaining felony arrest reports toward the office of the "area deputy" for Condenado.

Among the felonies, Hawk brought to the office a fairly routine arrest of a male Negro in his mid-forties for the possession of marijuana (Calif. Health and Safety Code Sec. 11530). The arrest was one of the 3234 felony arrests made in Vario County in 1969. Of these arrests, 757 were, according to the California Bureau of Criminal Statistics, released without prosecution, 51 were transferred to other jurisdictions, 416 were prosecuted as misdemeanors, and the remaining 2010 were prosecuted as felonies? The police report in this case described the substance of the offense in typically abbreviated fashion:

RO [reporting officer] and Officer Jones at approx. 0030 hours observed Suspect vehicle traveling slowly westbound on First Avenue. Followed vehicle approx. 2½ blocks and observed vehicle execute illegal left turn onto Broad Street. Officers proceeded to [turn on flashing red light]. Vehicle stopped after traveling approx. 1 more block. S [Suspect] exited vehicle and produced driver's license upon RO's request. RO then observed a package of "Zig-Zag" cigarette papers protruding from S's shirt pocket. After informing Officer Jones of this fact, both RO and Officer Jones proceeded to search vehicle. Search produced a matchbox containing green vegetable matter found under the passenger side of the vehicle's front seat. S was then arrested on suspicion of violation of H & S 11530.

Sergeant Hawk had no particularly strong feelings about the case. The suspect, Homer Jennings, gave the officers a residential address in a town fifty miles north of Vario County, and as far as Hawk knew, Jennings had not had any prior contact with their police department. Until the district attorney's office received a copy of the suspect's "rap sheet," a list of an individual's arrests and their dispositions compiled in Sacramento and sent upon their request to law enforcement agencies, neither the officer nor the prosecutor had any particular reason to believe that Jennings was, to use one of the phrases common to police and some prosecutors, a "bad ass."

Normally either the police department or the district attorney's office requests the rap sheet in the process of preparing for the preliminary hearing in felony cases held in the municipal court in the arresting jurisdiction. The prosecutor may use the rap sheet in determining whether to insist on the initial charges or, when the defense initiates the idea, reducing the charges in exchange for a plea at the time of the hearing. As a general rule, the longer the list of previous offenses, the less likely will the prosecutor consider a reduction, but we shall see that prosecutors do not attach uniform weights to prior offenses and do not agree on the significance of arrests without convictions indicated on the rap sheet.

If Jennings had been known as a "bad ass," someone with a record of repeated police contacts and arrests and in many cases a reputation for uncooperativeness after arrest, Hawk probably would have advocated issuing a felony complaint more vigorously. A "cooperative" suspect is not necessarily one who gives officers information with which to seek other arrests. The patrolman who makes the arrest normally does not participate in the investigative function in which informers play an important part, and he does not judge cooperativeness in terms of a willingness to give information but rather in terms of the extent to which the suspect submits to arrest peacefully and does not unduly insult the officer. As things stood, Hawk did not especially care how the office disposed of the case. Since most cases become routine events in the officers' experience, and since most officers—although by no means all—who take reports to the district attorney realize that the prosecutor is usually busy and appreciates a minimum of rhetoric, and because most officers realize that if they "cry wolf" they will lessen their credibility on serious crimes or repeat offenders, Sergeant Hawk approached the case casually. Besides, the arrest happened during the night shift, and Hawk, assigned to the day shift, had not discussed with the arresting officers whether they cared how the case was prosecuted.

To understand the process by which the office issues complaints on arrests like Jennings's requires a detour into the structure of the office. When reduced to the neat boxes of an organization chart, the office seems to respond effectively to its geographical and jurisdictional setting. A range of sparsely populated hills running roughly east and west divides the county geographically so that getting from the southern population center, Condenado, to the northern section containing many newer suburbs takes at least twenty minutes by car. The district attorney's main office occupies the top floor of the Superior Court building in Centerville, the county seat north of the hills, where the district attorney, Robert Nolan, spent nearly all his time. Because of the range of hills, the office also maintains the Condenado branch, where twelve of the thirty-six deputies worked. Except for the three

30

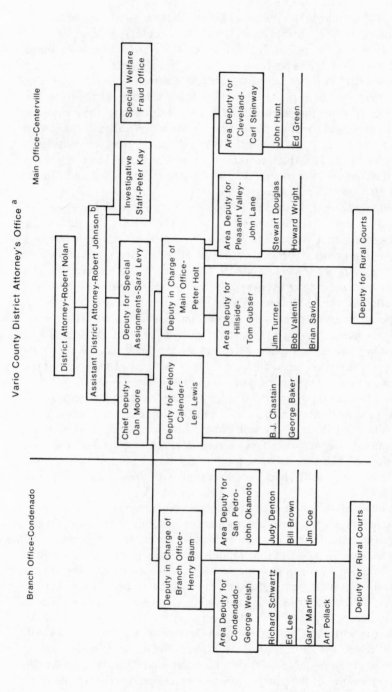

Figure 2-1. Organization Chart

Vario County District Attorney's Office [a]

Branch Office-Condenado

Main Office-Centerville

District Attorney-Robert Nolan

Assistant District Attorney-Robert Johnson [b]

Chief Deputy-Dan Moore

Deputy for Special Assignments-Sara Levy

Investigative Staff-Peter Kay

Special Welfare Fraud Office

Deputy for Felony Calender-Len Lewis

Deputy in Charge of Main Office-Peter Holt

Area Deputy for Hillside-Tom Gubser

Jim Turner
Bob Valenti
Brian Savio

B.J. Chastain
George Baker

Area Deputy for Pleasant Valley-John Lane

Stewart Douglas
Howard Wright

Area Deputy for Cleveland-Carl Steinway

John Hunt
Ed Green

Deputy for Rural Courts

Deputy in Charge of Branch Office-Henry Baum

Area Deputy for San Pedro-John Okamoto

Judy Denton
Bill Brown
Jim Coe

Area Deputy for Condendado-George Welsh

Richard Schwartz
Ed Lee
Gary Martin
Art Pollack

Deputy for Rural Courts

a. This chart designates positions held for the bulk of 1970 by the prosecutors discussed by name below

b. Position created August 1970

deputies who handled welfare fraud and related cases in separate offices in other towns, the remaining deputies worked in Centerville. The three deputies in the "family support division" rarely if ever played any part in the disposition of cases outside their field.

The office has organized the bulk of the personnel in both Centerville and Condenado to handle cases from the several municipalities and unincorporated areas on each side of the hills. The Condenado branch contained, in addition to the deputy in charge of the branch, two "area deputies" with five years experience, each of whom supervised personnel assigned to the two major municipal areas in the "south end," and a third younger deputy in charge of the smaller municipalities and unincorporated areas that make up the rest of the south end. The office organization chart specifies a simple chain of command: within their first six months, new deputies are assigned to an area; they are supervised by the area deputy, who in turn reports to the deputy in charge of the branch. The main office follows a similar organizational pattern, although superimposed upon it are the deputies who handle felonies during the pretrial preparation and negotiation phases in the superior court in Centerville.

The only significant question facing Hawk and the prosecutors was whether to file a felony complaint or a misdemeanor complaint against Jennings. The office handles felonies (cases that may be punished by a fine of $1000 or more or by state prison sentences) and misdemeanors (for which lesser fines and/or county jail sentences may be imposed) by different procedures, and the felony/misdemeanor distinction, like the county's geography, dictates the office's organization of manpower. The office by law prosecutes misdemeanors only in the nine municipal and justice courts, some of which, like Condenado's, handle the full range of crimes that occur in urban areas—thefts, drug offenses, traffic violations, batteries, and so forth—while others, like the rural justice court, in the small town of Clover, ninety minutes' drive north from Condenado, handle only the community's occasional public drunk or speeder. In 1970 areas with a population greater than 40,000 had municipal courts; those with less had justice courts (California Constitution Art. VI, Sec. 11). Six of these local courts consist of one judge, two of two judges, and one (Condenado) of three municipal court judges. Since prosecutors in Vario County file six out of every seven cases as misdemeanors, the office assigns most deputies in both branches to an area defined by the jurisdictional boundaries of the municipal and justice courts and assigns them responsibility for cases arising in those jurisdictions. A municipal or justice court judge also screens the remaining seventh of the cases (felonies) at a preliminary hearing held in the local court for the area in which the crime occurred. The preliminary hearing tests whether, from the evidence the prosecution presents, there is reason to believe that a crime has been committed and that the suspect committed it (Calif. Penal Code Sec.

872). In a few instances, the grand jury performs the same function by indictment. Once a felony complaint has survived the preliminary hearing, the office files the "information" of the preliminary hearing with the superior court and transfers the case file to what in 1969 was called the "felony division," where the prosecutors in that division, who had not previously seen the case, would guide it through the proceedings in the superior court in Centerville. In fewer than one in twenty cases does the judge find the evidence insufficient at this stage, and the municipal court judges appear to differ in the quality of evidence they deem sufficient at this stage. The roughly three to five dozen grand jury indictments each year put these cases directly into the superior court, thus bypassing the municipal court proceedings altogether.

George Welsh, a quiet man in his late thirties who had attempted unsuccessfully to set up a private practice in a small town two hundred miles to the north of the county before joining the office in 1964, served as area deputy for the Condenado jurisdiction and supervised the three deputies who handled the bulk of Condenado's proceedings for felonies. Normally Hawk took his felony reports to Welsh, and Welsh, a man whom most subordinates, police officers, and defense attorneys respected highly for his sense of "realism" and, on occasion, his compassion, would decide whether to file the case as a felony or as a misdemeanor, or to refuse to prosecute altogether.

In 1969, Welsh and the office were trying to adjust their approach to marijuana prosecutions to the increasing evidence of marijuana's widespread use and to the fact that juries seemed increasingly reluctant to bring in convictions for felonies even in clear-cut cases of possession of small quantities. By that time the sons and daughters of several police officers and one superior court judge, as well as of other "prominent" county figures, had been arrested for marijuana possession. Furthermore, several of Vario County's career prosecutors had heard that state prison administrators had objected to the state's judicial council that to make room for the rapidly increasing number of marijuana convicts they were forced to release prematurely individuals whom they considered far more potentially dangerous than marijuana-users. Legally, prosecutors had three options in charging someone found in possession of marijuana. If arrested with a "large" amount, the suspect could be prosecuted for "possession with intent to sell," a felony. In the absence of direct evidence of sale or attempted sale, the amount must be large enough to convince a jury that the suspect could not consume that great a quantity himself, a charge obviously ruled out in Jennings's case. Possession of any quantity of marijuana, down to a few "seeds and stems," may be charged as a felony under Health & Safety Code Sec. 11530, and this is where the office's real difficulties arose. While the charge was permissible in Jennings's case, some prosecutors doubted that possession of one or two cigarettes' worth of marijuana deserved felony treatment, and these prosecutors preferred either to charge the suspect with the misdemeanors of possessing marijuana "paraphernalia" or of being present knowingly in a place where marijuana is used (Sec. 11555 and 11556). (Three prosecutors volunteered to me that they had used marijuana themselves, and since I made no attempt to canvass them on the issue, others may have done so as well.) Or they could charge him with 11530 but add a note to the file to instruct the deputy to accept a plea to one of the two misdemeanors at the preliminary hearing.

In this regard Jennings's case was somewhat ambiguous. The matchbox contained more than enough for two cigarettes but less than enough to convince most juries that he intended to sell it. Furthermore, Jennings technically did not violate Sections 11555 or 11556, and if the attorney chose to do so, he could threaten to take the case to trial and force the office to go through the process of refiling the case as a felony. To force the prosecutor to have the suspect rearrested and to refile the case as a felony because the misdemeanor charge is unsustainable both exposes the client to a greater charge and requires him to pay bail a second time. For these practical reasons defense attorneys normally encourage clients to accept an unsustainable but more lenient charge where they see no clear way to defeat the more serious charge.

Then, too, the case contained some legal problems. It was not clear that a search for marijuana based simply on the observation of Zig-Zag cigarette papers was reasonable, since presumably some people still roll their own tobacco cigarettes. The California Supreme Court in 1955 adopted the "exclusionary" rule whereby evidence seized without a search warrant cannot be admitted in evidence unless the officer can demonstrate that the suspect might rid himself of inculpatory evidence before a search warrant could be obtained. On the other hand, while the prosecutors knew virtually nothing about Jennings, the fact that he was picked up in a "high-crime" neighborhood, as well as the fact that he was an older man found "committing" a crime that, when it is done experimentally, is usually done by the young, might make it wise to file the felony and then wait and see whether the rap sheet revealed previous arrests for possession and sale of marijuana.

How Welsh would have resolved the issue in 1969 is problematical, for while in theory officers take their cases to the more experienced area deputies, Welsh was that morning trying a felony in Centerville, so that Hawk could take the case to any of Condenado's less experienced deputies. Hawk took his files to Ed Lee, a twenty-eight-year-old deputy with about six months' experience in the office. Lee, the only Condenado deputy in the office at the time besides the complaint deputy, filed the case as a felony under Sec. 11530 after Hawk satisfied him that the two arresting officers were honest and diligent and had no motive to hide anything. (Had Hawk approached not Lee but David Snow that morning, the results might have been different, for Snow, who used marijuana himself, felt strongly that such cases should be prosecuted only as misdemeanors, and not at all when the case contained legal problems.)

Lee did not file the case without first checking with a superior. The office at irregular intervals circulates lists of those deputies who are experienced enough to authorize issuing felonies, although due to the rapidity of turnover the list is often outdated, and the deputy may simply turn for advice to any more experienced deputy. In this case Lee found John Okamoto, the area deputy for the neighboring San Pedro area, and secured his approval of the felony filng. The consultations to secure authorization of felonies can be cursory, especially in the rather frequent instances in which Welsh, generally attentive in this regard, was unavailable. This cursoriness was particularly evident in Jennings's case, because Okamoto preferred to let the inexperienced deputy "use his own best judgment" rather than dictate the deputy's decision.

In actually filing the case, Lee filled out the following form, suitable for both felony and misdemeanor charges, which he then sent together with the copies of the arrest and crime reports to a secretary:

(JUSTICE)
IN THE (MUNICIPAL) COURT OF THE_____JUDICIAL DISTRICT
(SUPERIOR)
PEOPLE OF THE STATE OF CALIFORNIA

vs   CRIMINAL COMPLAINT
_____   (Felony)
                                                      (Misdemeanor)
_____
(Defendant(s)
STATE OF CALIFORNIA) ss.
COUNTY OF VARIO   )

_____ being sworn, (ON INFO & BELIEF)

deposes and accuses _____

_____ defendant(s)

                (Felony)
of the crime of   (Misdemeanor) to wit: VIOLATION OF CALIFORNIA

_____ CODE SECTION _____
                                                 (number and description)

committed as follows, to wit: That said defendant(s) on or about

_____ at _____
in Vario County, State of California, did then and there unlawfully and wilfully (and feloniously)

She in turn typed out a formal complaint form, which Lee later signed, and she also prepared a manila, legal-sized folder on the Jennings case, into which she placed copies of the reports and the complaint. The secretary then took the signed complaint down the hall, together with the other felony and misdemeanor complaints initiated that day, and filed them with Condenado's court clerk.

The secretary routed Jennings's manila folder, along with the other felony folders she prepared that day, to the desk of the deputy in charge of the Condenado branch, Henry Baum. Although Baum did not have time to review each file carefully, his seven years' experience in the office had taught him to spot problems and loopholes quickly. Occasionally he would add a note to the file pointing out possible difficulties. More often, if he had any questions or suggestions, he casually mentioned them to the deputy who issued the case. The search problem in Jennings's case may have raised his eyebrows, but he did not advise, as he would in some cases with possible search problems, to "deal it out." Baum, although he did not insist upon it, since some deputies argue that "overfiling" constitutes legal blackmail, generally preferred the strategy of filing "high" and dealing down to a final settlement, and he occasionally recommended that policy to deputies.

Jennings's manila folder then moved from Baum's desk to Welsh's. Since Welsh did not file the case himself, he followed his general rule of assigning the task of "putting on" the preliminary hearing to the issuing deputy, in this case, Lee. Since the preliminary hearing normally follows the arrest by about two weeks, occasions arise in the multijudge courts when the issuing deputy already has a trial scheduled for the time set by the court for the "prelim."[5] Often these schedule conflicts don't reveal themselves until a day or two before, and deputies can find themselves putting on another deputy's prelim at the last minute.

No such conflicts arose in Jennings's case, however, and Lee's job of putting on the prelim seemed to present few problems. He would simply put the two officers on the stand and, using their reports as his guide, ask them to recreate for the judge what they had recounted in the report. Lee anticipated correctly that Dennis Childers, Jennings's twenty-six-year-old public defender, would probe the search question at the preliminary hearing, but he planned to rely on his background knowledge of the law in that area, since the municipal court judge scheduled to preside at the preliminary hearing, Judge Bailey, was generally regarded as impatient with such legal technicalities. While many prosecuting and defense attorneys agreed in interviews that most, though not all, municipal court judges are reluctant to throw out a prosecution at this initial stage, the defense bar seemed generally uncritical of this tendency. Section 872 of the Penal Code states that if "it appears from the examination that a public offense has been committed, and there is sufficient cause to believe the defendant guilty thereof," the judge must hold the defendant to answer. Most defense attorneys feel that this law is so loosely worded as to permit wide judicial discretion at the preliminary hearing, and they believe the police do generally succeed in making out a *prima facie* case against the suspect, which is all that is required to support holding the defendant to answer.

The preliminary hearing usually provides prosecuting and defense attorneys with their first chance to discuss the possibility of settling the case short of trial, and this is particularly true when public defenders represent the defendant, since their work load prevents them from looking carefully at a case until a day or two before the prelim. The defense does not present its case at the "prelim," and defense attorneys have little reason to research and prepare the details of their case then. Some private attorneys do, however, adopt the strategy of seeking dispositions as early in the case as possible, since they reason that the thinner the file and the less the district attorney has thought about the case, the less dangerous he will consider the suspect. Other defense attorneys, however, will adopt the opposite strategy of "settling on the courthouse steps," settling at the time of trial, on the theory that only at the last minute will the prosecutor so thoroughly investigate his case as to be aware of its defects. Both of these strategies, depending on circumstances to be examined below, may succeed.

Jennings's case, as we have seen, did not dictate any obvious solution. The amount was sufficient for perhaps six joints, and the suspect was old enough so that, if he used marijuana at all, Lee thought it plausible to conclude that Jennings used it regularly and conceivably could be a dealer with a small supply at the moment. Whether to accept a misdemeanor plea, or at least to promise that the D.A.'s office would not press for a state prison sentence, depended on Jennings's rap sheet, but that also was ambiguous. The rap sheet revealed two convictions for passing forged checks (the amounts were not specified) and revealed that Jennings had done 120 days of county jail time for the second offense. But the rap sheet dated the first of these offenses in 1961 and the second in 1963, and since Jennings had apparently stayed "clean" since then, Lee did not foreclose the possibility of reducing charges if the defense suggested it.

Meanwhile, Jennings's attorney, Dennis Childers, decided to tackle the legality of the search head on. His client had firmly maintained his innocence and had explained the presence of marijuana in his car to Childers with a story that was not in itself terribly convincing but which Childers tended to believe because of Jennings's sincerity and because of his ability to provide many details, none of which were contradictory. Jennings, who was free on bail, also told Childers in their conference the day before the hearing of his reluctance to plead to a misdemeanor charge that involved some jail sentence, for fear of losing his job. The fact that Jennings held a job did not automatically disqualify him from public representation. In his initial contact with the interviewing secretary, in the public defender's office, Jennings indicated that he had no personal financial assets, that his job as a janitor paid $105 per week, part of which he sent to his wife, from whom he was separated. Since family size, financial debts and assets, and other factors affect the public defender's decision to take the case, no single personal income amount qualifies or disqualifies all applicants from aid. One of the supervising public defenders, Joe Ryan, indicated to me that the average cut-off was probably around $5000 annual income, but he agreed that, since the office cannot afford to investigate the financial claims of most clients thoroughly, perhaps a quarter to a third of the clients exceeded that amount.

Most settlements at the preliminary hearing stage involve a reduction of the charge from a felony to a misdemeanor. While at later stages felonies may be compromised when the prosecutor eliminates some of the felony charges or promises not to recommend a state prison sentence, promises of this kind are not worth much in municipal court, because they require the informal approval of the superior court judge who will impose sentence on the remaining felony charges, and no superior court judge will do so until the file is put before him. If, on the other hand, the felony charges are reduced to misdemeanors, the municipal court judge will impose sentence, and he can and does in chambers indicate his position on the sentencing before the defendant would enter the plea at the time set for the preliminary hearing. In short, the defendant and his attorney need to be assured of the outcome of a plea before entering it, and in municipal court no one is in a position to assure the sentence disposition on a plea to a felony because the sentencing judge has not yet seen the case. Furthermore, Childers knew of cases where felony division prosecutors had refused to accept felony plea arrangements in municipal court, and he would not, regardless of the potential strength of his case, plead his client guilty to a felony without some indication of the position of a felony division deputy. Following Jennings's wishes, therefore, instead of discussing a reduction with Lee before the prelim, Childers decided to challenge the search.

At the preliminary hearing Lee examined the two officers, who, with little elaboration, repeated the substance of their report. On cross-examination Childers established, to Lee's surprise, that when the officers searched Jennings at the time of his arrest, they found no package of Zig-Zag cigarette papers. The reporting officer testified that he had seen the package of Zig-Zag papers and denied that he might in fact have mistaken a red package of Pall Mall cigarettes for the red package of Zig-Zags, the position Jennings took at his trial. Armed with this new information, Childers pressed the legal arguments against the search before Judge Bailey, who, as expected, held Jennings to answer but indicated to Childers in chambers that the search issue should be pursued in superior court.

As a legal matter, the fact that the officers could not produce the Zig-Zag papers in court did not invalidate the search, since the reasonableness of the search hinges on the question of whether the officers, though mistaken, reasonably *perceived* the situation as one requiring a search. Besides, the officers indicated on the stand at the preliminary hearing that both of them had taken their eyes off Jennings while they searched his car, a practice, Childers pointed out, that violated routine police procedures, so that Jennings might have thrown the Zig-Zags to the street unnoticed. That testimony may have reinforced the finding that the search was reasonable.

After the preliminary hearing, Ed Lee sent the Jennings file, in which he put a note about the missing Zig-Zags, to the felony division in the main office in Centerville. In 1969 the felony division was simply the designation given four prosecutors who, on the basis of their experience and reputation, handled the pretrial preparations and negotiations in all felonies. The members of the division had virtually complete discretion to dispose of cases as they wished, especially because the district attorney for the previous ten years, Roger Savich, had just taken his newly won seat in the California senate. Dan Moore, the chief deputy district attorney and a man with twelve years' experience in the office (the longest of any deputy), supervised the office, but he did not intrude on the decisions of the felony division, since both he and two of the deputies in the felony division each had hopes that the County Board of Supervisors would appoint himself to the vacant position.

One or more members of the felony division would normally have guided Jennings's case through the routine of arraignment (the formal reading of the charges to the defendant and the entering of his plea, which in Jennings's cases was a firm "not guilty") to the pretrial negotiations with defense counsel, negotiations in which the superior court judge in charge of the criminal calendar for that year, David Shapiro, actively sought to push the parties to a settlement short of a trial. By law the trial must take place within sixty days of the filing of the information or indictment unless the defendant requests an extension. Most defendants who make bail prefer extensions, and many defendants who do not make bail do not disapprove of such extensions, since they often receive credit against their sentence for the time they serve prior to conviction. In Jennings's case these proceedings took not sixty days but twelve months, for following the arraignment and a postponement to prepare his arguments, Childers filed a motion in superior court to challenge the legality of the search, to which Len Lewis of the felony division responded. Childers moved under Penal Code Section 1538.5, which permits the defense, following arraignment, to move to prevent the introduction at trial of any evidence illegally seized. In this case, a ruling to suppress the evidence of the seized marijuana would, of course, require the prosecution to dismiss the case. Judge Shapiro rejected Childers's arguments in June of 1969 and concurred with the prosecution's argument that Zig-Zag papers were so commonly associated with the making of marijuana cigarettes that officers who discovered Zig-Zags incident to a lawful stop procedure could reasonably institute a search for marijuana on that basis.

Childers then appealed to the California Court of Appeals. In late October of 1969 the appellate court also rejected Childers's motion, and due to the approaching holidays, the parties agreed to postpone the setting of a trial date until after the new year, when a new superior court criminal calendar judge would replace Shapiro. In January of 1970, the new criminal calendar judge, William Jensen, set the trial date for Monday, March 16.

Meanwhile, in late August of 1969, the Board of Supervisors had appointed Bob Nolan, a former prosecutor, the new district attorney. Nolan, at the beginning of 1970, abolished the felony division and created in its place a "superior court calendar division," headed by the Chief Deputy Dan Moore, to handle felony preparations. One purpose of the new arrangement was to improve communication between the municipal court and superior court deputies by including the area deputies in an office conference, held before the opening of pretrial negotiations, in which the office would determine the position to take on the case regarding a "deal." This conference met from three o'clock to five o'clock each Thursday afternoon. The conference, supervised by Moore, determined the office position on each of the cases to be discussed with defense attorneys in Judge Jensen's chambers eight days later at what was called the "pretrial conference." Judge Jensen, who was continuing the form if not the substance of practices established by Judge Shapiro, in turn scheduled the pretrial conference a month in advance of the trial date. The conference in the district attorney's office, which Moore, Leonard Lewis (a man with ten years' experience), and his assistant (one of four different deputies who, due to high office turnover, assisted Lewis during 1970), and the area deputies attended, was informally named the "pre-pretrial conference." Lewis and his assistant actually performed the bulk of the pretrial preparations and presentations of felonies in 1970.

At the pre-pretrial conference in early February 1970, Moore, Lewis, and Welsh agreed that they could promise Childers they would concur in the probation report sentence recommendation and would not insist on a state prison sentence, but Moore did not feel the office could commit itself, regardless of the probation report, to a recommendation of no jail sentence whatsoever, which was the only condition on which Childers indicated Jennings might plead. It had become increasingly clear to Welsh that, despite even a fairly solid prosecution case, the jury might not convict Jennings of the felony, but Moore, whose administrative tasks had for the past few years prevented him from trying any cases, did not have Welsh's feeling for the sentiments of Vario County juries.

Moore made a number of arguments favoring insistence upon some jail time and for taking the case to trial: that marijuana possession "deserved" some jail time, that the office should not establish a precedent for agreeing to no-jail dispositions to felony cases when Bob Nolan faced the first election challenge to his position less than five months later, and that, in such circumstances, an isolated jury defeat would expose Nolan to less criticism than would a pattern of lenient and bargained dispositions.[7] Besides, he asked, how was Jennings going to explain away the presence of the marijuana in his car? While the reticent Welsh may have disagreed with these criteria for determining the office posture in the case, he did not challenge Moore's arguments.

Ed Lee, who by that time had gained enough misdemeanor trial experience so that his superiors felt satisfied that he was able to handle a felony, got the trial assignment from Welsh after the pretrial conference before Judge Jensen failed to change either the prosecution or defense position. Had Judge Shapiro presided at the pretrial conference, he might have engineered a settlement, for Shapiro felt strongly that superior court time should not be wasted trying either cases that the parties could resolve but for their need to save face, or cases that presented matters normally handled at the misdemeanor level. Since the filing of Jennings's case over a year earlier, the state of California had, through Section 17 of the Penal Code, permitted prosecution of marijuana possession cases either as felonies or misdemeanors, and some Vario County prosecutors had then begun to adopt misdemeanor dispositions in many cases similar to Jennings's. Thus, Shapiro might in rather blunt language have advised the prosecution that he would grant straight probation without jail time to Jennings to save a trial. Judge Jensen, for reasons to be explored more thoroughly in chapter 4, declined to influence pretrial negotiations on these grounds.

The case was Lee's first felony trial, and Lee speculated that Welsh probably gave it to him, rather than a more experienced deputy, because he sensed it was a "dog," a loser. At the trial before another superior court judge, the officers testified as they did at the preliminary hearing, and the reporting officer repeated several times his conviction that he had seen Zig-Zags, not Pall Malls, in the suspect's shirt pocket. Childers, of course, faced the task of explaining how the marijuana got in Jennings's car without Jennings's complicity. On the witness stand, Jennings told the following story: He had come down for the weekend to visit the apartment of some friends who had planned a party for that Sunday night. He had had some wine at the party, but had developed a headache and had gone to sleep in the bedroom for several hours. He had awakened around 11:30 and had, to clear his head, gone out on the friend's second-story back porch for some fresh air. From the back porch, he noticed what appeared to be several juveniles standing around his car, parked on the street below. He called his hostess, who came to the porch and observed the same thing. Since he had to return north in time to get to work the following morning, he decided to leave then and walked down to his car to investigate. As he approached, he noticed that several youths were actually in the car, and as he shouted at them, they all ran off. He said he smelled what he presumed was cigarette smoke in the car, but didn't think anything of it until his arrest. He then got in his car and was proceeding toward the freeway when the officers pulled him over. He denied any knowledge of the marijuana and said he felt the kids must have dropped it there when he scared them off. Childers also put Jennings's hostess on the stand, and she testified she had been out on the porch with the defendant and had also seen what appeared to be juveniles loitering around his car.

The jury acquitted Jennings after deliberating an hour and a half.

Ed Lee and I drove back to Condenado together after the jury brought in its verdict. Lee was of course disappointed after losing his first felony trial, although the jurymen with whom he and Childers chatted afterwards had assured him that they felt he had put on his case effectively. What persuaded the jury, apparently, was a discrepancy in the evidence that neither Lee nor Childers had noticed. The officer had testified on cross-examination that a search of Jennings's clothing at the jail that Sunday night failed to produce any traces of marijuana in the pockets. Yet one of the jurors observed that the matchbox of marijuana introduced as evidence had leaked its contents inside the plastic bag in which the police preserved it as evidence. The juror asked to examine the exhibit in the jury room and pointed out to the other jurors in the jury room that the two wooden matchbox parts did not fit together snugly and that when he shook the matchbox it would spill some of its contents. Lee, who at no point indicated to me that he doubted Jennings's guilt (he thought Jennings's explanation for the presence of the marijuana in his car was a typical "cock-and-bull" story invented to beat the rap) attributed the discrepancy to the likelihood that the matchbox had developed its leak during its year in the Condenado Police Department evidence locker as officers pawed over it in search of evidence in other cases or dumped heavier items on top of it. But, although I sensed that Lee could not quite bring himself to concede that the jury could entertain a reasonable doubt about Jennings's guilt, neither Lee nor his fellow deputies seemed terribly concerned about the loss of the case. In fact, as we shall see in chapter 5, the few deputies who worried about the case at all worried about why the case went to trial in the first place, not the fact that it was lost. What concerned these deputies about the case was that it illustrated an office tendency to get "locked-in" to taking cases to trial that might well be lost.

Implications of Jennings's Case and
Outline of Following Chapters

Jennings's case might have concluded differently if different people had handled the case at different stages. Had Hawk initially consulted the experienced Welsh rather than the inexperienced Lee, Welsh might have insisted that the police produce the Zig-Zags before initiating the prosecution. Had Hawk found Snow rather than Lee, Snow might have issued the case as a misdemeanor. Had Judge Shapiro rather than Judge Jensen presided at the pretrial conference, the case might have been settled by a plea and disposition that Jennings could accept. The disposition of cases regularly depends on the knowledge and preferences of actors, and the diversity of knowledge and preferences among actors is one of the several kinds of diversity and uncertainty that make it difficult for deputies responsible for managing the prosecutor's office to impose standard practices for uniform disposition of cases.

Critical evaluations of the operation of criminal administration in the United States have frequently employed pejoratively the metaphor of the assembly line to characterize the disposition of criminal cases. An assembly line has a considerable capacity to turn out products of uniform quality by controlling or programming the types of inputs, their rate of movement, and the sequence in which they are combined. The assembly line gives little room for improvising, innovating, or learning as the task is performed, and it is this characteristic of assembly lines that leads critics to use the term pejoratively, because the fact-finding procedures of a trial are designed to encourage learning and open-mindedness and discourage premature conclusions based on inadequate information. The law specifies a process of establishing guilt through trial in which it is presumed that the characteristics of a case evident at the outset cannot capture its full complexity. Law presumes innocence and limits the introduction of certain kinds of evidence, hearsay evidence, for example, because human perceptions are rarely synoptic and generally reflect personal needs and experiences. The devices of adversary presentation before a jury of laymen and rules of evidence collectively seek to prevent the simple categorization or pigeon-holing of cases. As the American Bar Association's Joint Conference report of 1958 put it, an "adversary presentation seems the only effective means for combatting this human tendency to judge too swiftly in terms of the familiar that which is not yet fully known" (Report of the Joint Conference, 1958, pp. 1159-60).

Jennings's case illustrates that, in Vario County, at least, the prosecutor's handling of cases does not resemble an assembly line because, unlike the assembly line, prosecutors cannot fully specify in advance what materials they will have and how they will combine them. The "constants" on an assembly line are the prosecutor's "variables," both among different cases and within one case as it proceeds to disposition. To the attorneys and judges of Jennings's case, both the law and the facts were ambiguous entities the character of which changed as the case progressed.

The following three chapters review the characteristics of the prosecutorial process in Vario County that resisted programming, a review that describes the explicit and unsuccessful attempts of several members of that office to program the decisions of their subordinates. By "programming" I mean the process whereby management personnel prescribe for production personnel an objective or objectives to be achieved and, on the basis of information available at the beginning of the production process, specify the actions production personnel should take to achieve the objective.[8] These chapters will analyze the characteristics of the Vario County office that collectively encouraged individuated case dispositions and discouraged a programming or hierarchical style of management. (See figure 1-1.)

3

Prosecutors' Backgrounds and Expectations

What kind of men become prosecutors and why? How do their backgrounds, their personalities, and their expectations influence the decisions they make? In Vario County at least, men and women in similar legal and official roles did not possess similar family histories, personal preferences, or interpersonal skills. This diversity complicated the task of programming office decisions to achieve uniform case dispositions. The characteristics prosecutors did share—a legal education and, for most, a desire to enter private practice—also inhibited managing deputies' capacity to discourage nonconforming behavior.[1] This chapter describes both the shared and the diverse characteristics of prosecutors that together reduced the degree of managerial control of prosecutorial behavior. However, analysis of questionnaire results concerning backgrounds, career goals, and attitudes of prosecutors obscures the critical point that many prosecutors dispose of cases and define their obligations to one another largely in terms of their perceptions of "whole" personalities. Prosecutors think that the decisions they make depend heavily on the personalities involved.[2] This chapter therefore combines the statistical results from questionnaires and interviews with short biographies of several Vario County prosecutors. Perhaps the chief deputy, Dan Moore, is the most instructive personality, since he held considerable managerial responsibility and since he attempted at several times during the year to control felony dispositions, both by making rules and by deciding personally which position the office would take on many felonies. The contrasts between the backgrounds, career motives, and tasks of supervising deputies like Dan Moore and those of operating deputies help explain the inability of supervising deputies to program decisions.

When Dan Moore graduated with honors from Hastings College of Law in 1951, most of the men who were to work under him in 1970 were still in elementary school. And when, at the age of thirty-four, Dan Moore joined the Vario County office in 1958, after a brief and unsuccessful stint in private practice followed by five years with a title insurance company in Los Angeles, the majority of 1970's prosecutors had not yet graduated from high school.[3] Moore was atypical not only in his age and length of experience but because he entered the career relatively late in life. Only three other prosecutors had had any experience in private practice, and only one of these, District Attorney Nolan, had had extensive experience as defense counsel in criminal cases. For two-thirds of all prosecutors in Vario County, and for nearly all under the median age of thirty, prosecution was the first and only job since finishing law school.

The six senior deputies, although not formally designated as "senior" or "superior" by the office, were District Attorney Nolan, Robert Johnson, the assistant district attorney whom Nolan appointed in the summer of 1970, the two branch supervisors, Henry Baum in Condenado and Peter Hoff in Centerville, superior court calendar deputy Len Lewis, and a "special services" deputy named Sarah Levy, whose role remained somewhat undefined during the year. The senior deputies averaged forty-two years of age; their length of service in the office varied from Johnson's few months to Moore's 144. Moore, like the six other senior deputies, rarely tried cases himself. By his own recollection, he had not tried more than a half dozen cases after he became the chief criminal deputy in 1963, and he had tried none in the last five years. In 1970 only two of the six other senior deputies tried any cases. Johnson, Lewis, and Baum took no cases to trial in 1970. Hoff took two cases, and Levy took one. The area deputies (like Welsh), whose average age was thirty-four, tried cases more frequently, on the average of roughly one per month. But men in their middle and late twenties with less than two years' experience handled all the misdemeanor cases and handled the initial screening of most felony complaints. Because Moore's administrative duties cut him off from contacts with judges, defense attorneys, and with the complexities of cases, younger prosecutors tended to discount his recommendations, because they felt he was "out of touch."

Dan Moore grew up in a working-class family in Fresno; his father was a railroad brakeman. Like Moore, most deputies were neither born nor raised in Vario County; as we shall see later, this contributed to the absence of any strong ties between the office and any local party or interest group.[4] Unlike Moore, however, Vario County's prosecutors did not come from predominantly working-class homes. Four prosecutors listed their father's occupation as distinctly professional—two physicians, a lawyer, and an architect—and seven more listed occupations safely classified as executive and/or managerial positions in large businesses. Seven listed farming or other manual labor, and the remainder was hard to classify: a college football coach, a furrier, and a tavern owner, for example.[5]

Ten of the prosecutors received their bachelor's degree from the University of California system, three from the California state college system, and three more from private universities in California. The majority of the remainder graduated from nationally known out-of-state colleges. Two were Dartmouth graduates, and Northwestern, Carleton (Minnesota), the University of Wisconsin, the University of Pennsylvania, Rutgers, and Lewis and Clark College (Oregon) each produced one. Sixty-three percent of the prosecuting attorneys received their law degrees from one of the University of California system's law schools (Boalt Hall, Hastings, or UCLA). Three more graduated from the University of San Francisco, five from Golden Gate School of Law, and one each graduated from Loyola, University of Indiana, and the University of Chicago. An identical percentage, 63 percent, of private attorneys sampled received their degrees from one of the University of California system law schools. Although I did not attempt to discover the law school class ranking of the prosecutors, I sensed that most prosecutors had not done work in law school substantially above the average. Several admitted to me how pleased they were to discover that they did not have to submit a transcript of their grades when they applied for a position in the office.

Dan Moore had by 1970 made a career of criminal prosecution. When the county supervisors passed over him for the position of district attorney, and then a year later in 1970, when Nolan did not appoint him to the new position of assistant district attorney, he talked briefly about leaving the office, but felt he could not, with a family of five, afford to take the cut from his $24,000 salary. (Beginning salary was approximately $11,500.) At his age, with his specialized skills, he probably would have had difficulty finding a law firm that would offer him a comparable salary. Most men who joined the office, however, had little or no expectation of making it a career, and most deputies listed purely pragmatic reasons for taking the job. Twenty-one deputies said they wanted trial experience; nine indicated it was an "available" or "secure" job where "nothing else looked better." Only seven indicated either they were attracted to law enforcement or public service. Two-thirds of those interviewed indicated they could imagine themselves having begun work in the public defender's office instead of the district attorney's office, and only four, including Moore, rejected the possibility of leaving the office to work for the public defender. (One of these four, late in 1970, did in fact do so.) Only seven of thirty prosecutors questioned indicated that they expected to be in the office in 1975. Five of these were, like Moore, senior deputies.

Although most senior deputies expected to complete their professional careers in the office, none rejected the possibility of becoming a judge, though less than 20 percent of the county's judiciary had any prosecutorial experience, and the office is not known as a stepping-stone to the bench. None of the younger deputies reported any active interest in a judicial position. Most had either given it no thought or said they would find the work, especially at the municipal court level, tedious, repetitive, and frustrating. Of the remaining deputies, most expected to be in private practice in the county or in the area within five years, although a substantial number (seven) said they really had no idea where they would be. All of those anticipating entering private practice planned a general, essentially civil practice, a realistic expectation, since the criminal volume in the county supported only a half dozen private attorneys who devoted more than half their time to criminal matters.

A review of the careers of seventy-four prosecutors employed in the county who have left the office since 1959 tends to confirm that the expectations of the younger deputies are realistic. Twenty-five prosecutors (including two Negro ex-deputies) now practice privately in the county, and seventeen more do so in the general area. One has become a superior court judge in the county and one is a judge in a small county in the Sierras. Six are in private practice outside the area; one is deceased; one is retired; two are in business; one returned to his earlier career of police work; and five could not be located. The remainder are now in some form of public service. Six became public defenders; one is with the attorney general's office; one, a Negro, and Nolan's political opponent in 1970, heads the Legal Services office in the county; one works for the Securities Exchange Commission; two are prosecutors in other counties; one works with a city attorney's office nearby; and former district attorney Savich is now a state legislator. Len Lewis described one more prosecutor as a "big bullshitter; he's now got some cushy job with that T.V. Repair Board in Sacramento." Since the office has constantly expanded since 1959, it is difficult to calculate a turnover rate per year, but eleven of thirty-six left the office in 1970.

In some respects these characteristics of the Vario County district attorney's office and its members resemble characteristics of most purposeful organizations: age and educational background separate superiors and subordinates, and occupants of different roles see different slices of organizational operations and develop conflicting priorities and preferences that must be constantly reconciled. In the prosecutor's office, however, several factors tend to magnify the divisive or pluralizing effect of these differences. First, age and educational background particularly differentiate superiors and subordinates in law, because the assumptions about crime and the requirements of due process changed rather dramatically in the 1960s. Younger deputies, the majority in Vario County, had very recently completed an educational experience in which both the classroom and the informal discussion among students tended to legitimate the due process requirements articulated by the Warren Court in the 1960s. Furthermore, legal education in the 1960s encouraged criticism of assumptions underlying military policy in Vietnam and domestic economic and social policies that in turn fostered the habit of skepticism about other policies, including assumptions about the causes and treatment of crime. Henry Baum, Peter Hoff, and Dan Moore did not appear to share many younger deputies' implicit appreciation for the legitimacy of due process or their skepticism about social affairs and processes. In part because of the differences in educational experiences, the senior deputies' preferences for case strategies and dispositions struck some young deputies as questionable. More important, at least Hoff and Baum understood this difference and therefore did not seek to impose their own point of view on younger deputies. They tended to let deputies "use their own judgment," both because they sensed their own educational referents had been undercut and because they did not welcome the implicit criticism from younger deputies that they were incapable of adjusting to newer professional norms themselves.

Second, as we have already mentioned, the career goal of the deputies themselves, the desire for a successful private practice, gave the private bar and the judiciary a capacity to reward attorneys for their honesty, candor, and "realism" that at times undercut the preferences of supervisors.

Finally, the work of the office itself, unlike the work of many organizations, places the bulk of discretionary judgments at the bottom of the organizational hierarchy. James Q. Wilson describes how police administrators face a similarly inverted pyramid of discretion that distinguishes their administrative setting from that of a business executive.[6] The executive makes the major discretionary decisions on which organizational performance and success depend. The behavior of their subordinates can be effectively programmed by rules to fit the needs of executive decisions. But it is the patrolman and the deputy prosecutor at the lower rungs of the organizational ladder who make the decisions on which organizational effectiveness depends, and there are few clear cause/effect guides for programming the behavior of these subordinates to realize goals a superior may have.

Contrasting Approaches to Criminal Prosecution

The distinction this section draws between Dan Moore and a younger deputy, Richard Schwartz, parallels the distinction between order and learning drawn in chapter 1.

The Formalist: Dan Moore

Dan Moore performed a variety of administrative duties. He supervised the selection of personnel,[7] he coordinated the needs of the attorneys with the resources of the clerical staff, he collected, tabulated, and analyzed the statistics concerning the office's performance, and he supervised the "pre-pretrial" conferences. He approached these duties, especially the gathering of statistics, in a way I have designated as "formalistic." Moore believed that human events and behavior ought to obey both legal rules and generalizations or theories about human motives, and he seemed frequently irritated and frustrated by events that he thought ought to conform to some generalized rule, theory, or norm but that failed to do so. He was a formalist in the sense, then, that rules, theories, and generalizations guided his behavior, and these guides often displaced search for concrete information. Consider:

1. He was inclined to respond to what he perceived to be an office problem by making a rule to cover it. When at one point he observed four deputies chatting in one office, he ruled that no more than three people could be in an office at one time, a rule the deputies completely ignored. And to encourage efficient case settlement, Moore ruled, with Nolan's approval, that

the office would not accept a plea in the last seven days before trial, a rule that was also honored in the breach, as we shall see.

2. But Moore did more than make rules to cover problems; he searched for generalizations and theories to explain events and guide action. He kept in his desk two pages of rules of "good management," rules that included such directives as:

Let each employee know how he is getting along.
Tell an employee in advance about changes that will affect him.
How to handle problem:
    Determine objectives.
    Get the facts.
    Review the record.
    What policies, rules, regulations apply?
    Talk with individuals concerned.
    Get opinions and feelings.
    Be sure you have the whole story.
    Weigh and decide: What possible actions are there?
    Check each action against objectives weighing effect on individual, group, and pro-
      duction. Don't jump to conclusions.

The irony of these pages of good management rules was that Moore did not in fact follow them himself. His belief that he could manage effectively by referring to a list of rules of good management in his desk indicated the type of mind that often failed to "get the facts" and that tended to "jump to conclusions."

3. Moore believed that the prosecuting attorney and the legal system could and did operate as an administrative system to realize moral values by applying general cause/effect statements to concrete problems. During a conversation with me he said:

Justice is something we always try to achieve. We don't always succeed, but there is a goal here we all try to reach. . . . I don't think you can have a legal system that's not based on a moral code, that has a moral sense. . . . As a prosecutor I'm completely above board. I will justify anything we do. I wouldn't be in this job if I didn't feel I could justify publicly every bargain I make. I have never yet heard of an innocent defendant being convicted by this office. Of course, some people claim that they're innocent, but the facts show otherwise. We lean over backwards in this office. In fact, we just about go so far as to offer a polygraph to anybody who wants one, on the only condition that if it shows they're guilty, the results can be admitted. We've got two very good polygraph operators. One of them has been at it since World War II. You can't run a machine that long without being very good at it.

Moore's belief that the criminal administration system could achieve goals by rational analysis, e.g., by using the polygraph, led him to minimize the importance of the presumption of innocence. He believed that guilt and innocence were factual, not legal, constructs, and he justified jail and prison sentences because he assumed that incarceration can rehabilitate. He strongly agreed, for example, with the statement: "Where there is doubt about an individual's guilt, and he is merely fighting the case on its technicalities, this can indicate a lack of contrition on his part that will influence our feelings about the punishment he deserves." Moore commented in the follow-up interview:

There's no doubt about this. If he holds back or if he doesn't give a shit, I don't have any hesitation. If he's fighting the system, well, it's hard to think how he can be rehabilitated if he's fighting the system. Of course, you can say he's just exercising his rights, but the system would break down if everybody pushed every possible loophole to the ultimate.

In my interviews and conversations with Moore, he seemed frequently frustrated or irritated by those factors that he felt interfered with rational case dispositions: irritations with appellate court decisions, with political hassles with the Board of Supervisors, with the idiosyncrasies of local judges, with the tactics of defense attorneys, and with police sloppiness or deliberate ignorance of legal and evidentiary rules. Moore had taken steps to remove police officers by threatening to prosecute those who were discovered violating the law. "I personally eliminated several police officers, one with eighteen years of experience, for taking a sack of charcoal. That doesn't seem like much, but in 365 days that can add up to a lot of charcoal." Although Moore does not condemn the courtesy system, in which police officers do not ticket other officers, judges, or prosecutors for any but the worst traffic offenses ("If they stop a guy and let him go, that has a definite deterrent effect. I don't want the guys over at highway patrol to think I'm an ass"), he does condemn the code of silence whereby officers refuse to reveal or volunteer information concerning another officer's transgressions. "I don't think you should have men as police officers who operate under that code, but we do have that code in police forces. That's bad."

These irritations reflect real constraints within which prosecutors must operate, but they also illustrate a personality and a quality of thought that, because others perceived them as critical or threatening or simply unrealistic, led deputies to discount the significance of instructions and suggestions Moore made. Moore's frequent use of generalized cause/effect statements made him look at times inconsistent and foolish, because these statements so frequently ignored the complex and practical difficulties of cases with which his subordinates had to wrestle.

Moore did not think of himself as having a decision-making or policy-making power different in any way from the authority of other senior deputies in the office. He did not sense that he held any veto power over the decisions of other senior deputies. Senior deputies, including Moore, assumed that the "boss" bore the authority for overall direction of the office, and the boss's actual reluctance to do so in 1970 did not prompt others to assume the role of court of last resort. Thus, in describing how he felt about office practices, Moore expressed frustration with the necessity of coping with events and compromises that were essentially beyond his control. For example, with respect to filing and prosecuting cases raising questionable evidentiary issues, Moore noted:

Of course, we've got two problems here: how I feel about things and how they're actually done. I'm absolutely opposed to filing charges to further investigation, for example. The police like often to do this, and a lot of people in the office do it. I think it's wrong. . . . We've had differences of opinion on what to do about searches and seizures. Should we go ahead and issue and let the judge decide, or should we refuse to issue and go to the police departments and get some corrective measures going? And there's been disagreement on whether we should file the case to shake down people—I shouldn't use that expression on tape—and try to use this as a means for getting a guy to plead, which is a form of intimidation I don't believe in. . . . But there are differences in personal philosophy. John Lane would be less likely to issue on something than Jim Turner. Turner is young and gung-ho, and he tends to look at things from a police point of view. I think he'll change; you have to be here a while before you learn, and pretty soon you begin to look at the case and say, "What's the evidence?" My philosophy is that if it won't fly, don't try to make it fly. . . . If you can't pin it on the guy, don't charge him on the assumption that you'll make the case later. But a lot of people charge with the police theory in mind, which is just the opposite of mine. All of this has been to my detriment. My political acumen has not been too great on these things.

Moore is most critical of those aspects of prosecution, particularly the filing of cases, for which he has least responsibility. Regarding the disposition of felony cases in which he does participate, Moore is generally reluctant to dismiss cases or to reduce them for fear of embarrassment to the office. He said, "I think that once it's filed as a felony in superior court, we better be able to prove it's a felony." In one case in which a defendant was charged with the rape of a girl and the kidnapping of her boyfriend, whom he forced to leave the scene of the rape (Penal Code Sec. 207, the kidnapping section, covers any moving of a person against his will, and hence is frequently charged in addition to robbery, rape, or other violations that involve a short-term, short-distance moving of a victim.), Moore refused to drop the kidnapping charge despite the suggestion that to do so would more likely avoid a trial and would probably not affect the sentence. He argued, "Where you have the boy and the public to think about that would look very bad. After what he did, the press could make us look very sick for dropping the kidnapping charge on a boy who was held at knifepoint. . . . We try to give the public the feeling that we're a good honest outfit that makes some sense of the criminal justice system, so people can go out of their houses at night and feel secure."

Moore does not feel comfortable in interpersonal settings that call for easy camaraderie and compromise. An intelligent man, his ability to analyze the subtle legal strengths and weaknesses of a case is at times hidden behind an appearance of gruffness and occasionally of suspicion that tends to put those who do not know him on the defensive. I experienced this facet of Moore's character during my first meeting with him, and I observed it later when he interacted with others whom he perceived as "outsiders," a defense attorney or a police officer who had had little previous contact with Moore, for example. With those who work with him Moore does not really shed his aggressive but rarely belligerent gruffness, but those who work with him perceived that gruffness not as a threat to them—Moore is not a spiteful or begrudging man—but simply as evidence of the kind of man Moore is: a man regularly frustrated and irritated by a world he thinks ought to be rational and predictable but which regularly proves otherwise. He had relatively low regard for the skills and attainments that he imputed to politicians, and it is perhaps this aversion that accounts for his lack of success as a private attorney and for his satisfaction with his present position. He was not a particularly tactful person; he disagreed sharply with Sarah Levy's belief that the office should concentrate on analyzing and dealing with the social causes and consequences of crime and stop wasting time on "legal games" as she called them, and the two rarely spoke to each other.

Moore, a chunky redheaded man (who some deputies called "Carrot" behind his back), struggled with his weight during much of the year 1970 by eating a miniscule lunch at his desk. He thus cut himself off from the informal and relaxing conversations with the other deputies he previously had joined for a few hands of bridge at noon, and he cut himself off from contact with the younger prosecuting and defense attorneys who regularly headed for the various small restaurants and cafes in Centerville on their lunch hour. Although he realized that he isolated himself from much of the informal discussion about office problems he did not believe that office decisions should depend on friendships or informal lobbying.

Finally, by substituting generalization for information, the apolitical Moore worried regularly about the necessity of avoiding "public criticism" of the office and of avoiding decisions that "could hurt the reputation of the office." His very tendency to reason from generalization seemed to lead him repeatedly to overemphasize the "public's" capacity somehow to harm the office.

How did Moore appear to outsiders—to the police and defense attorneys? One of the more common complaints was that Moore did not appear enough, that attorneys did not see enough of him to have a firm feeling for who he was. Several public defenders referred to him as the office's *éminence grise* or "unknown quantity." One experienced public defender, James Pepper, who defended several homicide suspects during the year, said of Moore:

The thing with Dan Moore as far as I'm concerned is that he can't speak from strength. Anything Dan Moore says with reference to defendants or trials or almost anything, we look at with absolute abject horror and say, "Write it off," because Dan Moore as a guy has been written off in our estimation. Dan Moore has not exhibited, as far as I have been able to discover, anything about anything which is valid. As a human being, as a man, you know, I never see him at the Village Inn, I don't think I've ever seen him in the coffee shop. I've never seen him on the street more than twice just walking to his car in two years. I've never seen the guy in a restaurant, and I've never seen the guy at all except I think I've seen him maybe eight or ten times in two years, say twice on the street, twice in the elevator, and three or four times in the office. So right off Dan Moore is almost like Red China; he doesn't exist to a lot of people, you know. He's a big red blob of something, but he's not really there except when you hear the deals he's offering, and you know very well he's there, unless Nolan is a ventriloquist. And then we know we never see him in court, and that's subconsciously very important. Anyone I've ever talked to has nothing good to say about the guy as an attorney. Also, he is much older; he went to school and grew up with the pre-Warren Court. Everything he learned about law is out of date. As a guy I think he's out of date, and just about everybody else I've heard thinks he's out of date.

When Moore did interact with defense attorneys, it was usually to resolve a specific problem, and he tended to do so by creating and applying cause/effect premises to facts rather than by seeking an accommodation. Thus, many defense attorneys learned to consult someone other than Moore whenever possible, which only increased his isolation. Among the defense bar, several stories circulated about Moore. One had it that Moore was irritated because a deputy left the district attorney's office to join the public defender's office. When he found that the man had taken a copy of the Los Angeles district attorney's manual on search and seizure belonging to the district attorney's office, he threatened to prosecute him for petty theft when he refused to return it. Moore backed off only when another deputy threatened to quit and defend the "wrongdoer" if he followed through. Later, Moore threatened to seek a contempt of court holding against a public defender for waiting until trial to reveal a confession from the brother of his client exculpating the client. Another defense attorney, a former prosecutor, recalled a story in which his client, awaiting trial in jail, was found to possess

either Sleep-Eze or NoDoz, I can't remember which. Well, they charged him with a felony for possession of drugs in jail, and I had a big fight with Moore. Dan said something to the effect of "NoDoz today, heroin tomorrow." Some poor deputy was going to have to try that dog! It was finally dismissed when somebody in the crime lab said it wasn't a drug. But Moore said, "I remember a case up in some northern county where they convicted a guy of possessing aspirin in jail." That kind of attitude is always a danger.

To defense attorneys Moore often seemed rigid and unrealistic. To deputy prosecutors, he often seemed to behave inconsistently as well. One young deputy indicated to me he was perplexed to hear Moore "cry for greater office efficiency one day and then the next day insist on trying a case *because* it was a good case—when the facts indicated the guy would get the same sentence whether we dealt it out or not. I don't know, maybe it was for his statistics."

I witnessed another incident in which Moore tried to console a deputy who had just lost a jury trial on a charge of receiving stolen property. Moore said that this case, which involved the theft of a car, should never have been filed as a felony in the first place. But one of the area deputies, Carl Steinway, who had sat in on the pre-pretrial conference for that case, overheard their conversation and said, "Now wait a minute, Dan. I told you that was a crummy case, but you kept saying 'No, no, we should go. That's a good case!' I don't want to hear any more of this crap about we shouldn't go on dogs like that if you're not willing to deal them out." Steinway, a pleasantly vocal man from Brooklyn with two and a half years of experience in the office, did not hesitate to speak this way to the office's most senior deputy.

Len Lewis, who worked daily with Moore on felony dispositions and who felt some empathy for Moore, spoke of him this way:

Moore sometimes seems more rigid than he is, but occasionally he'll just get his back up, like on that case today. If you have a cold armed robbery, obviously you don't play games with it. But today, where you end up depending on an eleven-year-old boy to come through for you, yet you could take the plea and be done with it, well, I think if we lose that case it won't bother Moore. We've got him charged with the thing he did, and the fact that the jury may not convict is something Moore can't quite understand sometimes.

By contrast to Moore, Len Lewis, whose ten-year tenure was second in length to Moore's, appeared to most defense attorneys and deputies as unfailingly accessible, reasonable, affable, and above all knowledgeable concerning sentencing alternatives, about which he is considered, according to an official of the state's Bureau of Criminal Statistics, an expert not only in the county but in California. Educated at Dartmouth and Boalt Hall, Lewis, though he agreed with Moore in several respects (including his dislike for the civic club luncheons and rounds of golf and other maneuvering that a successful private practice seems to require in Vario County) appreciated the pragmatic nature of his job. While Moore found the job similar to that of a baseball umpire, Lewis listed the "union bargaining representative" analogy on the questionnaire. Moore mildly disagreed with the statement that "by and large, the defense attorney who is not familiar with the personalities and policies of this office usually does less for his client than the attorney who 'knows the system,' " but Lewis strongly (and during the interview emphatically) agreed. Moore mildly disagreed that "sometimes I have the feeling that we are just too busy to stop and look at the long-range implications of what we do," but again Lewis strongly agreed.[8]

Dan Moore perceives the world around him in terms of the cause/effect relationships of abstractions and generalizations: fighting a case on technicalities indicates lack of contrition; jail can deter if not rehabilitate; a concession in a case can arouse public resentment; and laws and rules provide clear guides for behavior. He is happiest working with quantities that he can control and manipulate in a predictable way and impatient with the unpredictable demands and compromise of principle inherent in building effective and influential interpersonal relationships. From his perspective, the feelings, emotions, and perceptions of people who see the world from a different angle are simply not relevant data. Moore's gruffness and his irritations, although some people interpret them as evidence of personal antagonism, really indicate that for Moore personal relations simply do not matter. Dan Moore did not appreciate that persuasion depends on credibility and trust, and that credibility and trust require learning the expectations of those to be persuaded.

Richard Schwartz, whom we shall consider next, proved adept at influencing those whom he wished to influence because of his empathy for their individual needs and perceptions and because of his ability to live with the ambiguities inherent in effective interpersonal relations. I have contrasted these two prosecutors with the adjectives *formalist* and *humanist* because Schwartz's effectiveness derived from his sensitivity to human emotions and factual subtlety and variety and from his belief that generalizations and rules, strictly followed, block learning and adjustment and the consequent capacity to influence.

The Humanist: Richard Schwartz

Richard Schwartz and Dan Moore had little in common. Schwartz, who earned a master's degree in English from Berkeley after he graduated from Boalt Hall, understood thoroughly the cognitive limits on rationality, the subtleties and ironies that perplex any human group, and the subtleties of social psychology. Unlike Moore, who spent considerable effort gathering statistics and who several times went out of his way to praise my questionnaire, Schwartz, convinced of the world's complexity, refused to fill out questionnaires of any kind, including both mine and the census questionnaire he received in 1970. He believed that a single sentence that attempts to capture anything real can only mislead through oversimplification. This section describes Schwartz at considerable length for two reasons. First, his story is worth telling, because Schwartz has perceived what I believe is an essentially accurate understanding of the patterns of relationships in Vario County. Second, Schwartz's story illustrates the contextualizing quality of his mind that differentiated his prosecutorial behavior from Moore's.

We begin with Schwartz's perceptive verbal autobiography, which in turn begins in Neah Bay, Washington, where he lived until he was fifteen:

Neah Bay is a town of about five hundred people in the middle of an Indian reservation. One of the reasons it made such a big impression on me, I guess, was that in that kind of town you grow up getting to know how everything works. That's something that most children who grow up in urban areas never get. It was an interesting place, in that a white patriarch more or less ran the town. He owned the general store that was also the post office, and he was the postmaster. There was a tribal council, which consisted mostly of drunks, and there was an Indian agent who did nothing but serve out his time in order to get his federal pension. In the five years he was there, so far as I know, he never had an Indian in his home and never went to an Indian function. I guess he felt there was something demeaning about that. He lived in a large white house on a bluff overlooking the Straits of Juan de Fuca, and always had a flag flying in his front yard. Our home was in the middle of the village. My dad was a jack-of-all-trades. I suppose basically he was a minister, but the ministry couldn't support a full-time minister there, and of course the Indians couldn't support a full-time jack rabbit. He taught school one year and acted as a liaison for the government. He worked as a butcher in the local store and spent one season fishing with an Indian. We were really the only white people in the village. There was a logging company that ran a company town nearby, but it was a real company town. The whole place was surrounded by a ditch and piled railroad ties so that no stray Indian horse could get in. It was socially self-enclosed. They had no contact with the Indians to speak of. And there was a Coast Guard station there, but the Coast Guard had a policy that anyone caught fraternizing with Indian girls would be sent to the Umatilla Light Ship to serve out their term. There was an Air Force base nearby, but the Air Force people were supposed to stay on the base. Sometimes they'd come into town and knock up an Indian girl. If they had any honor, they would marry the girl and take her back to New York. That usually lasted about two months and then the girls would be back on the base alone. I suppose boys would take the girls back to their Irish or Italian mothers and they wouldn't want any part of an Indian girl in their family, and they'd make life pretty miserable for the girls. And sometimes the Air Force men would come into town and get drunk and start fights and wander back to the base, which was two and a half miles away. Sometimes they would shoot animals on the reservation, where the only time you could shoot would be with permission from the tribal council. So lots of times my father acted as a referee between the Air Force and the council.

There was another church in town, a Presbyterian church manned by a drunk who always felt that he was passed over and shunted off. He tried to limit his congregation only to whites, but without too much success, because the Church had established a mission school there some years back. But in that kind of vacuum, my father became pretty tightly identified with the Indian cause. He always kept penicillin in the house, even though it was illegal, but what doctor would want to make a one-hundred-mile trip out to a reservation on a gravel road? I remember one time the road washed out and the only food we had for three weeks came in by seaplane. It was really pretty primitive. Over in Vancouver Island, the Indians still believed in some form of voodoo. Sometimes they would come over and dance and cause hell. I remember one time we came back and found Vancouver Indians dancing around our house. They were trying to cast a spell on us because they thought we were the symbols of the white man bringing all the trouble to the Indian nation. None of the local Indians were involved in that, though I have seen some of the Indians in Neah Bay having dances in which they would fight with butcher knives and actually cut each other up. And I've seen women writhing and frothing on the floor so that it took six men to hold one woman down. Once I remember peeking through a window and watching my dad take a gun away from an Indian man who was threatening to shoot his wife, when everyone else was too scared to go near the place. And I remember once when a three-hundred-pound Indian woman chased me into a corner, where she said she wanted to kill me. (Did you ever see *Treasure Island* where Jim Hawkins is trapped in the crow's nest and the guy is climbing up the ladder after him? Well, I felt like Jim Hawkins.)

Well, throwing a kid with any intelligence into a setting like Neah Bay would have to have an impact on him, and I don't have to spell it out for you. I developed a tremendous sympathy for the Indians and their problems, but unlike a lot of liberals, what that kind of experience teaches you is that you never see anything as a block idea. It's hard for me to see people in terms of ideas, and this is carried over into my feelings about blacks in the ghetto. And I suppose it has made me distrustful of surveys and surveyists as well.

But to finish the story, when I was fifteen my dad was killed in an automobile accident in which my mother got a broken neck and I broke my elbow. I was in the hospital for a month, and some friends moved us out of our house while I was in the hospital. So I never set foot in that house again. I've gone by it and I've wanted to go in, but someone else is living there. I'd hate to walk in and say, "Hi, I used to live here." But I left that house without the lingering looks that people like to have when they leave something for good, because I never knew that I wasn't going back to it.

Schwartz spent a year earning a master's degree after graduating from the law school at the University of California, Berkeley, and then began work with the Legal Aid office in Vario County. In 1968, at the age of twenty-eight, he shifted to the district attorney's office because he felt he could learn no more from handling the repetitive contests between merchants and consumers that made up the bulk of his work. He could not predict where he would be in five years, but said he was considering full-time work related to the affairs of the Presbyterian Church in which he had become very active in Condenado.

Schwartz predicted he would not stay long in the district attorney's office, for he found it intellectually unsatisfying:

I have never been around a group of people that have attained as much formal education as these people have who are as unscholarly as these people. Most of them can't make a decent literary allusion. They don't know literature. They don't know anything about classical music. Most of them are very pop-culture people. Their idea of great music is Mantovani; their idea of a book is what's on the best-seller list. Most of them don't read that much. They're not even scholarly about the law. It's depressing to me that the judges are no more scholarly about the law. Most of our deputies don't know the law. They panic when they get into court against a really competent defense attorney. They've got all the polish, but they don't have any of the real know-how. They know how to act. They know where to take the papers. They know how to put on a case, but they don't know the law. . . . One problem is that the criminal law is one of the more exciting parts of the law. It's a fairly narrow field, and in our office we handle very special kinds of problems, like search problems and admission problems. It doesn't take that much to know all there is to know about such problems without getting into real nebulous areas. Most deputies don't want to go beyond the West key system [the basic indexing system for legal research] because for their purposes they don't think it's necessary. So you breed a lot of sloppiness in the deputies. . . . I think most of them would be puzzled by my concern for the corrosive effect of the West key system on the common law. That would puzzle them. It's surprising that people with seven or eight years college aren't that scholarly. . . . The way you make scholars is having the younger scholars watch how the older scholars work, not by going to school, but there isn't much of that scholarship in this office.

Schwartz is wary of attorneys who seek principles of law in the West key system, in which the legal findings of often complicated judicial opinions are reduced to short statements, because he is skeptical of most rule-bound decision making. He does not oppose the existence of rules, but he insists upon their flexible application:

I don't say that a rule is completely unnecessary or senseless, although sometimes they are. Usually the rule is there as a majority case thing, a guideline. But we shouldn't be straight-jacketed with things like Moore's seven-day rule. The reason they give for the rule [the "rule" stated that no defense attorney could plead his client within seven days of a trial] is to put pressure on the attorneys to get the clients to plead before the last minute. Well, that's a bunch of malarky. Most private lawyers don't talk to their clients about pleading until the last week before trial. . . . They're worrying about other cases until then. And the public defender a lot of times doesn't get in touch with his client until a day or two before trial. So it's O.K. to say we've got a rule like that, so the attorney can use it to help beat his client over the head. But when we get a deal, we should take the deal and settle. You see, there are rules that are nice to have that aren't really rules. . . . Rules are good because you don't have to fight with guys. You can say, well, we've got this rule, and they understand it.

At staff meetings, Schwartz argued against making any fixed rule separating felony and misdemeanor marijuana filings. He explained: "I was against drawing lines because what do you do if you catch a big dealer at a school who just happens to be a bit low? You'd want to file a felony on that kind of case and you shouldn't have rules preventing you from doing it."

In contrast to Moore, Schwartz believes that the strength of the common law lies in its inherent uncertainty, an uncertainty that permits tailoring case dispositions to their unique facts:

Look at the common law. You've got two lines of argument on all kinds of issues. Now it's very predictable in the sense that the lawyer knows how to put his case in one line of authority, but it's confused to the extent that should the equities demand, although the judge may not make it explicit, they can gerrymander that thing into the other line of authority. It's confusing to the layman, who won't have any sense of this at all, but a good lawyer will. He can predict because he's predicting more than just on the confused state of the law. He's predicting on the personality of the judge, on the facts of the case, and he's predicting on the basis of the community reaction to the defendant at that particular time. So the law can be confused and at the same time be predictable.

David Riesman has written that lawyers "learn not to take law seriously."[9] By taking rules seriously and by invoking rules and generalizations to justify his actions, Dan Moore suffered in two respects. He did not search for information that might permit him to better resolve a problem. More damaging, his failure to search for information cut him off from the collateral benefits of searching: the growth of interpersonal trust and knowledge of the values of those whose behavior he hoped to change. Moore, for example, had on occasion refused to prosecute cases the police felt were extremely serious, because the police investigation had not been complete. By simply invoking the rule, Moore appeared to the police to be challenging directly the validity of their judgment, and opposition by several north county police chiefs to Dan Moore's appointment to district attorney contributed to the Board of Supervisors' passing him over.

Schwartz, on the other hand, understood thoroughly that the exercise of influence upon police required winning their trust, and that winning their trust prevented him from directly challenging the validity of police judgments. Schwartz similarly recognized the importance of the trust relationship between prosecuting and defense attorneys. He lamented how, while Centerville had a "lawyers' bar," the back room of the Village Inn Restaurant, where prosecutors and public and private defense attorneys could meet over a drink to get to know each other and to test informally the strengths and weaknesses of their cases, Condenado had no such common meeting place.

By "not taking law seriously," Schwartz succeeded in solving or averting what might have been difficult problems for his office. For example, when Tom Gubser took over as head of the Condenado branch in September of 1970, he announced that he did not approve of the practice of "overfiling" cases, a practice that police might interpret as a softening attitude toward crime. Seeking to persuade the police of the wisdom of his position, Gubser, upon arrival, began to contact the chief and the two deputy chiefs of the Condenado police department. Schwartz, however, knew that, as he put it:

There are about three men in the Condenado police department [he named three sergeants] who aren't the police administration, really, but they have earned everybody's respect, so that if the other men see them respecting you and trusting you, they'll all do it, and a word or two from one of them over coffee about you being chicken-shit, and you're dead.

Schwartz sensed that Gubser had not adequately cultivated these three, and he also sensed that Gubser's pleasantly efficient but somewhat antiseptic approach came across falsely to these officers as evidence of Gubser's effeminacy. Schwartz, therefore, both advised Gubser to get to know the three sergeants personally and simultaneously stressed to them and to other influential officers his enthusiastic support for Gubser. At the end of the year Schwartz told me that he was not running into any more of "this limp-wristed shit about Gubser in the police department."

The contrast between Moore and Schwartz parallels the contrast between order and learning developed in chapter 1. Moore tended to perceive the world in terms of the relationship of plausible but universal abstractions, and he tended to assume that collecting and weighing the relevant abstractions would provide necessary and sufficient information for action. He did not persistently seek concrete information, because if the abstraction is the key to action, further information didn't matter. Schwartz, on the other hand, found abstractions and rules suspect because they could displace continuing inquiry, inquiry that Schwartz valued, both because he found it intellectually satisfying and because the knowledge he gained from inquiry increased his capacity to influence.

This contrast raises three points that require further development. The first, which chapter 5 develops, concerns the consequences of Dan Moore's presence upon office management. Dan Moore represents a strategy of management that was unsuited to the technological and environmental circumstances constraining the prosecutors' office in Vario County. The second point, which chapter 6 develops, concerns the ethical implications of this contrast. Dan Moore had a certain freedom to attempt to correct the worst abuses of the system of criminal justice, which Schwartz, committed to maintaining effective interpersonal relations, did not have. The ethical question directs us to the normative question of what responsibility we believe prosecutors ought to assume for improving the quality of criminal justice, and it directs us to the pragmatic question of designing the prosecutor's working situation to meet whatever responsibility we assign to him.

Finally, the contrast between Moore and Schwartz illustrates that the job of prosecutor does not, at least in Vario County, either attract men who do the job similarly or mold them into common ways of behaving. But a sample of two is hardly conclusive in this regard, and the final section of this chapter reviews further, to paraphrase James Q. Wilson, the varieties of prosecutorial behavior.

Four Prosecuting Styles

In *The Lawmakers*, James David Barber writes of the seductions of fourfold tables, of the danger that such typologies can obscure much of the world's richness and complexity.[10] With that warning in mind, the following four categories of prosecutorial styles should serve only to illustrate that considerable variation among prosecutors' preferences and behavior may exist under one roof. I do not want to suggest that all prosecutors may be placed in one of the four categories or that the placing of any one prosecutor in one of these categories describes and explains all aspects of that prosecutor's behavior.

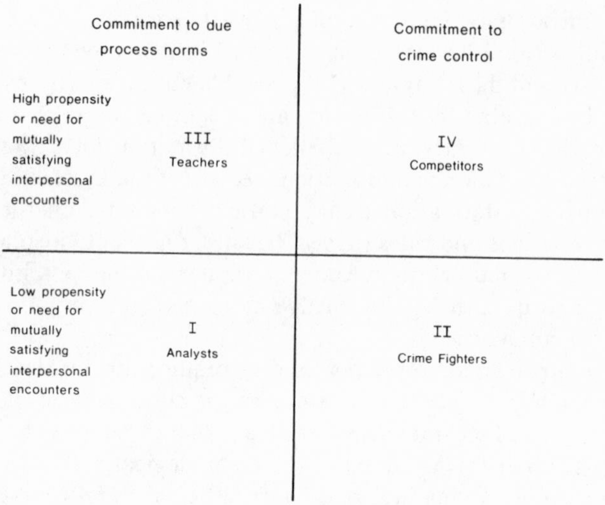

	Commitment to due process norms	Commitment to crime control
High propensity or need for mutually satisfying interpersonal encounters	III Teachers	IV Competitors
Low propensity or need for mutually satisfying interpersonal encounters	I Analysts	II Crime Fighters

Figure 3-1. Typology of Prosecuting Styles

The first axis—a continuum, in reality—that defines the four categories of prosecutorial behavior is marked at one end by a commitment to the due process norms of legal practice, and at the other end by the extent to which a given deputy conceives his role as that of controlling crime.[11] The crime control model presumes that the most important function of prosecutors is to preserve public order by securing as quickly as possible convictions of all offenders, while the due process model focuses on the compliance with formal limits on state power, at the expense of efficiency if necessary. The second axis is marked at one end by a low, at the other end by a high, propensity or need to engage in mutually satisfying interpersonal encounters[12] Peter Blau has written that a "basic reward people seek in their associations is social approval, and selfish disregard for others makes it impossible to obtain this important reward."[13]While prosecutors with low propensities for mutually satisfying interpersonal encounters may receive internalized rewards—the satisfaction from legal craftsmanship or from ridding society of criminals—others with higher propensities tended to define their objectives in terms of how others with whom they deal—the judge, the defense attorney, or the defendant himself—will respond. Satisfying interpersonal encounters dilute adherence to both legal craftsmanship and crime fighting.

The feeling of intellectual anemia that systems analyses of politics often produce in readers arises from the failure of systems analysis to incorporate the perplexing and occasionally terrifying absence of predictability or "systemness" that flesh-and-blood actors in political affairs confront. The purpose of this table is to illustrate that criminal prosecution need not, and in Vario County did not, resemble any of the "models" or "systems" of criminal administration. Rather, what may characterize the process of case dispositions is that to its participants it does not look like a system at all. Those charged with the daily responsibility of trying to make some sense out of the procedures they supervise confront not a due process model or a crime control model or a series of mutually satisfying exchanges, but something that is from a practical perspective very different: a system with the capacity to be all these things at once.

The following descriptions of individual prosecutors indicate the extent to which different styles coexisted in one office, but the labels I have given the four cells deserve some further explanation. Those I have designated "analysts" in Cell I accepted and acted upon the legitimacy of formal legal procedures. They viewed the practice of criminal prosecution essentially as the extension of the analytical habits they developed in law school. They tended to give relatively little thought to the accused himself, either as the subject of punishment or as a human being in need of assistance. These prosecutors are designated analysts because they believed their work required the orderly disposition of cases in the light of the best available scholarly knowledge. What distinguished them from "crime fighters" is that the analysts tended to reject ideas that have not been legitimated by some formal process of inquiry. The analysts' commitment to due process stemmed in part from their respect for the formal process of judicial inquiry from which these concepts have emerged. Analysts therefore tended to reject generalized theories of retribution or of deterence, since penology, a formal school of inquiry, today questions such theories. Crime fighters, on the other hand, appeared to base their premises for action upon influences from nonacademic sources, from the popular retributive culture of movies and television, for example.

The analysts' respect for formal knowledge and the crime fighter's concern for "protecting society" tended to displace mutually satisfying interpersonal relations. Analysts and crime fighters placed less emphasis on interpersonal accomodations because adherence to the abstractions of legal norms and of social protection may dictate results that displease those with whom they deal. Analysts and crime fighters valued making decisions that are in some abstract sense "correct," and they valued being correct more than manipulating or influencing others.

"Teachers" (Cell III) also valued formal knowledge, but they believed that knowledge becomes useful only when it is transmitted. Prosecutors so designated sought to transmit an understanding of legal requirements to police and an understanding of the social consequences of illegal behavior to suspects. Prosecutors in this category accepted the necessity of making intellectual concessions in order to gain the trust of those whom they sought to influence. They believed that some circumstances called for mercy because they believed that benevolence may win allegiance.

Mutually satisfying interpersonal relations reward "competitors" but in a different way from the rewards given teachers. Indeed, a prosecutor may not be a competitor because he believes in the necessity of crime control; he may believe in the necessity of crime control because he enjoys competition. Competitors may elevate the importance of crime control because the crime control perspective gives them a clear measure of what they have won from effective bargaining. A relatively severe sentence is a more tangible measure of success than the observance of legal formalities. Like teachers, however, competitors realized that they must persuade those with whom they deal that the results of the exchange would satisfy both sides.

Cell I: The Analysts — Tom Gubser

Tom Gubser was raised in Riverside, California, where his father was a successful building contractor. He received both his B.A. and his LL.B. from the University of California at Berkeley. He was an amiable man of thirty-two who analyzed cases carefully and who worked diplomatically with others, but who as prosecutor adhered firmly to positions once he decided they were correct. Until Nolan rewarded his careful work with promotion to head of the Condenado branch, Gubser was the area deputy for the rapidly growing Hillside community near Centerville.

Despite his amiability, Gubser made few interpersonal commitments. He said of himself, "I'm not a joiner. I haven't made the effort that some at my level in the office have, and I suppose that's a question of my personality, although I'm sure it helps if you eat and drink at the Elks Club with Judge Scott and Supervisor Coles." Gubser did not spend much time cultivating members of the legal community. He indicated that most of his close friends were nonlawyers and said that the couple he and his wife most frequently saw taught and worked in a museum.

Like the teacher Schwartz, Gubser was concerned with the quality of legal work in Vario County. When asked whether his work as a prosecutor had changed his personal philosophy of law or of life, he answered that he had become more aware of both the strengths and weaknesses of the legal system, and he continued:

It's hard to put it in words; maybe it's the county, maybe it's the office, maybe it's the system in general, maybe I only see it with blinders because I see it only from this office, but I suppose I am disappointed in the quality of work the average lawyer is doing. Now that includes both deputies in this office and attorneys in private practice, and judges, and myself, and I don't know where the blame, if any, lies. Maybe the average lawyer in this county isn't all that sharp, maybe the practice doesn't demand it, maybe this county is no different from any other county. In this office I know we have too much volume. I think this is something I have just become aware of: the criminal law is limited to accomplishing certain limited goals, and we're trying to do too much.

Gubser on the questionnaire listed "maintaining a high level of professional legal performance" as an office goal he personally felt was most important but rated degree of goal achievement only "sometimes but not very often." He analyzed the obstacles to improving legal performance:

We could do something, but it's like everything else. People are too busy doing it to learn how to do it. There are lots of things that militate against success: turnover, the volume of work. You know, in the minds of the most liberal district attorney, success is often measured in terms of outfoxing the other side, sort of a bluffing game without enough attention to the meat and potatoes. . . . Most deputies do a half-assed job of preparing the file when he issues the complaint. He figures he'll worry about it at the prelim when he tries to outfox the defendant into a plea, and often that plea is obtained because the defense is more ignorant than the deputy in the law and the facts, and the defendant doesn't have the money to go to trial anyway, and for a number of reasons that don't have anything to do with the quality of legal work.

Gubser thought of his own work largely in terms of the legal quality of case handling. He did not seem particularly concerned for the lives of specific defendants nor on the other hand did he express any desire for retribution. Gubser had little faith in the capacity of the system to reduce the crime rate. He felt the prosecutor's ability to do so is very much limited by the decisions that the police make, and that police decisions have the primary impact on crime rate. He did not embrace any theory of punishment terribly seriously, and felt that the only impact on crime rates derived from the fact that the incarcerated can't do much damage while confined. To Gubser most cases were depersonalized. "I don't really get close to any defendant. It rarely goes beyond a name on the file, because ethically we don't have any connection with them." Unlike some prosecutors, he did not assume that a defendant was irresponsible and undeserving because he had been accused of a crime. He did not, for example, believe that defendants regularly lie to defend themselves. "I would say many defendants tell stories that they have convinced themselves are the truth but that clearly are not the truth." Unlike his immediate superior for most of the year, Peter Hoff, Gubser did not believe that prosecutors should "overfile" cases:

My feeling is that the single most important decision to be made on any case is whether and how to file it. Once we've filed, everything else seems to fall into place. . . . We've got a big advantage over the poor cop on the beat. He's got to make a decision in a split second. So the law gives him a higher degree of flexibility than it gives us. We have a higher burden of proof, and we ought to take our own sweet time about filing. . . . The police are very upset about this for very good reasons. After all, if they go to the bother of arresting someone, they hate to do it all over again, but I think it's better that we move carefully. . . . But there's a growing feeling, principally among the younger deputies in this office, that we ought to file felonies and take misdemeanor pleas later. I agreed with Joe Busch of the Los Angeles district attorney's office. I went to the Criminal Law Institute's conference up in Reno last month, and Busch called overfiling "legal-blackmail," and I agree. If the D.A. is saying he'll take a misdemeanor, how do you convince the defense when you're serious about the felony? He'll say, "Well, the last time you gave me a misdemeanor," and then we have to say, "But this time there are five joints instead of one," and he says, "Well, what difference does that make?" I disagree with Hoff. I think this lowers our credibility to the vanishing point if we overprice our goods on the market. The younger deputies want to get the plea, but I keep pointing out that if the defendant doesn't take it, he has three cracks at the search. But he has only one crack before the municipal court judge [on the misdemeanor charge], and you know the judge is going to give you the benefit of the doubt whenever he can.

In short, Gubser's actions and beliefs derived from an application of abstract principles and analyses to concrete problems. If law specifies that a man is innocent until proven guilty, the legal system should be prepared to prove guilt rather than rely on coercive measures to induce a plea. If the accused is presumed innocent, then his "fighting the case on its technical-ities" is unrelated to the capacity of the accused to be rehabilitated upon conviction.[4] If criminal administration seeks to prevent individuals from harming other individuals, then crimes without victims are a mistake. (Gubser favored legalization of marijuana.)

Of all Vario County prosecutors, then, Gubser, both in appearance and attitude, most resembled the stereotype of a corporate lawyer. He did not seek to engage in mutually satisfying interpersonal relationships, because he found the rewards of intellectual thoroughness and legal craftsmanship satisfying in themselves. He accepted legal premises, both substantive rules and the professional norms of craftsmanship, which led him to reject the advantages of overfiling, but the rewards of legal craftsmanship also dis-placed any feeling of responsibility either for the improvement of social conditions or for the welfare of either individual victims or individual sus-pects. Gubser, then, hardly resembled the stereotype of the aggressive pro-secutor. But Brian Savio, a crime fighter, did.

Cell II: Crime Fighters — Brian Savio

Brian Savio, the only deputy to describe himself politically as "ultra-conservative," was one of three deputies whom most prosecutors believed did not somehow "work out very well." All three of these deputies were strongly committed to the crime control perspective. To most defense attorneys, they seemed unrealistic, inflexible, and unduly dogmatic in their handling of cases. The three also had several other things in common. Their fathers all held blue-collar jobs, each prosecutor was strongly religious, and each was unmarried. Savio repeatedly filed the most severe possible charges and did not regularly "deal them out." He was raised in Los Angeles, where his father, a laborer in a tool and die company, died when Savio was in grade school. Savio attended the University of San Francisco and received his LL.B. from Hastings College of Law. He was one of the seven prosecutors who listed as a reason for becoming a prosecutor a desire to be in public service; he was the only one in the interview who volunteered that he chose the job because he felt he was psychologically well suited to the work.

Savio, unlike his immediate superior, Gubser, chose "maximizing sentences," "keeping the cases moving," and "reducing the crime rate" as his preferences among office goals. Savio, although he seemed more resigned than frustrated about it, nevertheless complained about what he believed was the office's lack of aggressiveness or commitment to the control of crime. He felt that the office "knuckles under to what other groups want politically." Gubser, on the other hand, felt politics were virtually irrelevant in office operations. Savio believed the office was unnecessarily solicitous of defense counsel interests and that cases were therefore dealt out at the police officer's expense:

Nobody goes on radio or television and says anything about the crime problem when a jury finds somebody not guilty when he's really guilty or when a police officer is shot and nothing is done. It's incumbent on the district attorney to get up and say that we've had some Supreme Court decisions that are unrealistic and don't protect officers or victims.

Savio identified strongly with the police and their problems. He listed "patrolman" as the only occupation similar to his, and he rode with police officers in Hillside frequently. While most deputies felt they really had no client and did not think of themselves at all seriously as lawyers for "the people," Savio felt that both the police and the state of California were his clients:

You're only as good as your client, and if you can identify with someone sitting in the courtroom with you, well. . . . I've always felt that society, the people, are personified through its employee, the police officer, because the police officer is the only thing separating the innocent citizen from the criminal.

Savio supported the police strongly because he believed in punishment for its own sake. "I think putting people in jail to teach them a lesson is the best way to handle it. They're not rehabilitated, so it should be purely a punitive thing."

One of his colleagues, Art Pollack, analyzed Savio's difficulty in terms of what Pollack called his "super gung-hoism," which Pollack believed most judges, juries, defense attorneys, and other prosecutors did not appreciate:

The attitude of "take the conviction any way you can get it despite the state of the evidence" doesn't help the office with other agencies we have to deal with, and it doesn't achieve any sense of justice, which I think we should be striving for. . . . Our ability to judge how one case is going to affect anybody, including the defendant, is so slight that basically you can't be so gung-ho public.

Most prosecutors and defense attorneys perceived crime fighters like Savio as unsuited to their work because that orientation blocks search for, and adaptation to, new information. Openness to new information can yield tangible payoffs to prosecutors, but more important, by presenting himself to others as a "persuadable" or "flexible" person, the prosecutor generates trust that expedites the handling of cases. The due process perspective, even when coupled with a low regard for satisfying interpersonal relations, does not similarly block openness and trust, because that perspective is itself, as we have seen, a model of information search. Put more concretely, Gubser succeeded and won promotion because he anticipated and responded to the kind of problems—identification of legal weaknesses in cases, the preparation of reluctant witnesses, or the presentation of complicated sequences of evidence—that carried some tangible payoffs that those around him could identify: winning good cases and avoiding the prosecution of losers. The crime-fighting model, as Pollack pointed out, has no comparably concrete payoff for the organization.

Cell III: Teachers — John Lane

Analysts and crime fighters employ abstract premises in determining their positions on cases. Teachers and competitors consider and react to individuals: defendants, defense attorneys, judges, and police. Like Gubser, John Lane listed "maintaining a high level of professional legal performance" as one of the goals he personally thought the office should be trying to achieve, but he also listed as personally important a goal that he added to the list of goals: "Concern for long-range impact that convictions and/or sentence may have on defendant, i.e., proper rehabilitation and maintenance of status in community." The occupations he listed as similar to his job stressed the element of teaching and persuasion: "coach," "salesman," and "union bargaining representative."

Lane described his approach to his job this way:

I would say I've become more liberal. Some of my friends might be disappointed to hear me say that, but one of the things about our office, and I think it's something a lot of the younger deputies, and even some of the older ones, don't take advantage of, is this power really to do something for a person. There's no question that we call the shots; we make an offer, and if it's not accepted, it goes to trial. But I like to be able to evaluate a person in terms of what a plea may mean in terms of his stature. I think to the extent I've learned that, I've become more liberal. This has happened largely through my contact with actual individuals and their defense attorneys.

Lane did not attribute his philosophy to any influence from the office itself. Lane worked, and became area deputy during the year, in the Pleasant Valley area, the county's wealthiest area, where the bulk of suspects come from "respectable" families and cases tend to involve relatively minor offences: marijuana and pill possession, drunk driving, etc. Judge Hanrahan in Pleasant Valley had worked closely with Lane since he began work as a prosecutor, and Lane adopted Hanrahan's perspective, which Lane described:

Hanrahan is a very equitable judge. It used to be commonly thought that some attorneys got preferential treatment, but from personal experience I've learned that's not true. I've learned a lot of things from him—simple things like how to mark exhibits to get them into evidence. I'll try a jury in front of him, and then we'll go out for a beer together, and I'll ask him what I did wrong and he'll tell me. That's great. He's clearly not the best legal mind, and he would be the first to tell you, and he's not a hanging judge the way Judge Coughlin is in Hillside. But I would say Hanrahan is the best. He's an equity judge.

Responding to the equitable model of Judge Hanrahan, Lane early in his career as a prosecutor broke explicitly with orders from his superiors in the office regarding a drunk driving case. He described the instance and the long-term impact it had on him:

It was a bus driver, forty years old and the sole supporter of an invalid daughter. I just said "screw it," and went ahead and reduced it to reckless driving. And I wasn't so much worried about what they would say back at the office, but I was worried about whether it would open the floodgates. But I made it very clear to the judge and the defense attorney that I didn't want anybody to hear about it. I think about that case whenever I think about reducing cases, and often I do, so maybe it did open the floodgates. It was against my better judgment, because at the time I was aware that it might be the start of something big, and as a matter of fact it has been—not necessarily something big, but something that didn't used to happen. . . . Now I have attorneys tell me they talked to somebody in Condenado, for example, and the deputies there won't budge, whereas maybe I would. So the net effect is that somebody is getting screwed. If he gets caught in Condenado, he would be treated differently than if he drove another ten miles and then got caught in Pleasant Valley. And that does kind of bother me. Taking a reckless in a drunk driving case, you know, runs contrary to a pretty strong policy in our office. I have justified—at least I feel I have justified—every disposition I've made on the facts. There's no doubt that many of my superiors have disagreed, but I don't lose any sleep over that. Hoff is probably least flexible in terms of reducing cases he personally handles, but when [a deputy] does it, and talks with him about it—and we've gone around and around on a lot of cases—he has made it very clear that you're the attorney, you do what you think is right, because you're responsible. He says, "I might not have done what you did, and here's why . . . ," but he makes it very clear you're responsible.

Lane, like Hanrahan, sought case dispositions that he hoped would instruct rather than punish the defendant. He also played the role of teacher to police officers and those prosecutors whom he supervised. It was, in fact, in his relationships with police officers where his respect for the legal model as opposed to the crime control model became most apparent. Lane was fairly strict about filing only charges that look solid. I observed a situation in which a police officer requested the filing of charges against two men for illegally discharging a weapon inside a dwelling. Lane refused to file charges because the police had not been able to determine which of the two men had actually fired the shot. He explained the legal reasons for his decision carefully to the officer, and then expanded his explanation to me afterwards:

[The officer's] argument usually is that it's my job to look for the elements of the crime and leave the question of facts up to the judge and jury. But I don't see it that way. . . . The reasonable doubt in this case is clear to me. . . . You've to to prove that a given man shot a specific gun in a specific inhabited dwelling intentionally to get a conviction here, and on the face of the police report, we just can't do that. I had no choice. It's part of my job to look at the facts in the case as well as the legal elements. Otherwise the police could arrest everyone and give the argument "tell it to the judge." I hear that all the time. We've got to take the place of the judge and jury on skinny cases. Maybe this is our function only because the case load is so high, but as I see it, the biggest part of our job is to keep the legal system running smoothly.

Like Gubser, Lane had reservations about overfiling but reported considerable disagreement in the office about that policy. He described the approach of deputy Bob Valenti in Hillside:

In Hillside they have a large vice squad, and they spend a lot of time busting people for grass. Perhaps from overzealous patrol, they have more legal issues, so Valenti overfiles, and maybe he avoids the legal problems by taking a plea later. . . . To me that isn't right all the time. I do it sometimes, but why, if you know he's going to plead to a misdemeanor, do you file the felony on him and cause him to pay more bail and make him sit in jail longer? To me it's not fair. A lot of people say we ought to stick 'em, but that offends my conscience. And another way he can get stuck is that his attorney will charge more.

Competitors Bob Valenti and Jim Turner, like Savio, worked under Gubser but did not share his approach to the job. Because Gubser did not personalize his feelings, he did not teach his subordinates to follow his pattern. Lane, on the other hand, succeeded in transferring his perspective to his subordinates. Stewart Douglas, a newcomer in 1970, explained how Lane had worked with him when he first began to work in the office:

The first time I was down in municipal court in Pleasant Valley I heard there was all this wheeling and dealing going on, and I didn't know what to make of it. John said,

"Well, everybody in the office kind of has a different attitude. You're going to have to take your own attitude. It's up to you, but I always try to think, not 'let's get this guy' but in terms of being reasonable." And I like that. I think that's a good attitude. You have to be reasonable in every case. I know a lot of people call him "Santa Claus Lane," but I know all the dispositions I've seen him make I've always agreed with. When he deals, it's because he's being realistic and looking at the facts.

Cell IV: Competitors — Jim Turner

Jim Turner was raised in Chicago, where his father was a vice-president of a large department store. He decorated his office with large *Sports Illustrated* posters of the Cubs' Ron Santo, race cars, and an eight-oar shell under way. At one time he kept a bulletin board to which he pinned a statement of a professional quarterback, "Winning is everything. . . . You do anything you have to to win. Everything else is crap." He also pinned a strip from "Pogo," a conversation between two characters best identified as "Mole" and "Spiro Dog":

> *Mole:* Now as to these two prisoners, you must recall the law considers each man innocent until—
>
> *Spiro Dog:* Caught.
>
> *Mole:* A fascinating new interpretation of the law. How'll it hold up in court?
>
> *Spiro Dog:* Excellent. . . . Any reasonable judge who listens to reason will reasonably agree.
>
> *Mole:* Listen to *whose* reason?
>
> *Spiro Dog:* Ours. . . . Whom else's is there?

Turner no doubt put these items up primarily for amusement's sake, for he enjoys being amused. Shortly after he arrived in the office he labeled the rather flamboyant Carl Steinway "Superjew," and Steinway responded by designating Turner as "Sluggo," since Turner mildly resembles that pudgy cartoon-strip character.

Turner had a reputation both among fellow deputies for being hardnosed, yet he suffered none of the social handicaps or criticism that Savio received, for he recognized the importance of maintaining amiable personal relationships with defense attorneys and judges:

A guy who can't get along with defense attorneys will just kill you. No matter how you slice it, even when you stick it to those guys, you've got to come away so they don't dislike you, because you're going to deal with them again. You can say you're going to screw somebody, but you can say it in several different ways.

One of those ways, Turner explained, was that during Nolan's election campaign he had

rationalized to defense attorneys why I had screwed them. It's the perfect out. It's like the public defender's "my client won't do it." There's no way either of us can find out. I say, "The heat's on: it's an election year." But really it's just a reason that I don't feel like discussing any more with them, or I want the guy to get out of my way and stop bothering me.

Turner keyed his behavior to specific individuals with whom he interacted, but, unlike Lane, these rarely included the defendant. Primarily he keyed his behavior to the judge or the defense attorney in the case. His view of interpersonal relations was rather simple. "Some guys are winners and some are losers.... If the judge likes you, he'll grant you a favor; if he doesn't he won't." Regarding the defendants, Turner listed "maximizing sentences" as one of his preferred office goals and adopted the straightforward deterrent theory:

There are differences between the way superiors feel and the way I feel on some of these goals. . . . I sort of believe in the deterrent effect even though I know it's not supposed to be in vogue right now. I think it does affect [that is, punishment affects] a peer group, especially regarding younger defendants. If a guy sees he can commit ten burglaries and spend ten days in jail, it will affect his friends. It's like the speeder. He knows if he gets caught he'll pay a fine. If the burglar gets caught, he should pay a penalty too. . . . But you really have to work hard to get in jail. The first offender, even the second or third time around, gets the benefit of the doubt.

Turner did not hesitate to justify the convictions of those who may have good legal defenses. He believed that guilt is almost always a question of degree, and he did not criticize taking a plea from someone who "may only have been on the fringe." He continued: "They may not have done it at all, but they're guilty to a certain degree. Whether they're guilty 100 percent or not may not always be true. But that's separated down mostly on taking lesser pleas. If a guy isn't completely guilty, that means his case will be weaker and you'll try to deal it." Unlike Lane or Gubser, Turner followed what he called a "loose filing" strategy: "I probably tend to be a looser filer than most people. If nothing more, it'll put the guy to the expense of getting an attorney and going to court, and that in itself may be enough to keep the guy going straight in the future. And often you'll win."

Turner joined the office to build up trial skills, and he enjoyed striking an advantageous bargain, but he respected the "professionalism" of defense attorneys who met him head on. He said he knew which defense attorneys were "afraid to go to trial. They stand out like a sore thumb, and you know you're gonna screw 'em in the end, just for the trait that he has. The guy who comes across straight to you, who tells you what the situation is, he's the guy who you'll listen to when there are equities in the case, because you can believe what he's saying." Turner felt the prosecutor should "file high and deal down" because that encourages the bargaining, which he enjoyed:

Some [prosecutors] feel we should start out realistically, but my feeling is that for a defense attorney to get his guy to plead, you've gotta give him something. The defense attorney is selling a service, and if his client feels he hasn't done anything for him, then it's not being fair to him. You just file high and then deal it down a notch to what it should have been all along, and everybody's happy. We get what we want. The defendant thinks his attorney is great. The attorney gets his money. . . . It's not our job just to go on the ironclad cases.

Most deputies had little difficulty distinguishing Turner's behavior from Savio's. One deputy contrasted the two by pointing to what he felt was the eternal conflict in the office between "doing your job for society" and "not screwing up the court calendar."

The guys who don't make it around here are the guys who push too hard, like . . . Savio. They stir up more trouble than it's worth. But there are people who can be real tough without making waves, like Turner. . . . He makes very few deals and is very stiff, and he's willing to take his lumps on a bad case when he gets caught at it. And he has the personality to carry it off without pissing people off too badly. So, it can be handled, but it takes an unusual person to do it.

One of the teachers, Howard Wright, who worked under Lane said: "Turner has the kind of personality where he can tell an attorney to stop bullshitting him right now. He gets better plea bargains, and he's probably a better poker player than I am, too. He likes to bargain. I personally don't like to fart around with that."

What causes such diversity? In one sense the absence of courses in law school that focus on the processes and assumptions inherent in the task of prosecution accounts for it. (Only four deputies felt law school had given "fully adequate" training for their job.) But common experiences in Vario County also failed to give prosecutors common answers to the questions they must answer in their work. In chapter 5 we pursue further the explanations for the organization's failure to reduce this diversity: why, when prosecutors disagree with their superiors, they do not, like John Lane, feel constrained to substitute their superior's judgment for their own. But we must also address ourselves to the consequences both of the fact of diversity and the consequences of each of these styles. Is one style preferable to another? Is the analyst's commitment to legal craftsmanship preferable to the compromises a teacher makes to influence others? Might we prefer, on the other hand, the approach of crime fighters or competitors because these approaches at least can preserve genuine adversariness? Chapter 6 returns to these questions.

4

The Prosecutors' Working Environment

Their working environment presents prosecutors in supervisorial positions with four kinds of obstacles that inhibit their capacity to program the decisions of their subordinates.[1] The first of these obstacles may be called *segmentation of information*. Even if Vario County contained only one police department, one municipal court, one superior court judge, and one criminal defense attorney, the prosecutor would still need to cope with the sometimes conflicting cues about the offense and the offender that the officer, the defense attorney, and the judge communicate to him at different times and in a sequence largely beyond the prosecutor's control. What may look like a strong case when described in a police report may become weaker at a later stage when the defense offers to present a witness with a credible story that contradicts the police report. Although a supervisor might program case dispositions by instructing the deputy how to react when the complexion of the case changes, segmentation makes the task of programming decisions more cumbersome and encourages in practice a "wait and see" strategy.

The second obstacle, *heterogeneity*, requires the prosecutor to adjust to conflicting requests and expectations from the environment.[2] Again, even if there were one police department, one defense attorney, one judge, and one expression of public expectation toward the office, the prosecutor would still have to balance the desire of the police that offenders receive punishment against the defense attorney's expectation that the prosecutor view mitigating factors realistically and against the judge's desire for the efficient processing of cases. The prosecutor must accomodate these positions rather than accept one and reject the others, because he needs to maintain his capacity to influence people with mutually inconsistent expectations. For example, the prosecutor must retain the capacity to encourage police to improve the accuracy of their reports and at the same time be able to persuade defense attorneys to accept the validity of the prosecutor's position.[3]

But Vario County contains a variety of police departments, judges, and defense attorneys. Not only do police departments vary in the quality of the information they bring the prosecutor, police officers within one department often vary in this respect. Defense attorneys employ different strategies for influencing the prosecutor, and personal values and preferences cause judges in identical roles to treat comparable cases differently. This third obstacle, *diversity*, discourages programming by increasing the number and possible combinations of categories into which a case may be classified in order to program its outcome. A policy directing prosecutors when to accept at the preliminary hearing an offer by the defense attorney to plead his client guilty to a misdemeanor would not only need to instruct the deputy how to interpret a potentially enormous factual variation, it would, in order to dispose of cases uniformly, also need to instruct the prosecutor how to adjust to different judges. It would need to instruct him to reduce in Judge X's court but not Judge Y's because Judge X imposes stiffer sentences than does Judge Y. Like all intensive technologies, the cost of making rules of sufficient detail to govern all possible case outcomes exceeds any benefit to the organization from doing so. A policy broad enough to encompass the complexities of all cases only restates the necessity of discretion, and a detailed policy always runs the risk of ignoring the unique but critical element.

Segmentation, heterogeneity, and diversity increase the impact of the fourth obstacle, *unpredictability*. In combination, these factors mean that most managing deputies know that they are less capable than the deputy or deputies directly preparing the case to assess just how the case should be handled. But in addition to the combination of these three factors, prosecutors face the additional unpredictable element that a judge or a police officer or defense attorney may individually behave in unpredictable ways. The police, defense attorneys, and judges in Vario County created for prosecutors a segmented, heterogeneous, diverse, and unpredictable working environment, but a fourth element, the dynamics of local politics, amplified these environmental characteristics.

Prosecutors and Police

Twelve different police departments as well as the sheriff's office and the California Highway Patrol brought cases to the Vario County district attorney's office. They ranged in size from fewer than two dozen employees to Condenado's 150 officers, and most prosecutors, defense attorneys, and judges believed that the quality of the work of these departments varied considerably. The Riverdale police department, in the small upper-middle-class community near Condenado, seemed to the prosecuting and defense attorneys who worked with it to investigate thoroughly, to observe due process requirements in field work, and according to prosecutor Judy Denton, who worked with them regularly, to "treat the defendants like people." Miss Denton continued:

They don't scream at them or call them names, and they get better results than those that do. The Riverdale police usually shake hands with the defendant after a prelim, and Dennis Childers [who was assigned to Riverdale in 1970] just can't get over that. In the last case I had, the defendant made a dollar bet with the officer that he'd beat the rap. Some public defenders get real uptight about that. They think you should just *hate* police. I don't blame them, either, because with some police departments some of the things you hear are true.

Cases in which "some of the things you hear" are more likely to be true arose five miles away in San Pedro. The community of San Pedro has attracted a disproportionately high number of white "immigrants" from the rural Midwest and South. The community appears to combine Baptist moralism and a propensity to brawl, and the police force there reflects the same combination of traits. The sergeant in charge of criminal investigations in San Pedro appeared almost daily in the Condenado office requesting felony complaints for trivial and/or poorly investigated cases. To the prosecutor, legally similar cases may be worth "more or less," depending on the police department involved. Judy Denton had no hesitation to file charges of interference with a police officer (Penal Code Sec. 148) when Riverdale officers requested it. They made "148" arrests rarely, and those they made held up in court. But Gary Martin, assigned to Condenado, knew that officers there had provoked or misreported acts of interference with police, and he scrutinized these arrests carefully. (Schwartz left to Gary Martin, a former police officer, the task of resolving all "148" charges in Condenado. Schwartz believed that if he handled them himself, he would sacrifice his capacity to influence departmental operations when he refused to issue complaints for charges against Condenado officers.)

Police departments also varied in the degree to which police chiefs, deputy chiefs, and lieutenants attempted to pressure the office into filing questionable cases. The Highway Patrol, because it had no entrenched office or constituency in the county, rarely intruded into the prosecutor's decision-making process. The Centerville police chief, on the other hand, and the police chief and lieutenants in Hillside seemed to the area and branch deputies for that region to complain rather frequently and sometimes bitterly when they believed the office had refused to prosecute a case they thought serious. Because police who complained to superiors could in certain circumstances extract compromises, and because, in anticipation of complaints, some superiors tried to avoid taking steps that would offend officers who frequently complained, the office dealt with these police officials in an accommodating rather than an impersonal and rule-oriented way.

Most prosecutors agreed that within any one department, police officers differed considerably in the accuracy of their reporting, their ability to give convincing performances on the witness stand, and their observation of procedural protections. One Condenado officer, the thoroughness of whose investigations frequently amazed Schwartz (Schwartz believed that this officer could match from memory the license plate number and the owner of every car he had ever stopped) also had, as Gary Martin put it, "a tendency to beat on people." Martin and several others referred to him jokingly as "148 Jones," and Martin generally refused to file 148 arrests that he made. After a brawl off-duty in a bar, Jones resigned in the summer of 1970.

In addition to considering his reputation, prosecutors weighed other rather subtle cues from officers. Howard Wright, who worked under John Lane, believed that he could tell from the way the officer presented the case to him how strong it was:

They come in and tell us when they've got bad cases. Or maybe they hate to tell you, but you can tell the way they present the case that they expect a misdemeanor all along but just decided to take a shot at the felony anyway. And there are other cases where they come in and they're all excited and they fire facts at you, and then you know they're serious.

As a result of police variation, prosecutors could not assume that the police report would prove accurate throughout the prosecution. Nearly all prosecutors and defense attorneys agreed that most police reports themselves are inevitably inaccurate in some respects, though they disagreed about the reasons for the nature of the weaknesses in reports. Gary Martin believed that police reports "are weak in that they don't give all the facts both ways. They give all the prosecutor's facts and not the other facts. They're building a case just like us." Half a dozen prosecutors believed also that police reports omit critical facts or "put matters most favorably to them" or will "skirt an issue," and they believed that these omissions were for the most part intentional. Others believed that the omissions were unconscious, caused by ignorance not bias, and supported this argument by recalling instances in which the police omitted information that would have strengthened the prosecution's case. Carl Steinway, who felt many deliberate police omissions hurt his chances of success, described a typical instance in his jurisdiction, the semi-industrial area of Cleveland:

They leave out something because they know it's not part of the game. Like they won't give a suspect the Miranda warning and they'll just stand there in the hall and shoot the shit with the guy and elicit a great statement. But they don't put the statement in the report. That causes all kinds of problems at trial, because then when the defense finds out about it, they can claim that anything the police did afterwards, they did because of the statement.

Steinway was referring to the so-called "fruit of the poison tree" doctrine, which prevents prosecutors from introducing at trial any legally obtained evidence the existence or location of which the investigating agency discovered by virtue of an illegal search, arrest, or interrogation.[4]

The police and their reports, then, presented prosecutors with informational diversity and unpredictability, but additionally police officers developed relationships with some prosecutors that strained toward mutual accommodation and compromise and therefore discouraged prosecutors from consistently screening out cases where they *knew* of defects in the arrest and investigation of the case. Accommodation and compromise also led most prosecutors to shun any responsibility for encouraging police to cease practices that violated constitutional standards, even when these practices complicated the prosecutor's task of winning convictions.

Four factors explain why relations between police and prosecutors encourage accommodation and compromise.[5] These factors, by encouraging prosecutors to file some weak cases, further mitigated against programming, because the office had to maintain some capacity to identify and "deal out" weak cases. First, most prosecutors, including many who fully accepted the legitimacy of due process standards, empathized with the police. Their empathy derived partly from the fact that they collectively sought essentially the same goal: the imposition of sanctions upon those who had committed crimes. Most of those prosecutors who reported in the interviews that their work had brought about some change in their philosophy of law or of life indicated only that they sympathized more with the officers' reactions to the frustrating nature of their work. Empathy for police officers also derived from frequent contacts between specific pairs of officers and prosecutors and from the fact that prosecutors often observed firsthand some of the sources of police frustration: the release without punishment of those whose factual guilt of a serious crime is unquestioned, perhaps because the police erred unintentionally, perhaps because the police deliberately obeyed legal requirements and refrained from making an arrest; the acquittal of someone whose factual guilt of a serious crime was unquestioned, perhaps because a defense attorney succeeded in confusing one or two jurors enough to hang the jury, perhaps by blowing up out of all proportion an insignificant inconsistency in a police officer's report or testimony. Most prosecutors believed that procedural errors freed defendants or forced them to reduce charges much more frequently than did defendants with conclusive legal defenses plead guilty. Although most prosecutors abstractly approved recent innovations in criminal procedure, repeated observation of these frustrations favorably disposed many prosecutors to "give the officer the benefit of the doubt," as one deputy put it.[6]

The few deputies who rode with officers reported seeing the heckling and the danger and the hatred that might be directed irrationally at an officer whom the deputy knew to be one of the more benevolent and restrained officers on the force. Art Pollack (a member of the liberal Peace and Freedom Party), who worked in the Condenado area and who strongly approved due process norms, reported an experience while riding with the Condenado police one night:

A call came out over the radio that someone had been shooting at a police car, and so we all started tearing over in that direction. The car ahead of us was going eighty miles an hour and hit a puddle or something and went over the edge of the road into an embankment. I guess the officer was in the hospital for about a week. Anyway, a crowd gathered and started hooting and catcalling that, you know, the pig got his, and all that, and you could see the police about to pull the batons out of their pockets and start cracking some skulls. If I had had a baton myself I probably would have started to crack some skulls too. So I had a good feeling for the kinds of pressures that can happen out there on the street, which, when you get into an antiseptic courtroom, you say, "How could a police officer do something like that?" You call it "over-reaction," but when you're out there, it's nothing abstract or artificial. You can really feel it. It's not imaginary. It's a real vibration in the air. I can understand how the cops react. That's not to say it's justified. It shouldn't happen, but it's understandable.

John Hunt, another young deputy with progressive political opinions, indicated he would have no hesitation about working in a public defender's office, but he did not feel he could do so in Vario County because of the strain being a public defender would put on the friendships he had made with police officers:

Police officers believe what they're saying. They may have a different interpretation of the facts than we do, but they really believe their side. And as a D.A. you work with the police so closely to present their side of the story that, to turn around and say, "No, I don't think you're right," well, it's just a personal thing I couldn't do. They're friends.

Prosecutors differed in the extent to which their empathy for police influenced their decisions. Prosecutors like Schwartz and Steinway, who spent considerable time with the police departments in their areas, used their relationship of trust with police to prevent officers from pressing for prosecution of cases with legal or evidentiary weaknesses and to encourage them to improve arrest and investigation practices. Crime fighters and competitors, however, tended to act as advocates for the police. Bob Valenti played soft-ball on an amateur team with many police officers from his area and indicated that he filed questionable cases in order to "deal them out":

I sit around with the police and shoot the shit. They're concerned. They don't want to lose a case when a crime has been committed. If I can find any evidentiary support in the code, I'll file on it, because I think the police deserve a hearing on it. If it's a clear out-and-out police violation, I won't file, but otherwise I will. I tend to file more than others and get more deals than others in the office. I don't know how the others in the office feel about it. I know the police leave things out [of police reports], but I've never found them saying things that were deliberately untrue. They like to leave things out, and I don't blame them. You hate to play poker with your hand on the table where everybody can see it.

Crime fighters and competitors believed that their advocacy of the police perspective would not endanger innocent citizens. B.J. Chastain, a trans-planted Oklahoma farmboy, argued that the prosecutor does not need to concern himself with the possibility that the innocent citizen will be caught up in the snare of a mistaken prosecution. He felt that police departments press cases with serious evidentiary problems only when they involve what he called "real criminals," and he added, "There's no question who the criminals are. To some extent you can tell by the crime and their rap sheet, but you can always tell from the cops, because the cops *know* who the criminals are." And Ed Lee argued, "If an officer comes in and says, 'We know that X is a pusher, a big man, but we haven't been able to nail him until now,' and he's only got a few joints on him, then I'll nail him for the felony." Thus, some prosecutors do more than give the officer the benefit of the doubt. For those prosecutors who believed their primary responsibility was to control crime, the police were the primary source of information about how to do it. Crime fighters valued police work highly and sought to reward it with aggressive prosecution.

The second reason that most prosecutors did not aggressively check police behavior is that they could only rarely determine conclusively that the police engaged in deliberately illegal practices. Pollack, for example, insisted that if he ever learned of a police officer deliberately rewriting the facts of the arrest to make it fit constitutional or evidentiary requirements, "I would write a letter to his police chief and get it out that day." But although Pollack said he had some suspicions, he said he had never been "totally sure" and therefore had not written such a letter. One prosecutor, however, did recall an instance in which he and another deputy succeeded in forcing the resignation of two police officers in their area.

We became suspicious of two police officers who were bringing in a lot of 148s because they were telling the same story over and over again. We got suspicious and started riding with them, and when we figured that a lot of the things they were doing just weren't too cool, we let our recommendations be known to the chief, and eventually they resigned.

The example suggests that only after gaining firsthand knowledge would a prosecutor willingly take such a step, and only those few prosecutors who regularly rode with patrolmen or joined in investigations gathered such concrete proof.

Third, most prosecutors valued mutually satisfying solutions with police because they had no institutionalized method for arbitrating differences. Prosecutors and defense attorneys may disagree because the rules of the game permit it and because the judge is ultimately responsible for the outcome or the resolution of their difference. But a conflict between a prosecutor and a police officer risks escalation into mistrust and hostility, because the parties themselves must engineer the solution to the problem.

Senior deputies were particularly conscious of the necessity of maintaining trusting relationships with police. When Robert Johnson moved into the office in September of 1970, he immediately began to introduce himself to police administrators in the county:

I've made it a point since I got here of going around to each police department, introducing myself and saying, "I'm Bob Nolan's new assistant. What problems should we talk about?" So there's that kind of politicking in my job. . . . I think that [getting to know the police] is absolutely imperative. . . . I think personal relations in this business are one of the most critical things. If you can't engender confidence in the people you're dealing with, you're just going to be fighting a losing battle. We have enough difficulties without throwing personality conflicts on top of it.

Dan Moore hesitated to take any step that would disrupt police coopera-tion. He would not, for example, permit a lie detector test to be given to a suspect charged with interference with, or assaulting, a police officer. Moore explained:

It's bad policy any time you have to question the word of a police officer. Any time the polygraph will flatly question the word of a police officer, I think the polygraph is not being used as a proper tool. All you've got to do is come up one time and say the guy is innocent, which the polygraph will do, and we have no way of proving [otherwise.] In other words, it's the word of our operator of the polygraph against the police officer, and as soon as you do that, you have the whole police department saying that the D.A.'s office doesn't trust them. As soon as you start running police officers on the thing, you have a complete split in the cooperation necessary. As soon as you put the guy on the other side of the thing on the polygraph, you're questioning the police officer, aren't you? Because the next step is to say, "O.K. let's run the police officer."[7]

Richard Schwartz refrained from directly challenging police concerning their practices. Like Schwartz, Carl Steinway explained, "If you play cop, you play cop. If I see something I shouldn't see, I usually look the other way rather than get into a big argument with them. They'll resent you if you overdo it." Both Steinway and Schwartz agreed that where they knew of a police violation, they would not file the case, but they did not interfere with such practices when used to gather information from an informer or to recover stolen property without prosecution. David Snow, a former deputy who continued to ride occasionally with police officers when in private practice, told me:

I strongly agree that there's all sorts of illegal searches and seizures. [The police] just do it to destroy contraband or recover stolen property or just to harass people. The Condenado police know the bad guys from the good guys at sight. They see a bad guy go by with a tail light missing, and they'll harass 'em. I've seen a lot of that, but I don't say anything. I may tell 'em afterwards that I didn't think it was necessary, but I don't try to interfere because I don't want to get involved in a big dispute that will prohibit me from riding with 'em again.

In order to legitimize in the police officer's mind the right of the prosecu-tor to refuse to prosecute, the prosecutor may agree to acquiesce in a "street policy" of the police department in which constitutional norms of arrest, search, and seizure are not followed. For example, Schwartz explained how, in the middle of 1969, a group of white residents near a park began complaining frequently to the police department that teenagers, mostly Negroes, frequently came to the park to drink and, some people alleged, to smoke marijuana and to engage in promiscuous sexual practices. The police department attempted at first to make mass arrests in the park, but the linking of any given suspect to any given act was often tenuous, and many of the first prosecutions failed. At this point Schwartz and Baum agreed with the police not to question their practices of correcting the problem in the park, but they insisted that they would only prosecute strong cases. Schwartz explained:

Some of the cases we were getting were really chicken-shit cases. You know, an arrest for littering on a guy who throws a cigarette butt down on the ground. So last year, we threw out about 90 percent of them, but there was no problem because the police were breaking up the nucleus in the park. ... But our position will remain the same. We will only file on good cases. That way we don't educate these guys that they can beat the system. If we prosecute a bunch of bummers, then they start getting the idea that the law can't touch them. If they sit in jail for twenty-four hours and then go home because somebody tells them the D.A. has decided not to prosecute this time, but he'd better be careful, then they're not so sure.

The final reason why prosecutors provide no consistent check on police behavior, a reason closely related to the third, is that the police can put pressure or "heat" on prosecutors when they do not like a prosecutorial decision. Prosecutors disliked pressure partly because they did not welcome the disruptions that they knew an irate telephone call from a police official could cause in their boss's schedule, and partly because they knew the police could convert such pressure into public criticism. Prosecutors believe the public expected stern law enforcement from them (in part because they heard most frequently from this segment of the public), and the police were the only group in the prosecutor's daily environment that threatened to reinforce or amplify this criticism.

Both the branch supervisors, Peter Hoff and Henry Baum, seemed particularly concerned about criticism from the police, and this concern was one of the factors that led Nolan to reverse their assignments in the summer of 1970. Stewart Douglas indicated he felt his new superior, Henry Baum, tried to avoid dismissing weak cases in order to keep the police happy:

Henry told me just the other day—there was a case that looked just hopeless to me, and I dismissed the case outright. It was ridiculous, and I don't know why it was filed in the first place, and Henry said, "We should try to get something on these things." I try to do that in most cases, but there are some cases I'd just laugh at if I had to put them on in trial. In a case like that I think it's our duty to dismiss, not to try to stick the guy with something. . . .
Just last week there was a bad situation with the Hillside department. They came in and wanted a search warrant. It was a cut-and-dried case as far as they were

concerned, but I saw the problem that the evidence on which the search warrant was to be based was, in my opinion, tainted because the earlier search that had turned up the stolen property was bad because the officer had lifted up a tarpaulin [without probable cause to believe that stolen property was beneath it.] This was the first search warrant I was going to write. I pointed this out to the officer, and he said, "You know you're right." But then the sergeant came in and threw the report down on my desk and said, "God damn it! What can a policeman do these days if you don't give me these things?" And about twenty minutes later Captain Richards calls up Henry, and it turned out I had to write a memo, and it got to the point where Henry was worried that the police were going to go to the victim and say, "Look, we know where your property is but the D.A. won't let us do anything about it." I know Henry was worried about it if it ever reached the papers, and I think that was the real trouble. The police couldn't see the legal problems in the case.

In the end, Baum sent the case to Robert Johnson, who decided against drafting the search warrant.

Thus, empathy, uncertainty, the necessity of maintaining trust, and the fear of criticism encouraged some prosecutors to become advocates for the police and discouraged most prosecutors from screening out aggressively the errors they perceived in police practices.[8] The absence of effective screens increased the frequency with which they had to make unanticipated adjustments at later, and usually more awkward, stages of the case.

Prosecutors and Defense Attorneys

Criminal justice research has reviewed more extensively the relations between prosecuting and defense attorneys, the process by which they dispose of the bulk of criminal cases without trial, than any other aspect of postarrest activity. These interactions, private and unreviewed, can and do encourage injustice, and we shall return in the final chapter to the question of how we might minimize these instances. For the moment, let us describe the dimensions on which defense attorney behavior, and the prosecutors' reactions to it, can vary.

First, defense attorneys in any jurisdiction vary in their capacity to present a persuasive case at trial, and in a county the size of Vario County, most prosecutors learned within their first few months on the job which defense attorneys had a reputation for exceptional persuasiveness before a jury. When an attorney had such a reputation, most prosecutors agreed that, on cases that received no sizable press coverage, they would be more likely to dismiss or reduce charges because they believed, apart from the strength of their case, that the alternative of a trial would prove time-consuming and very possibly fruitless. Thus, Len Lewis reported that Don Smith, a former Oklahoman whose "country" style proved particularly effective with juries in the north end of the county, "has had more cases washed out of this office than any other five attorneys in the county put together." (Smith was also, by general reputation, the wealthiest attorney in the county.)

But Vario County has few attorneys with Smith's forensic skills who handled criminal cases regularly. The public defender's office processed between 50 and 60 percent of the county's criminal cases. The bulk of the remainder of cases proceeded either through attorneys who so rarely appeared in criminal matters that whatever trial skills they possessed suffered from a lack of experience in criminal law, or through private attorneys who, like the public defenders, handled a large volume of cases and depended on negotiated settlements to dispose of that volume efficiently. The bulk of attorneys thus did not rely on their trial abilities but instead resorted to a variety of strategies to settle cases out of court where possible. One lawyer insisted that his effectiveness depended on his capacity to move very quickly: "You get to [the prosecutors] before the file gets thick when they think they have to fight. Before it goes down the pike too far, before they get sworn statements at the prelim, et cetera, it looks less serious." Other defense attorneys preferred to settle at the last minute when the prosecutor, in preparing for trial, would discover the defects in his case.

Defense attorneys also disagreed concerning the extent to which they should advocate legal issues forcefully. One public defender believed that he improved his chances for benefitting his client when he avoided direct negotiations with the prosecutor, which might affect his judgment:

More and more I've found that I'm at a disadvantage if I talked it over . . . because [the D.A. and the judge] are going to say, "Well it's fine, Pete, that you feel that way, but if he goes to trial, he'll probably get six months. If he pleads now, we can talk it over." But if I just walk into court and go crazy, he can't soothe me.

Another public defender followed the opposite course:

The more I piss and moan on the record, the more I get hurt. But the more I can go into chambers and argue, you know, how bad that county jail is and things like that extraneous to the case, the more likely I am to come out with some sort of favorable thing.[9]

Regardless of the strategy the defense attorney chooses, the prosecutor adjusts to cues from the defense attorney, the most important of which is the defense attorney's trustworthiness. When asked what characteristics define the best defense attorneys, most prosecutors in Vario County denied that either trial ability or interpersonal friendship mattered nearly as much as trust. When asked, "If you trust a defense attorney more, are you willing to consider the equities in the case more carefully?" all but analysts Gubser and Steinway answered positively. (Most analysts believed cases were decided primarily on the facts and the law.)

While in some instances in Vario County the trust relationship between prosecutor and defense attorney arose from the general reputation of each, the establishment of the trust relationship did not regularly depend on general reputation. Instead, trust arose between specific pairs of attorneys from their personal experiences with one another. Because of the nature of the trust relationship, it introduced additional diversity to the prosecutor's work. The trust relationship, although it did not depend on sharing common personal values or agreement about the objectives of penology, did require that the pair agree on the criteria of professional competence. Since, as the previous chapter suggested, attorneys vary in their definitions of competence, we would expect to find that case dispositions might depend on the accident that the attorneys handling the case had or had not developed mutual trust. Thus, Miss Denton, a teacher, said of a black attorney with a reputation for radicalism, Cutter Smith, "I wouldn't trust him as far as I could throw him." But Richard Schwartz and Gary Martin, who valued legal strategy and procedure more than Miss Denton, reported having no difficulty negotiating with Smith. Schwartz described the process by which he and Smith came to trust each other:

The first time we opposed each other, the first question Cutter asked was objection-able, and I objected. So he knew I knew the rules, and vice versa. Now we let each other get away with a few minor objectionable questions rather than fight them. Once I was making a point in a prelim in cross-examination and got a statement that was crucial to our case but was on a question entirely outside the scope of direct examination [and therefore objectionable]. Cutter was really cool about it. He was sitting over in the jury box, and he just looked over at me and said quietly, "That's a no-no." And that was the end of it.

The essence of the trust relationship is that it reduces uncertainty for both attorneys. Men need not share each other's personal values or substantive beliefs in order to trust one another. Schwartz and Cutter Smith disagreed fundamentally about many aspects of penology, but each could predict what the other was going to do and felt confident he could determine truth (defined in part by his own values) from the statements of the other.

Trust developed on the basis of the "match" of characteristics of a specific pair of attorneys, so that a teacher, like John Lane, might consider trustworthy information about the background of a defendant that a crime fighter would reject. But the trust relationship in all cases required that each perceive the other as honestly seeking the truth, as avoiding, to use the most common phrases, "blowing smoke," "playing games with the facts," or "bull-shitting." Most prosecutors gave no credence to those attorneys who routinely sought lenience for their clients on the basis of general statements about the defendant—his family had had "tough luck" or the defendant would get a job or join the army, for example—that they could not substantiate. This is one respect in which the private attorney may have the advantage over the P.D., for he can credibly say in some circumstances, "Your honor, I've known this boy's family all my life, and...." Public defenders cannot usually do so, and those who earn a reputation for "always poor-mouthing" for their clients tended to be ignored. Apart from formal courtroom proceedings, where most attorneys agreed they and their opponents could legitimately employ any strategy not condemned by the Canons of Ethics, the attorneys who appeared openly hostile or uncooperative to prosecutors lost their credibility. One defense attorney routinely advised his clients to say nothing either at citation hearings or to a probation officer (to the amusement of several prosecutors, who felt the wiser strategy was to tell all to the probation officer and thus seem contrite), and one prosecutor said of this strategy that it "leaves us no alternative but to go ahead and push."

The significance of the trust relationship in the disposition of cases of course presents several dangers. One of these is that because the defense attorney cannot make implausible claims and remain credible, he is often reluctant to press an innovative point of law at the initial stages of a case. Perhaps more serious, the requirement of candor, of "being realistic," can and did lead some attorneys to downplay legitimate claims for their client. B.J. Chastain remarked, for example:

I get so damned pissed off and tired of these guys who come in and cry, "My guy's got a job" or "My guy's about to join the army," when he's got a rap sheet as long as your arm. His guy's a loser, and he's wailing on my desk about what a fine man he is. What really wins me is the guy who comes in and says, "O.K., what are we going to do with my criminal today? I know he has no redeeming social value. He's been a bad son of a bitch all his life, so just let me know your position. But frankly, you know, my feeling is that this is just not the case to nail him on. We all know if he does something serious, he's going." And before long the guy who approaches it this way has you wrapped around his little finger.

But the trust relationship is simultaneously a prerequisite for getting the prosecutor to consider mitigating circumstances. Because prosecutors soon discover that the defense can easily create a plausible story that, in trial, proves false, they are generally inclined to disbelieve a defense claim raised in negotiations without some reason for believing it apart from the story itself. Most believed not that the defense attorney has his client lie, but that before hearing much of the client's story he guides him toward the best position to take. As one deputy put it:

As soon as the client has outlined a few facts of the case, say it's an assault, the attorney will stop him and say, "From what you've told me so far, I can think of several defenses, self defense, for example. Think hard, now, Mr. Client, did you see a shiny object or anything that might have looked like a weapon in the victim's hand? Did he make any sudden movements? Is there anything you can remember along these lines, Mr. Client?" And before you know it, he's got the client half-believing his own lie.

Because prosecutors tend to downgrade the truthfulness of the defense position, many defense attorneys believed they could maximize the benefits to their clients as a group by being candid at all times. Miss Denton recalled dismissing a case because of her trust of the defense attorney. It was a sex case, and the suspect had a prior sex offense on his record.

We looked at it pretty closely because it was a serious crime. He had a fantastic story, and when I first saw it I was sure he did it. But the lawyer seemed to be telling it straight; he really seemed to believe his client. So we took a closer look and then some of the facts began to come out that cast a doubt. The demeanor of the defendant made a difference, too. He was scared to death, and he was also very handsome. He was so scared that if he did it, I'm sure we scared him so much he wouldn't do it again, so I think justice was done.

While candor and honesty need not in theory prevent an attorney from pushing the prosecutor to consider the legal, factual, and equitable merits of the defendant's case, this inhibition is often the practical result, and the final chapter will suggest reforms to minimize this danger.

Prosecutors and Judges

In interviews defense attorneys and judges were asked if "differences in personalities and personal preferences of judges" seemed to correspond to the communities that they served. Nearly all respondents, including most judges, believed that judicial styles and preferences did not seem to reflect clearly community needs or patterns. One superior court judge went so far as to doubt whether "the same judge on the same day" would necessarily behave consistently with himself, let alone with judges in his own community. Jack Evans, an attorney in Nolan's old office, stated:

I have no doubt that, everything being equal, if you ran a case through the [different] courts, you'd find almost as many dispositions as you have courts. I think work load, the area, and the personalities of judges all enter into it. In Hillside, you have Coughlin, who is likely to give you a pretty good shaft, whereas down at the other end of the same hall with Sam Speegle you have, well, if I were a citizen I'd say it was some of the most outrageous dealing that goes on, just because I think Sam's basically lazy. In Pleasant Valley you have Martha West upstairs who's just an unknown. The woman's nuts. . . . You know that on a drunk driving upstairs Martha is going to give the same fine that Dick Hanrahan does downstairs, but he's also going to get five days suspended and he's going to get sent to traffic school, which just isn't going to happen downstairs. In Condenado Judge Bailey will take a colored guy and just rap hell out of him. But Henry Williams [also in Condenado], maybe because he's colored, tends to be a lot more lenient.

To establish precisely the extent of judicial variation in Vario County would require an extended empirical review of case dispositions. To gather a sample of cases large enough to control for all potentially relevant variables would have required research resources not available for this project. What is significant for our purposes, however, is that prosecutors and defense attorneys, without benefit of computer analysis, believed that judges varied considerably and sometimes behaved unpredictably.

Municipal Court

The thirteen municipal court judges ranged in age from forty-three to seventy-two, and they became municipal court judges at different times and in a variety of ways.[10] The position is formally nonpartisan, and while several of the older judges, like Judge Bailey, earned the right to run for the office by serving what twenty-two years ago was a powerful Democratic machine in Condenado, few of the more recently elected municipal court judges had any strong party ties. Hanrahan had worked actively in the Rotary Club in his area. Judge Mason Dale, a Democrat, had few organizational or political affiliations but took advantage of an electoral fight between two older Republican lawyers in his area (the industrial town of Cleveland) and won election because the two opponents split the majority of the vote.

In one respect prosecuting and defense attorneys agreed that most municipal court judges were uniform; the quality of their legal analysis was poor. Because their legal education predated many of the constitutional innovations in the area of criminal procedure in the 1960s, and because most judges appeared case-hardened by their years spent reviewing daily life's sordid affairs, few municipal court judges (Mason Dale was an exception) seemed to take an active interest in ruling favorably on an innovative defense motion.[11]

The following typical comments from prosecutors and defense attorneys reflect their perceptions of the municipal court bench.

Carl Steinway: There are few judges who are *really* objective and few judges who know the law.

Tom Gubser: A judge is somebody who knew a governor.

Stewart Douglas: One of my biggest disillusionments concerns the quality of judges. Only a few know the law, and several are outright incompetents.

Richard Henderson, a former prosecutor who headed the public defender's office in Vario County: If you take the median group of judges, I would say they were unwilling to follow the damn law. They're not worried about reversals. They can get around reversals by finding the right things. . . . Municipal court judges are particularly blind.

Dennis Childers: I always thought the judge was supposed to know all the answers, not rely on the attorneys to tell him the answers, but a lot of them do that. Bailey's probably the worst, because he doesn't know the law.

Whether the attorneys do in fact inform the judge correctly is another matter. From what I could observe, prosecutors only bothered to check legal points when they prepared for trial or to resist a defense motion. They rarely bothered to research or discuss legal or evidentiary questions in negotiations or pretrial proceedings. The office tried to keep a file of the briefs that deputies had previously written on legal questions that had been raised, but the file was not kept up to date, and very few deputies consulted it. Some deputies did not know of its existence. One deputy complained that his work load prevented him from being of service to the judge. "Judges rely on us to a great extent to bring them the law that's applicable. But we just don't have time to help the judge." A public defender told me in his work in municipal court he did not bother to do much legal research because he felt the judges' ignorance prevented them from appreciating a sound point when he made it.

Of the thirteen municipal court judges (technically only nine are municipal court judges; the remaining four presided over what were called "justice courts" in townships of less than forty thousand), three and possibly four, in the minds of most prosecutors and defense attorneys, possessed questionable competence for the job. The first of these, who retired at the end of 1970, was a justice court judge in his mid-seventies.

Another justice court judge in the category of questionable legal competence, B.W. ("Gramps") Stevens, perhaps belonged there by preference rather than by virtue of his age, sixty-one. His jurisdiction, the rural and sparsely populated northwestern third of the county, presented him with a stream of minor cases, principally drunk driving and disturbing the peace, which he preferred to settle in terms of his own intuitive sense of justice. He liked to tell the story of the man he convicted for riding a horse on the freeway while drunk, despite the fact that the statute (Vehicle Code Sec. 23102) under authority of which Stevens imposed the fine refers specifically to vehicle and by strong implication, therefore, excluded horses. The defendant, representing himself, sent a series of outraged and partially incoherent letters of protest to the judge (one of which began "Dear Judge Your Honor Sir"), and Stevens, aware of the legal problem, explained, "He gave me such a bad time, I found him guilty anyway. He was such a knucklehead. Sometimes I think stupidity should be penalized, too." Stevens delighted in offering a cup of coffee and endless stories to anybody who made the long trip out to his office and courtroom in Clover's creaky gray "courthouse" that resembled a feedstore, because at one time it was. He was not embittered by his low level of judicial attainment and seemed to have genuine affection for Clover's slow pace. Stevens did not hesitate to employ the knowledge he had gained about his townsfolk in making sentencing decisions. He reported, for example, that he was more likely to treat Mexican than Negro traffic violators leniently:

We have a Fourth of July picnic here every year, and my wife always comments on the courtesy of the Mexican families at the picnics. But the colored people seem to feel they're always getting picked on. With the Mexicans, if they got hauled up on some traffic offense, they usually don't have a license, and I like to treat them simply as driving without a license. That way I can keep them on the hook so they get a license and learn the rules. But I'm not sure the colored are motivated to do that.

"Gramps" Stevens, because he was essentially a conciliatory man, did not stimulate criticism from the bar. His cases were inconsequential for the most part, and while his decisions provoked amusement, few if any would have cared to see him removed from office. Martha West, on the other hand, provoked frequent and sometimes bitter resentment, apparently because, unlike Stevens, she insisted that the parties before her adhere strictly to the formal trappings of courtroom procedure at the expense of attention to substance and to moving the cases. In part what irritated defense attorneys was her tendency to equate formality with impartiality, often by berating or taking over from an attorney (or witness) who departed from the required decorum. She was particularly proud of awards she had received from traffic safety councils for her efforts to punish traffic offenders, and a wall of her courtroom, a converted gymnasium, was lined with citations of merit. She described her approach to the job:

I realize I'm not the fastest judge in the West. I give individual attention to each case, and I don't cut corners. I leave the courtroom exhausted each night because I just don't believe in industrial, belt-line handling of cases. If I get out for lunch at all, or off before 6:00, I'm lucky. I'm careful to scrutinize cases if they ask for a reduction or dismissal. If I think it's because of who he is, I'll stop it. I treat everybody, politicians and attorneys, like everybody else, like people. If the attorneys in a case do something I don't like, I bawl them out.

Regardless of the sense of impartiality that she may have conveyed to defendants, attorneys resented the time it took to complete proceedings before her (she completed only about half as many cases as her cojudge "downstairs" in Pleasant Valley, Judge Hanrahan), and they resented her intrusions into their preparations and presentations. One defense attorney commented:

It's impossible to assess her intelligence because emotional factors get in the way. She has an ego that's like a part of the body that suffers from acute inflammation. It's grotesquely swollen and exquisitely tender. Everything she says or does is in terms of it, and it hardly matters what else is going on, or what she may or may not know about the law.

A public defender, a married woman whom her office assigned to West's court in hope of winning greater empathy from her than a previous male had done, made a similar point:

She is very nervous about disrespect. Often she'll jump on the young Jewish attorney from Los Angeles for the slightest supercilious nuance. She'll rant and rave and then get sorry and end up giving his client the break because she's sorry. I had trouble knowing what to say to her, because you never knew what she would react to. The kind of thing that's usually understood between attorneys and judges, that you don't need to spell out, like why you need a continuance, she would—and this is why so many attorneys can't stand her—make a point of, you know, "We're going to have all this on the record; now give me your reasons."

Fortunately, at least for lawyers who wanted to complete their work rapidly, Judge West shared the bench in Pleasant Valley with Dick Hanrahan, who was in many ways her opposite, a judge most attorneys found very easy to get along with. Instead of citations of merit for promoting traffic safety, he displayed various indicia of his prominent position as a Rotarian, and his judicial style seemed to reflect the Rotary Club's Four Way Test which he had framed on the wall of his chambers: "First . . . Is it the truth? Second . . . Is it fair to all concerned? Third . . . Will it build good will and better friendship? Fourth . . . Will it be beneficial to all concerned?" Since both prosecutors and defense attorneys preferred to work with Hanrahan, they agreed upon a procedure to avoid trials before Martha West, which a defense attorney explained as follows:

I arrange, as do many other lawyers, not to try criminal cases before Martha, and the way we do that is, if we have a pretrial [conference] before Hanrahan, we arrange to try the case before him. If we have the conference before Martha, we ask for a jury and then waive the jury at the last minute and point out that since she pretried the case, she can't serve as trial judge. She's quite aware of what's going on, and the D.A.'s office is aware of what's going on. Everybody goes along with it. Part of the problem is that she complains about her work load, although she probably disposes of only a third of the cases Hanrahan does, so she's happy to shove the cases off on him, and the D.A.'s office will suggest it. . . . Martha will automatically sentence a drunk driver with a prior to jail, even when the deputies drop the prior. Hanrahan doesn't do that, so it's Gresham's law at work. . . . Hanrahan is the kind of lawyer who could really only make it in a small community by being president of the Rotary Club and having fifteen kids and being a nice guy. Never any pretensions to knowing any law. He's temperamentally not ill-equipped to be a judge, but he's never going to be a bright guy.

Stewart Douglas had a slightly different image of Hanrahan:

Hanrahan is more an equity judge than a law judge. A lot of times I think he makes the right decision for the people involved, even if that's not what the law says. Take the guy who is going to lose his license for a fourth traffic ticket. He will say, "I think you're probably guilty, but the punishment [automatic license revocation] doesn't fit the crime, and I can't control the punishment. So I'll send you to traffic school and if you complete that I'll find you not guilty." I don't know if that's bad or good. . . . I like him personally—he's very fair in his decisions—but I've heard some rumors that bother me. [LHC: Like doing favors for friends?] Well, I've seen him do a few of those for a fact, and that bothered me a lot, but, you know, he drinks a lot and he's been picked up a few times, and his court reporter took a swing at a sheriff's deputy not too long ago, and we got him out of that. The attorneys he likes, you see it every day, he gives 'em anything they want. But if he doesn't like you, he can make it rough on you. I don't know if that's right or not.

The municipal court located in Hillside, a rapidly growing area adjoining Pleasant Valley, also had two judges whose styles differed dramatically. Judge Coughlin had the reputation as the "tougher" sentencer of the two, and of being "hard to do business with." His associate, Sam Speegle, was particularly eager to promote compromises. The same defense attorney who criticized West's ego said of Speegle:

Sam Speegle doesn't hate nothin' or nobody. As far as he's concerned, if nobody's mad enough to bother, he'll go along with anything you suggest, and it's a pleasure to go back in chambers with Bob Valenti and Judge Speegle, because you can settle things just like that and get it done. You can broker the thing to a conclusion. I don't know if that's justice or not, but you can do something for your client.

Most attorneys found Speegle likable but very indecisive. He rarely ruled on the objections of counsel, preferring instead to suggest alternate ways of phrasing the question that would satisfy both sides. When he found a man innocent in court trial owing to an error of the police officer, prosecutors reported that he often would not rule on the spot, but rather would take the decision "under advisement" for several weeks, then decide quietly so as not to hurt the officer's feelings. A public defender recalled an instance in which Speegle, apparently unwilling to offend either the police or the D.A., held a man to answer when he felt he had a good legal defense, then called "after he issued the holding order and told me, 'Look, I don't think your man should be held to answer. You've got a good 995 motion there.' "

Coughlin, unlike Speegle, prided himself on his fierce independence. In a newspaper interview during the election campaign (he was the only judge opposed for reelection in the county in 1970), he reportedly stated: "When I climb up in that saddle, I can sit there and decide a case the way it should be decided—and I couldn't care less who's on what side." While most attorneys confirmed that Coughlin was in that sense impartial, those who worked regularly before him in 1970 became alarmed by the extent to which a problem with alcohol increasingly affected his judgment, especially as the election approached, when some reported smelling hints of a three-martini breakfast in addition to his customary three-martini lunches. He took a long vacation shortly after the election, and upon returning seemed to have become more predictable than before, when some defense attorneys had found him at times amiable, at times irascible. One public defender recalled an incident in which Coughlin ordered his bailiffs to put the hand and leg cuffs on a prisoner awaiting a hearing "as tight as possible" because the prisoner, clowning, had attached his loose leg iron to the leg of another prisoner seated beside him in the holding cell. He also recalled another incident in which Coughlin had sentenced a prisoner to the maximum sentence of six months on a misdemeanor. On his way back to the holding cell, the defendant called the escorting bailiff "a pig." The bailiff told the judge, whereupon the judge recalled the prisoner and announced, "I know it's illegal and I can't do it, but I'm going to modify your sentence and make it one year." The public defender waited for him to cool off, went back the next day, and talked him into modifying the sentence back to six months.

A prosecutor recalled:

We had a chicken-shit case that we wanted to deal out—it was a bum speeding ticket. But the defendant went pro per [that is, represented himself] and challenged Coughlin. So the case was tried before Speegle. Coughlin came over to me and said, "I don't want you to dismiss this case." Speegle said he wanted to dismiss it, but he didn't want to piss Coughlin off, so we screwed around for a couple of continuances until Coughlin cooled off, and then dismissed it.

Three judges sit on the Condenado municipal court. Between Judge Williams, the only Negro on the bench in the county, at one end of the corridor and Judge Bailey at the other end was more than seventy-five feet of linoleum tile. Williams was a careful and scholarly judge about whom neither public defenders nor prosecutors had any criticism. In terms of "knowing the law" and "willingness to follow the law," most attorneys ranked him with Mason Dale as the best municipal court judge in the county. Judge Bailey, most agreed, had little inclination to adhere to the niceties of legal procedures. One public defender recalled catching Bailey signing the order holding a man to answer during a preliminary examination before the prosecution had finished calling its witnesses and hence before the defense had had a chance to complete cross-examination and disprove the prosecution's case. Bailey was the county's only judge whom prosecuting and defense attorneys regularly characterized as a racist, and he was the only judge, with the exception of Stevens's Mexican/Negro differentiation, who made overtly racist comments to me when interviewed. During a three-drink lunch of his own, he freely admitted he was simply sitting on the bench long enough for his pension rights to mature so that he could retire, which he planned to do shortly. After lunch, he told me that a prominent liberal black attorney, Cutter Smith, had said he was considering running against Bailey in the last election. Bailey reported that friends asked him if he were worried about being defeated, but that he had assured them, "Hell, no. I'm not worried. If that nigger can beat me, then I don't deserve the job in the first place." He continued:

That no good bastard. He [Smith] will cut corners to win cases. He got on my shit list but good. He tried to tell me he wasn't counsel of record once when the record itself showed otherwise. I'm mad at the son of a bitch for not running against me. We don't have a monopoly on these jobs. . . . Ethics don't mean anything to him. Win, that's it. He was a bulldog of a prosecutor. On the other side of the fence, he's begging. I'd say that nine out of ten attorneys realize that all they've got going for them is a reputation for being honest.

While some attorneys felt Bailey was a relatively lenient sentencer, others felt he was severe, but most would agree with Art Pollack's analysis: "If the client's black, there ain't no way he's going to find him not guilty."

Despite his candor concerning those Negroes he felt were lazy or dishonest, or about his colleague, whom he felt was too lenient (Bailey gave shoplifters an automatic five-day jail sentence and resented that Williams did not: "Christ, a kid goes before Williams and you'd think he was getting a medal"), Bailey was more of an old school Democrat than a racist, a man who was thoroughly aware of men's weaknesses and the things that could frustrate them. He had few illusions about the immutability of legal principles and preferred to rely on factual or situational assessment of guilt and of punishment. I asked him if he considered the economic status of the defendant when imposing sentence, and he answered:

I certainly consider their economic position. The trouble is, the fellow with the Cadillac, he knows somebody and gets off light, maybe he gets off completely. But the poor bastard with five or six kids, he can't afford it, he gets took because he doesn't know anybody. There's no question [that defendants sacrifice their opportunity to present a good defense], especially where the client runs out of money. I never made any money in private practice because I don't believe in playing all these games. If my client was guilty, I pled him. The clients with the money these days take it all the way to the Superior Court.

Bailey was resigned to what seemed to him to be the inevitabilities of the system around him, and, as he waited for retirement, he was in no mood to do much about it. His views of criminal justice after eighteen years on the bench are worth repeating:

Nobody's overworked around here, but it's a common complaint I hear all the time: "We don't have enough time to prepare cases." Dozens of times I've seen officers sitting around court after being up all night and wanting to go home and get some sleep, and the D.A. comes in and says, "I won't need you." Here's a guy wanting to go home and get some sleep! . . . They don't prepare, that's my only criticism of the D.A.s. There's too big a turnover for anybody to get expert. Nobody should stay in that office more than two years, just long enough to make some contacts with judges and other lawyers. Two years of contacts in the D.A.'s office is worth twenty years of contacts in private practice, especially for a stranger in the county. But he shouldn't stay there long because the experience is limited. . . . Now there's a flock of new D.A.s and P.D.s staggering around wondering what to do. Juries are won by argument, but they usually don't have any argument. All these new D.A.s and P.D.s, Christ, it's a never-ending battle. They have to learn by trial and error. We have to break 'em all in, it seems. We've just been muddling around for eighteen years. I can't tell them what to do, and they sure as Christ can't tell me what to do. That's the system; it's been going on that way for years.

I asked him whether he felt any political pressures on him, an idea he scoffed at. But he did say, "You hear so many lies and stories in this job you never know what to believe. . . . And you make so many enemies, hell, I don't know how I ever got elected. The winners, hell, they were right all along. And the losers blame you."

Judge Lucas, who sat between Bailey and Williams physically and in some ways philosophically, was a younger and more inquisitive man than Bailey. He was a bright but somewhat cynical iconoclast who enjoyed exposing the foibles of men and systems. While most attorneys believed he knew the law, whether he would follow it or not seemed to depend on criteria that attorneys had difficulty assessing. B.J. Chastain complained that Lucas would on occasion hold a man against the D.A.'s wishes to teach prosecutors and police not to bring such cases in the first place:

The trouble with Lucas—I hate that son of a bitch—is that you can't go in to him and say, "Look, judge, we shot this thing in the air and it came down full of holes; we better wash it out. Let's take a 415 plea or submit it on the police report." He'd just chew my ass out for wasting court time in the first place. He will hold to answer on anything. There are times when a D.A. goes in there and he wants to lose, and usually there are ways of signaling that. But you can't do that with Lucas, and he'll hang you up on some of the worst dogs imaginable and the flimsiest God damn things imaginable.

Lucas denied this motive, but he did admit that he believed that at the prelim the judge should not aggressively screen out cases.

How do you define the purpose of the prelim? Our approach is, is it reasonable that the defendant go through the expense and trouble of a trial? Any kind of case at all is generally reasonable. He may not get convicted on the exact crime charged, but that's second-guessing on our part.

For attorneys in Vario County, then, the municipal court bench posed several problems. First, though individually they may have been for the most part predictable, their preferences, attitudes, and behavior as a group did not provide predictable guides, guides by which the prosecutor or defense attorney could predict the decision regarding a case. Some judges (Coughlin was an example) sentenced more severely on some crimes than did the presiding superior court judge, so that in those instances the filing of a charge as a misdemeanor or the reduction of a charge to a misdemeanor would produce a longer sentence than the prosecution of the identical case as a felony. But this was true only of some judges and some classifications of cases, and judicial sentencing behavior was not uniform enough to permit the prosecuting attorney's office to make any policies regarding the reduction of cases.

Second, some judges, particularly those who intervened actively in the negotiation of cases, did not appear to prosecuting and defense attorneys to behave predictably regarding the practical questions for which the attorneys must have answers. The technology of law provides no clear and unambiguous guides or criteria for determining the significance of a prior arrest or conviction, the weight to be given the possible loss of employment, or—and this is perhaps the most critical from the defense attorney's point of view—the degree to which judges at the municipal court level ought to assume the responsibility for "making law," that is, extending beyond their precise facts and to their logical limits appellate court decisions concerning the rights of the accused. At least in Vario County, the variability among the lower-court judges suggested that as a system of behavioral control, the law itself did not succeed, either through moral suasion or through fear of correction and implicit criticism by reversal on appeal, in instilling in those who administered it common answers to the questions that matter most for prosecutors, defense attorneys, and their clients.

This review also suggests that a judge who meets all the qualities of a "good" judge may be a fairly rare animal, for each desirable quality *may* in a given case also have undesirable aspects. The considerate judge may be indecisive. The equitable judge may play favorites, perhaps to compensate for his lack of legal knowledge. The judge who insists on the observation of all formal legal procedures may be working out a problem of ego and self-identity that blocks him (or her) from sensitivity to factual variation and sensitivity to subtle but important cues. Besides Judge Williams (who neither returned a questionnaire nor submitted to an interview), only Judge Dale of Cleveland won consistent praise from the bar. One prosecutor described him:

Judge Dale is just tops. He's the perfect Renaissance Man: exceedingly fair, decisive, refreshingly open, and he enjoys [his work]. It's a pleasure to work with him. The last thing a judge can do is let his ego get tied up in a case, which is the negative thing about Coughlin.

The Cleveland area did not present Judge Dale with the amorphous problems of the rapidly growing communities of Hillside and Pleasant Valley. His was an older industrial area with stable ethnic groups—particularly

Portuguese, Italian, Mexican, and to some extent Negro—and traditions. Dale, partly Portuguese himself, delighted in the ethnic diversity and stability of the area, and on the days I spent in his courtroom he took me to lunch at several different ethnic restaurants in Cleveland. He campaigned for the job because he was dissatisfied with the bitter divorce battles that dominated his private practice and prevented him from spending time with his family. He took his annual one-month vacation to ethnically diverse places like Scandinavia and, most recently, rural Greece, where he was careful to look up the peasant parents of a Cleveland acquaintance.

His delight in human beings and their diversity translated philosophically into a respect for human life and opposition to violence. He defended the abolition of the death penalty with some genuine passion:

Without the death penalty, some people now have the idea that the defendant isn't getting punished, but I think that institutional killing may encourage violence. It diminishes everybody's respect for human life. There's a peculiar horror in the deliberate ritual killing. That's what makes Manson's case so horrible and that's what the state is doing when it executes, which is a ritual too.

At a later point he added:

We [in the United States] like violence. You know, television and all that. I don't believe in censorship, but if I censored anything it would be the killing in cold blood on TV. That's obscenity. We're perhaps the most violent nation in the world. I'm one of those who believes in no guns except for hunting. The .45 to protect the home is involved in seven out of ten murders. . . . The gun is a crazy symbol. There are sexual theories for it.

Judge Dale won the respect and admiration of those who worked before him because he combined an evident interest in individual suspects with a scholarly interest in legal analysis and a willingness to rule in the defendant's favor when the logic of law so dictated, without fear of public criticism. Judge Jensen, the superior court calendar judge in 1970, did attempt to conform to public criticism directed at the courts, and we turn to the subject of the superior court in Vario County next.

Superior Court

In 1971, the ten superior court judges, in response to increasing work load, chose two of their number to work as superior court calendar judges. (Traditionally the position has rotated among the judges who expressed a willingness to take the position. The post is not in any sense a particularly desirable one, and I was led to believe that the judges had at times had some difficulty agreeing on which one would volunteer.) With two judges on the bench, attorneys needed to adjust to the fact that the two differed rather substantially in their sentencing patterns. One, a sixty-year-old judge with nineteen years experience on the superior court bench in the first six months of 1971, sentenced felony offenders who pleaded guilty before him to terms in state institutions, state prison, Youth Authority, and the drug rehabilitation center or the Atascadero center for sexual deviants, for example, slightly less than half as frequently as did his colleague, a Republican in his late forties who had received his appointment to the bench only in early 1970 and who had had very little previous criminal experience. This difference, of course, gave knowledgeable attorneys (public defenders who work with the judges every day are especially aware of such things) some opportunity to maneuver their cases, and this disparity required some pragmatic adjustments from the prosecutors as well.

In 1970, however, only one superior court judge handled all criminal calendar matters—arraignments, motions, pretrial conferences, acceptances of pleas of guilty, and the sentencing of those who pleaded guilty—and the district attorney's office did not face the interjudge variability to which it had to adjust at the municipal court level. Judge Jensen did, however, pose several problems for prosecuting and defense attorneys. First, his judicial style differed significantly from that of his predecessor in 1969, Judge Shapiro, and the increasing severity of sentences in superior court itself required, as we shall see, some prosecutorial adjustment. Second, Jensen's reluctance to take firm positions on cases and his considerable sensitivity to potential political criticism produced its own variability and unpredictability.

Like the municipal court bench in Vario County, the superior court bench shared neither a single political tradition nor a uniform philosophy of the judicial role. The ten superior court judges ranged in age from forty-five to sixty-four. Two owed appointments to Governor Earl Warren, one to Governor Knight, five to Governor Brown, and two to Governor Reagan. Most of the Democratic appointments had been modestly active in party affairs, although predominantly at the county rather than the state level. Judge Thomas, for example, had served as the party's treasurer in the county and had, during his legal practice, acted as campaign manager for several candidates for the state legislature. Republican judges more likely earned the job through nonparty connections, primarily through the bar association, civic clubs, or business connections. Judge Rivers, a judge appointed in 1970 by Governor Reagan, claimed to have little or no party connection, but he was well known and highly regarded as an attorney representing various insurance companies in major personal injury cases.

The diversity of backgrounds, the even split in party affiliation, and the diversity of attitudes of superior court judges led Judge Thomas to describe relations among his nine colleagues:

Have you ever read C.P. Snow's book *The Masters*? It describes how the Fellows maneuver and manipulate toward the selection of a Master. And there's a great deal in there that bears resemblance to the way we have to live. [It's] kind of a monastic existence, and we only rarely really talk to each other. [There are] personal differences and political differences; we're kind of polarized. . . . There is a rebellion on the part of some judges, and a refusal to accept these rules. [He is referring to the recent innovations in criminal procedures.] They feel these rules are wrong, and they don't realize their obligations to accept them, and what they're playing is a game of poker: Will this case be appealed or won't it? . . . But there's no excuse for a judge not following the law because he doesn't believe in it, as long as the law is clear.

Personal differences among judges did not necessarily correspond to their differences in political affiliations or background characteristics. Judge Shapiro and Judge Jensen, both Brown-appointed Democrats, had worked actively in local affairs prior to their appointments, but their judicial styles, or at least the perceptions both prosecutors and defense attorneys had of their styles, varied.

Judge Shapiro was an aggressive, stubbornly independent, and occasionally theatrical judge who firmly believed that nearly all criminal cases could and should be settled without trial. As calendar judge, his leverage in influencing the disposition of cases lay in his ability to convince the defendant and his attorney that, upon conviction, the defendant would receive a sentence he considered "reasonable." In the bulk of felonies the defense attorney is far from confident of winning the case at trial. Because the calendar judge cannot preside at the trial and impose sentence in the event of a conviction at trial, the defense cannot accurately predict the sentence his client will receive if the case does go to trial. In fact, he will not know who the trial judge is until shortly before the trial begins. Because of these uncertainties, the defense attorney is usually willing to plead his client if he and the client believe they will receive an acceptable sentence.[12] Judge Shapiro so firmly believed in the efficiency of this procedure that in 1969 he committed himself in open court to a specific sentence in each case in advance of the sentencing analysis by the probation department, a procedure that appeared to irritate some probation officers, since it downplayed their usefulness. To this commitment Shapiro added the proviso that if the probation report uncovered information that required the imposition of a sentence greater than that originally promised, he would permit the defendant to withdraw his plea of guilty and proceed to trial without prejudice. Judge Shapiro himself initiated the mandatory pretrial conference in 1967. He preferred what he called the Scandinavian system of criminal adjudication in which all but the legal and evidentiary questions of guilt are settled by penal specialists, and he sought to adopt the features of that form of inquiry in his own handling of criminal cases. He also favored removing several of the "crimes without victims," such as gambling, prostitution, and minor drug offenses, from the category of crime altogether.

Most attorneys felt the procedures before Judge Shapiro handled the case load efficiently, and Judge Jensen continued this form in 1970. Judge Jensen, however, refused to commit himself on the record, and therefore publicly, to pretrial sentence positions. Unlike Shapiro's forceful management of pretrial conferences in chambers, Jensen often declined to commit himself to a sentence position even in the privacy of his chambers, preferring instead to defer until he had received the probation report. Jensen's preference apparently derived from his belief that he should conform to what he perceived to be a series of public demands for stricter law enforcement. The shift from Shapiro to Jensen contributed to the 275 percent increase in the rate of felonies that went to trial in 1970 over 1969.[13]

When I asked Judge Jensen if he would consent to being interviewed as part of my research, he declined, citing both the press of business and the concern that he might be quoted, directly or indirectly, in a way that would prove embarrassing. He recalled an acquaintance, a superior court judge in another county, had once been quoted to his embarrassment in the *Stanford Law Review*. My promise of anonymity did not change his mind, since, he reminded me, if someone knew the county and the year of my study, they could also figure out who had been the superior court criminal calendar judge. He did say he would look my questionnaire over and "give the matter some further thought."

This incident seemed to capture the three qualities of Jensen's judicial performance that irked both the prosecutors and the defense attorneys, particularly the latter: his considerable sensitivity to public criticism, his ability to justify and defend a position by giving "good" as well as "real" reasons (in open court this technique is known as "record building"), and his hesitancy to resolve problems conclusively.

Judge Jensen, a Democrat and formerly a partner in the law firm of the district's progressive congressman, had at the beginning of 1970 a reputation among the members of the county bar for being among the county's most knowledgeable and thorough judges. As Walt Tyler, a long-established defense attorney in Condenado put it, "Bill is extremely conscientious about his work. He eats, sleeps, and dreams nothing but good law." Jensen also had a reputation for fairness, both in his perpetually courteous attitude to defendants tried before him and regarding what most attorneys felt was fair and sensible sentencing. As 1970 progressed, and those who knew and worked with him became increasingly aware of what Judge Shapiro called Jensen's "flip-flop," speculation increased that more complex motives than devotion to good craftsmanship moved Jensen. Those with whom I talked advanced basically two explanations for Jensen's stiffer sentencing, his increased reluctance to grant defense motions, and his reluctance to approve plea bargains. First, some believed that Jensen hoped for an appointment to the appellate bench in California, and some attorneys explained Jensen's behavior in terms of his seeking the most likely strategy for appointment. Several attorneys indicated that Jensen had previously assumed that "keeping the bar happy" would best insure his appellate appointment, because the Reagan administration considers the recommendations of the local bar associations, but that, more recently, he had concluded that as a Democrat he would have to build for himself a reputation for firmness in criminal areas, a posture not widely welcomed by the local bar, to win a Reagan appointment.

A second explanation, more psychological than political, was that Jensen was personally unable to handle public or private criticism. This theory speculated that when criticism from the press, from the grand jury, and from police and probation officers exceeded the criticism he might receive from the lawyers who practiced before him, Jensen simply yielded to the greater threat and rationalized it, arguing that the public was demanding firm law enforcement and that he was obliged to conform to the dictates of public opinion. Although in the memory of those who worked there, no superior court judge had ever been seriously challenged, let alone defeated, for reelection, Judge Jensen was no doubt aware of the challenge and ultimate censure of Judge Glickfeld, a judge in San Francisco who imposed a seemingly lenient sentence on a suspect accused of attempted rape, and of the ultimately successful challenge to Judge Gitelson, who ordered the bused integration of Los Angeles schools in 1970. One local newspaper did threaten early in 1970 to print the disposition of every felony case in superior court, and Jensen may have felt threatened, although he did not face reelection for another four and one-half years.[14]

The prosecutors and public defenders fretted less about the explanation than about the fact that he sentenced rather erratically and did not provide clear-cut guides for case resolutions. Bob Stern, one of the most exasperated of the public defenders because he handled many of the public defender's felonies in pretrial negotiations, told me:

Often what happens in Jensen's court today depends on yesterday's paper. Once the paper picked up a story of a guy who was sent to county jail, and I might add with probation terms substantially stiffer than what he would have gotten if he had gone to state prison, but the paper picked up the fact that 173 counts of passing bad checks were dismissed against this guy as part of the deal. And of course they said nothing about the sentence. So somebody else—the day after this hits the papers, a guy with two checks, no priors, got a deal from the D.A. for county jail time. He comes up for sentencing before Jensen, and Jensen says state prison. He didn't even want to let him withdraw the plea. Well, the guy spent another thirty days in jail waiting for a trial after we withdrew the plea, and when he got it, the trial judge took one look at it and said, "Why is this guy going to trial?" We explained that Jensen wanted to send him to *state prison*, and he said, "No, it's not going to trial." The judge adopted the probation report, and the guy walked out. Here's a guy that was going to go to state prison because of bad press and because Jensen can't take the heat. This happens all the time.

Another public defender, Jim Pepper, described the exasperation of working before Jensen and said he would prefer to practice before a predictably prosecution-oriented judge, like Judge Scott, than to practice before the unpredictable Jensen. (I found Scott, though consistently conservative, a difficult interview subject because he turned each question into an ideological argument. One of his comments, in contrast to Mason Dale's feelings about the death penalty, was, "I don't see why people are so upset about the death penalty, when generally the manner in which the victim met death is usually so much more horrible than execution.")

Dick Henderson, the head of the public defender's office, said:

With Shapiro we knew where we stood from the very beginning. He'd lay it on the line at the start, and if you came in with a ridiculous request, he'd say "Baloney" or more likely "Bullshit." There's very little of that today, or his thinking will be one way one day, and then something will happen and the next day he's way over there. He's looking sheepish and not able to look you in the eye. And that's not a good thing.

Judge Jensen did not in 1970 sentence convicted felons to state institutions at a rate significantly higher than Shapiro's rate in 1969 (35 percent for Jensen and 33 percent for Shapiro). But most attorneys with whom I spoke indicated that they felt his county jail sentences were longer than Shapiro's and that he was very reluctant to rule in favor of the defense on any legal issue raising questions concerning the rights of the accused.[5] One private attorney reported that, while he felt that Judge Shapiro would recognize a well-researched legal argument,

Jensen can always find something in that transcript to overrule your [motion]. I had a case where some officers stopped some guys during the investigation of a robbery. It turned out the guys had nothing to do with the robbery, but the officers searched them, patted them down, and found a bulge in one of these guy's socks. So the district attorney asked, "Well, what did it feel like, officer?" and the officer says, "A bulge." "Can you describe it?" Well, the D.A. went on like that for three pages in the transcript trying to get the officer to describe the bulge. He asked what the officer was searching for, and the officer says, "I was searching for weapons, for contraband, for anything I could find." Well, that clearly is improper under the law. So on the basis of that transcript at the prelim, we hold a 1538.5 and put the officer back on the stand and the officer testifies to the same thing. He hedges around and he hedges around, and the D.A. keeps asking what he thought it could be, and he keeps saying, "Well, I don't know, it just felt like a bulge." The D.A. keeps asking him what it could be and finally he says, "Well, it could have been a weapon." And Jensen throws up his hands and said, "That's it." All it was was a wrapped up baggie with marijuana in it. It is patently unreasonable to think that that was a weapon. But just the fact that the officer said it was was enough for Jensen.

Further indirect evidence of Jensen's sensitivity to public criticism occurred late in 1970 in a case in which two youths, so press accounts indicated, set off a bomb in front of a police officer's home. Jensen denied the probation department's recommendation of moderate county jail terms followed by intensive probation supervision. This disposition seemed particularly appropriate for the younger of the two boys, since his involvement turned out to have begun only a few hours before the incident when he met an older boy at a party where both had been drinking and was persuaded to join him in the "crime." The "bomb" was not in fact a bomb but a dud military training device, a small explosive charge. When it was set off, the device had had glass and iron fragments driven into its side, but it was not clear that the younger boy had suggested they be used or helped to put them there. Indeed, whether the younger boy did much more than come along for the ride was never clarified. The damage from the explosion amounted to a hole in a hedge and a small crater in the ground, but it did no structural damage and injured no one. Jensen's refusal to follow the probation report came two weeks after he had received a letter from a local conservative "court-watcher's" group that criticized Jensen's decision in a more serious bombing case to make the state prison sentence on two separate counts run concurrently rather than consecutively. In open court, Jensen explained his decision not to follow the probation recommendation:

Well, I imagine a fair comment is that this is not one of the easier cases that comes down the pike. And the record may reflect that I have given a great deal of consideration to this case. You have in this case two individuals, both of whom in a great many respects differ from the type of person that we have in our court that is obviously criminally oriented, in that their backgrounds are different, and it's hard to explain actions of this kind.

I have always thought that just for the sake of punishment alone, that that wasn't a very appropriate subject for a criminal judge to engage in.

It seems to me that you have a situation here in which you have two conflicting interests of society: first, to protect itself; and, secondly is the need to do something in a constructive manner for those who have violated our laws.

I think we can't totally ignore the various bills that were in the legislature this year. Those bills, of course, are not effective and do not apply to this case. But I read them yesterday, and again this morning. For instance, Assemblyman Crown's Bill AB970, which is now part of the state law, and the Biddle Bill, AB1003, as well as others. There's obviously a great amount of concern in the legislative halls on all levels. And we have occasionally cases that require dispositions that are necessary to indicate to society as a whole, that our laws have to be complied with, and that we cannot have a society where people are going to take the law into their own hands, and that we cannot excuse at every level just because somebody didn't think about what they were doing.

After a great deal of reflection and a large amount of sober thought, in this case probation is being denied as to each defendant.

Jensen sentenced the older youth to state prison and the younger youth to the California Youth Authority.

Perceived public demands, which we shall examine in the next section, simultaneously influenced both Judge Jensen and the D.A.'s office. The present section has suggested that judicial variability—judicial diversity— required prosecutors to make pragmatic, situation-specific adjustments to judicial variation, which discouraged programming. In a sense the prosecutor/judge relationship demands the prosecutor maintain a greater capacity to adjust than does his relationship with defense attorneys or with police. Because prosecutors conceive of themselves as having at least as much legitimacy to decide questions as have police and defense attorneys, prosecutors may attempt to specify policies regarding transactions at this level. For example, Dan Moore felt it legitimate to make the "seven-day rule," although we shall see that it did not in fact produce the expected change in the behavior of defense attorneys. But most prosecutors do not believe that they have the same legitimacy as the judge to decide. When they feel it wise to attempt to influence a judicial position, they therefore believe they must employ the less formal measures of persuasion that depend on maintaining the trust and confidence of judges. Prosecutors must make delicate, situation-specific assessments of the measures that will do so.

Politics and Prosecution

Police officers, defense attorneys, and judges at different stages in the handling of a case give prosecuting attorneys cues. These cues both provide information concerning the seriousness of the crime and the kind and degree of punishment the suspect deserves and give the prosecutor tactical hints concerning the impact his position will have both on the outcome of the case and on his relationships with those with whom he deals. Because these cues are not clear at the outset of a case, the handling of cases must remain flexible enough to incorporate this information as it becomes available. In addition to these cues, both electoral politics and the perceived demands of members of the public outside the criminal justice process may provide cues both for the handling of specific cases and more generally for what character the district attorney's organization should assume.

We may dispose of one possible form of political influence on the office rather quickly. In Vario County, which selects deputies through conventional civil-service procedures, and where the position of district attorney is officially non-partisan, no evidence supported the proposition that prosecutors regularly used their position to advance in electoral politics. No deputies expressed an interest in pursuing an explicitly political career, and only four indicated any interest in holding even local nonsalaried positions on such bodies as a school board. While several of the senior deputies indicated an interest in a judicial position (Hoff particularly), they had no clear idea how that preference ought to translate into their behavior as a prosecutor. I saw no evidence of the kind of eager headline hunting described in Bernard Botein's novel, *The Prosecutor* (New York: Simon and Schuster, 1956). Hoff concluded that as a prosecutor he was cut off from contacts with the bulk of the bar that could promote him, either by election or appointment, to a judicial position, and he therefore entered private practice near the end of the year.

That partisan politics plays no direct role in the D.A.'s office is hardly surprising in a county whose population has nearly doubled in fifteen years, where most public offices are nonpartisan, and where there is no political machine. Vario County is the sort of county that could (and did) give conservative Republican Max Rafferty nearly twice the vote it gave Negro Wilson Riles in 1970 for the office of state superintendent of instruction, yet regularly returns a progressive Democrat to Congress by comfortable margins. The county contains several very loosely knit factions, but no party faction dominates or even tries to dominate county politics. Most public priorities are set within the county's administrative system, which, dominated by the civil-service ethic, has relatively few direct linkages to the community. Several of the county supervisors, a number of private attorneys, and Nolan are Irish or Italian Catholics who have ties to a local Catholic college and attend the same church. But some are Republicans and some are Democrats. The Democratic party itself, although it tends to coalesce around its congressman, is not deeply united and at times is torn by north county—south county tensions, such as occurred when some party members tried unsuccessfully to discourage Negro James Bates from running against Nolan.

The position of district attorney is not a focal power position in the county. Several prominent attorneys rejected suggestions that they accept an appointment to the vacancy when Roger Savich departed for the legislature. The supervisors, although four of the five were Democrats, chose Republican Nolan apparently because he had few, if any, enemies. One attorney commented simply, "You just can't get to know Bob Nolan without liking him," although by the end of 1970 some attorneys were beginning to grumble about Nolan's performance.

Nolan, although his victory was virtually guaranteed, campaigned actively beginning about a month before the June election date. (He spent about $30,000 in the campaign, slightly more than double his opponent's campaign budget.) He had the public support of virtually all the active members of the bar in the county, and he relied on his friendships in the bar to organize the campaign, which, except for Nolan's extensive speech-making, was rather casual. An attorney who handled campaign affairs in the Pleasant Valley area (but who only laughed and said, "I really didn't do anything," when asked what his job involved), explained that he supported Nolan primarily because he had become friends with Nolan through an accident of timing: "Nolan and I started out at the same time. His first jury trial in the D.A.'s office was my first jury trial, which I won. And then just a few weeks later, we each had our second jury trial against each other, which he won. And we've just kind of kept up with each other ever since." This example is typical of the casual nature of most political alliances in the county.

Court Reporter Dan Riccio provides the best example of the modal style of politics in the county. Riccio, a Democrat, ran Nolan's campaign. He came as close as anyone to being a political power in the county, and the explanations attorneys gave for his position bear retelling. Riccio ran the reporting service for most courts and attorneys in the northern part of the county, and many lawyers relied on him from time to time to aid in preparing litigation, both in the pretrial stage of taking depositions and in producing transcripts of hearings and trials for review and possible appellate litigation. Most attorneys therefore knew Riccio. Because of the exigencies of litigation's deadlines and, more important, because of the desire to show strength in negotiation through possessing superior information, attorneys often needed his services done accurately and quickly. Riccio had served his clients well in this respect, and they were grateful. He was also an organizer and a "doer." As one private attorney described him:

The fact that he's the court reporter for most of the county serving all these law firms . . . helps. But I think of his power more with respect to non-attorneys. I've seen him at all sorts of functions where he'll run it or be host or something. He makes things go. That's the best way to put it. And he's been generous with his money. He's not a Rockefeller, but around here, a hundred bucks here and a hundred bucks there is appreciated by politicians.

Because Riccio was a good organizer and because he made campaign contributions, politicians valued his support, but there was no evidence that he intervened at all frequently in policy making in the county. Riccio's reward appeared to be to maintain his profitable business monopoly.

The insignificance of partisan politics in Vario County, however, hardly isolated the office from influences outside the legal system. Several examples illustrate the kinds of influences which prosecutors, particularly the district attorney and his senior deputies, perceived as worth responding to during the research period. Several of these outside influences were relatively minor. The county's Board of Supervisors, apparently responding to criticisms from citizens about "the welfare problem," privately asked Nolan to devote more manpower to clearing up a large backlog of unresolved cases of welfare fraud and of the failure of divorced or separated fathers to provide child support, in order to give the supervisors a legitimate response to further public criticism. Nolan did so—the supervisor's control of his budget allocation as well as his debt for his appointment made it wise to conform—but this was the board's only request regarding prosecution itself during the year.

From the public itself Nolan received a few letters and newspaper editorials each week concerning the "crime problem" in the county. For example, after two teenage girls disappeared within three months of each other, one of the smaller local newspapers wrote in March of 1970 an "open letter" in its Sunday edition addressed to Nolan:

Dear Mr. Nolan:
What, if anything, can your office do to insure that our children can walk the streets safely during the day—least at [sic] night? Are we to put armed guards around our schools and on our school buses?
Since December many young girls have disappeared from our county, some have not been traced. The pattern may or may not indicate that one maniac exists in this

county and that our school girls are in peril almost every day. Can any parent be sure, with this situation, that their daughter will come home from school or is safe in her own home?

We realize that you have a difficult job, and with the ever-increasing spiral in the crime rate that your job is becoming more compound, more arduous. But something must be done. Granted, we can't watch every school bus, we can't stand guard in any home, therefore we must hit the source, the villain or villains that lurk in the streets, by an all-out concerted effort. Some type of pattern must exist in these cases if it is one man and they can be traced by other policemen spotting similar actions of persons loitering around. Parents should form, if necessary, to meet the school buses or at least house children until their parents should return home. The citizenry should be more alert to strangers in a neighborhood and keep some form of surveillance. Your office could encourage this and promote similar programs. Even an upgrading and expansion of the Block Parent program could be encouraged by your office through visits with the PTA and other groups.

We cannot tolerate the sufferings of families any longer when programs do exist that could give stronger protection to the area. Through your office you could "pressure" the Sheriff's office to patrol more stringently, especially when school is out. This may cost more, and you might have to battle with the Supervisors to get it, but what price for a life? . . . We don't ask for vigilanties, we don't ask for mob rule, we ask for deputized citizens, alert, informed, and directed. This will aid in the elimination of abductors or at least the apprehension of such vile persons.

Please, Mr. Nolan, let's start something today. [This newspaper] will do [its] part, whether it be written, oral, or door-to-door. We'll play our part if you will get the ball rolling.

Alone, these letters and editorials, nearly all of which expressed some expectation of and support for "strict law enforcement," did not appear to translate into any attempt at office policy making. Nolan, who agreed that "the public is poorly informed about the nature of our system of criminal justice," tended initially to dismiss such public cues as the product of public ignorance. However, during the research period, the district attorney, several of the senior deputies, and Judge Jensen did respond to what they perceived was a more legitimate and well-informed and potentially threatening criticism of possible lenience in law enforcement.

The most significant of these criticisms occurred in December of 1969, four months after Nolan took office, when the grand jury for the county delivered its final report for the year 1969 condemning what it felt was the lenience of felony dispositions that Judge Shapiro's pretrial negotiations had produced. The grand jury is appointed annually through a process in which superior court judges recommend several names. Jurors are chosen at random from this pool to sit for the following year. See Penal Code Sections 893-913. In addition to hearing and almost always approving requests for indictments from the district attorney, the grand jury reviews and reports through subcommittees on the performance of all county offices during the year. The report by the subcommittee on law enforcement at the end of 1969, the tone of which departed substantially from the reports submitted in both 1968 and

1970, apparently resulted from the lobbying of two "tough-sentencing" judges in the county, Judge Coughlin and Judge Scott. A close friend of Judge Coughlin's served on the grand jury and drafted most of the subcommittee's report. Judge Scott, meanwhile, gave a number of speeches to civic groups critical of the handling of felonies in superior court in 1969 and suggested his listeners complain to the grand jury.

The grand jury report for the year, a compilation of the various sub-committee reports, was as follows:

As victims, witnesses, and law enforcement officers testified before us, we more clearly realized what serious problems face the citizens of this county.

Time and time again the committee found that a repeat offender had been returned to the community with only token punishment for his crime. We criticize those judges whom we consider to have been unduly permissive in their disposition of cases; we commend those judges who have sentenced with the severity of the crime in mind, and with the thought that society's protection must be their first consideration. We ask that judges who hear criminal cases, when appropriate, be firm in their disposition. This is with the hope that possible offenders will be discouraged from committing crimes and repeat offenders will find it less profitable to continue. In this way the rise in the crime rate may be lessened, and perhaps may eventually show a decline. When an indictment is returned by the Grand Jury, it means there is sufficient evidence to bring a defendant into a public court for trial on the charges listed in the indictment. We feel it is not in the public interest to have indictments by a Grand Jury cancelled or changed by mutual agreement of the Court, the prosecution, and the defense attorneys in a pre-trial conference. We feel strongly about the disposition of indictment cases and firmly believe that in cases where the defendant has pleaded guilty, the sentences given did not fit the crime. We recommend to all judges, sitting on criminal cases, as a means of attempting to curb the rising crime rate that a philosophy of more stringent sentences be adopted. . . . We feel strongly that there should be an attempt made to establish better working relationships between the Probation Department and various Police Agencies. It is essential that they work together constructively for the benefit of all citizens of the county.

We have seen that Judge Jensen responded to this criticism by abandoning Judge Shapiro's practice of encouraging negotiated pleas by committing himself to a specific sentence in advance of the plea. Since Jensen refused to assume responsibility for a sentence commitment, defense attorneys began to turn to the prosecutor for a sentence commitment in the hope of giving their client a clearer understanding of the consequences of entering a guilty plea. Nolan and Dan Moore, however, were equally reluctant to adopt any formal procedure whereby they might appear to be ignoring the recommendation of the grand jury. Nolan and Moore therefore devised two policies. First, the office would refuse to agree explicitly to any recommendation that a felony suspect receive county jail sentence rather than a sentence in a state institution. While in the previous year the office had liberally approved such dispositions, Moore instead insisted that in 1970 the suspect must "plead and take his chances" with the probation report. Thus, if the probation report recommended a county jail sentence, the office would not oppose it, but the prosecutor would refuse to adopt that position on his own. Second, the office would refuse to accept a plea of guilty in the last week before trial, a rule additionally designed to eliminate the problem of deputies wasting time preparing for trials that literally plead out at the last minute, or alternatively not preparing at all in anticipation of a plea and then finding the case in fact did go to trial.

Implementing these policies proved more difficult than Dan Moore had imagined, and he and the other deputies who handled felony matters in pretrial negotiations soon faced an unforeseen consequence of their increasing inflexibility, which eventually forced an abandonment of the policies. In mid-February the public defender's office reacted to the decline of pretrial maneuvering and concessions from the district attorney with a "get tough" policy of its own. The office decided collectively that the public defenders would not plead a client guilty without some firm indication of the likely sentence from either the prosecutor or the judge and would simply plan on taking the cases to trial when no such commitments came forth. Bob Stern described his office's decision this way:

Actually, when the D.A. got tough we had no choice in the matter, because as a general rule we're not going to plead clients into state prison. It was pretty obvious what was happening, so I went in and told Dick [Henderson] that we were going to go to trial, and he said, "Fine." The conversation lasted maybe two to three minutes. Then at a staff meeting a week later Dick said, "We may be setting some trials back-to-back. Do you think you can handle it?" And the response was 100 percent "Yes."

Of the first sixteen felonies that went to jury trial against the public defenders after they made that decision, the public defenders won twelve, one of which was the Jennings case. Bob Stern commented, "Ninety percent of the cases we won would have been pleas to something reasonable. I think we taught them a little bit of a lesson, and I think they realized on some cases that the guy may be guilty of a misdemeanor, but that juries ... just didn't want to convict the poor guy of a felony." This rather dramatic shift in trial results (the public defenders generally expect to win approximately one jury trial out of every five) placed Moore on the horns of a dilemma. Continuing the present course appeared to open Nolan up to criticism on grounds of poor conviction rates. To resume the practice of making informal sentencing commitments, on the other hand, risked criticism from either the grand jury or the press (the editor of the one major newspaper in the northern half of the county, the *Vario County Tribune*, had given the grand jury's report considerable attention and editorial praise) or from what Moore felt was public opposition to the lenience of negotiated pleas, or from all three. Although he did not formally renounce the policy, Moore began to accept the necessity of some pretrial sentencing commitments. About the same time, late in April, it became apparent to Moore that trial deputies had ignored the second policy, the "seven-day rule," and that policy also evaporated.

The response to the grand jury report illustrates the first of two consequences its political setting had on the Vario County prosecutor's office. These political demands seemed to require of the office some form of centralized response, and the centralized response cut against the decentralizing thrust of the office's daily environment, so that subordinates tended to view superiors as complicating their lives. Furthermore, subordinates saw no justification for these complications. They knew that Nolan would win reelection, that a Negro had no chance of winning in that county. Indeed, Nolan was reelected by a three-to-one margin. While Moore, Nolan, Hoff, and Baum worried about public reaction, about "convincing the public the office is doing something about the crime problem," the office as a whole ranked this goal as less important than any except "maximizing sentences."

For most deputies, seeing superiors making policies the reasons for which were unclear and the application of which seemed to prevent sensible case dispositions (Jennings's case was so perceived) led to a "cheapening" of the management process by heightening the feeling that what superiors did was primarily for public consumption and therefore could be safely disregarded internally.

Why senior deputies in fact feared public criticism and responded to their perceptions of it raises the second consequence of the political environment. Public criticism in Vario County was a particularly keen sort of threat to senior prosecutors, because they doubted their capacity to predict its origins or control its consequences. A career deputy, especially if he hoped for a promotion, could easily imagine how, before an election, a seemingly innocuous decision—a refusal to issue a "desecration of the flag" complaint, a dismissal of a weak case in which the suspect commits a murder two days later—could stimulate an angry phone call or an embarrassing question at a Rotary Club luncheon. As a result, the senior deputies seemed to "freeze," as Stewart Douglas put it, in the months before the election, because Vario County prosecutors were in fact virtually incapable of assessing the political environment around them. They carried to their job vague notions about democracy and the validity of public sentiment, but lacked strong parties, political machines, or political institutions of any kind that could assess for them the threat from something like the grand jury report. Lacking these institutional conduits, senior prosecutors simply had no sense of where or how they might find allies or support if some serious public challenge erupted. Lacking the information to predict the likelihood of widespread public disenchantment with their performance, and lacking the information to decide how they would respond if it did occur, senior prosecutors tended to assume the worst. Assuming the worst, they responded in ways that further reduced their capacity to develop any shared perspective of their responsibilities among deputies, and we turn now to that management process itself.

5 Managing Diversity and Uncertainty

The previous two chapters have described a variety of circumstances that together inhibit the development of ordered or common attitudes and practices among those who administer justice. The argument thus far has implied several propositions about the circumstances in which organizations succeed in ordering or programming the decisions of their members, and the following summary of the argument now makes these propositions explicit. Chapter 1 suggested that two components of an organization's *technology* influence the degree to which men who manage the organization succeed in programming the decisions of men who daily produce the organization's output. The first component, the degree to which an organization operates with ambiguous "standards of desirability," suggests the following proposition:

Proposition 1: The more an organization's production process requires members to choose between several desirable but mutually inconsistent objectives, the less management personnel will attempt to program the decisions of production personnel, and the more effectively will production personnel evade attempts to program decisions.

Prosecutors who seek to reduce the crime rate by prosecuting and aggressively advocating incarceration for every suspect will not only increase work loads dramatically and slow the movement of cases, they will interfere with the maintenance of a high level of professional legal performance, since legal norms dictate that some suspects whose factual guilt is unambiguous go free. Conversely, the superior who insists that his subordinates prosecute only those cases that lack any possible legal defects will increase the potential for conflict with the desire of police and the public to remove "confirmed criminals" from their streets. Striking a fair balance between conflicting interests in specific cases may interfere with the uniform treatment of similar cases.

Standing alone, Proposition 1 is misleading. Virtually all purposeful action requires choosing among mutually inconsistent goals, but programming becomes more difficult where managers cannot isolate the act of choice from the production process itself. Where positively valued goals irrevocably conflict, superiors may nevertheless believe that they can specify with some confidence the effects of a given course of action on the achievement of a given goal. When they believe they can do this, managing personnel may simply choose one goal over another and then define precisely the steps necessary to achieve it. But where understanding of cause/effect relationships is

113

incomplete—this is the second component of technology—programming becomes more difficult. Hence:

Proposition 2: The more management personnel recognizes that its knowledge of cause/effect relationships is incomplete, the less management personnel will attempt to program decisions of production personnel, and the more effectively will production personnel evade attempts to program decisions.

If prosecutors could predict confidently that aggressive prosecution would in fact reduce the crime rate, or if they could specify in fact the criteria on which to measure the uniformity of case treatment, for example, they could choose such an objective and specify the behavior required to produce the desired outcome. But many prosecutors recognize the plausibility of the argument that incarceration encourages crime by exposing the suspect to other offenders and by preventing him from gaining steady employment and developing other stabilizing relationships in the community. At the more practical level it is difficult for prosecutors to predict whether trying weak cases and losing will discredit them in the eyes of a concerned public more than would a policy of bargaining down or dismissing weak cases. Thus, prosecutors not only face inconsistent goals in the handling of criminal cases, they may lack beliefs in cause/effect relationships that would permit choosing among them! It is not therefore surprising to find that Dan Moore ranked all but two of the questionnaire's nine goals (question 1-13) as "very important," and Nolan listed all but three "very important."

Chapter 1 also introduced the impact of intensive technologies upon the process of organizational control.

Proposition 3: The greater the degree to which only the production process itself reveals the information and cues on which organizational production depends, the less management will attempt to program decisions of production personnel, and the more effectively will production personnel evade attempts to program decisions.

Management personnel may program decisions that depend on information and cues from the *environment* if they can anticipate the categories into which this information will fall and can assess how different pieces of information in combination can affect goal achievement. To do so, however, requires a detailed knowledge of the production process itself, which management may not have the time to learn. In the prosecutor's case, the number of possible categories and their various combinations are so considerable that they discourage programming? Take, for example, the case of a parolee with a long record of felony convictions who commits another crime that would permit immediate revocation of his parole and reimprisonment. A rule specifying that those suspects with a certain level of prior convictions must automatically be reimprisoned would ignore many facts that ought to influence the revocation decision: How long has the parolee stayed out of trouble? Was the present crime one that indicated intentional retrogression, or might he have committed it while drunk? What does the parole officer recommend? Do the police have any reason to believe that the suspect has been involved in other unsolved crimes? What if all these factors indicate that parole should be revoked, but the suspect has promised to give the police badly needed information to crack a drug-selling ring in a local high school about which numerous parents have complained to the D.A.? From the standpoint of conserving organization resources, it is normally best to handle such cases on an individual basis rather than create a rule that imposes cumbersome appeals procedures to incorporate possible exceptions.

Chapter 3 indicated that Vario County prosecutors did not depend primarily on the organization for their rewards. Thompson notes that "one significant dimension on which jobs, considered as action spheres, can vary is the *opportunity to learn* skills, data, and attitudes which are appropriate for other, better jobs.... A second important dimension on which jobs can vary is the *opportunity for visibility*."[3] In most economic organizations the organization itself generates the opportunity to learn and the opportunity for visibility, and the organization itself rewards by promotion those who learn and become visible. Prosecutors, however, seek to learn and/or to become visible in order to gain advancement not in the organization but in the profession.

Proposition 4: In conditions of technological and informational uncertainty, the greater the capacity of people outside the formal scope of an organization to reward organization members, the less likely is management to attempt to program the decision of production personnel, and the more effectively will production personnel evade attempts to program decisions.

Since most prosecutors assumed they would enter private practice in the fairly near future, senior deputies tended to recognize that part of the inducement they could offer a young deputy included giving him the opportunity to develop skills and visibility that would make him a more successful private attorney. If a prosecutor enhanced his chances for a more successful private career only through appearing to the judge and to defense attorneys to be a pleasant and nonthreatening person, then deputies might welcome formal rules for programming their decisions, for they would then be able to ascribe decisions that defense attorneys did not like to the necessity of obeying a rule, thus avoiding personal responsibility. But the rules would simultaneously prevent the prosecutor from developing his own analytical and diplomatic skills, which the profession values.[4]

The last proposition reveals one form of environmental impact on the D.A.'s office in Vario County. Chapter 4 also reviewed the tendency of environmental diversity, heterogeneity, segmentation, and uncertainty to decrease the capacity of management personnel to predict the nature and the content of the information and cues on which production personnel depend. Put another way, environmental uncertainty makes the prosecutor's technology more intensive (see Proposition 3).

Proposition 5: The less accurately management personnel can predict the content of information and cues on which production personnel depend, the less likely is management to attempt to program the decisions of production personnel and the more effectively will production personnel evade attempts to program decisions.

Chapter 4 provided several examples of the instability of the prosecutor's environment. The change from Judge Shapiro to Judge Jensen, when coupled with a shift in public criticism, imposed a different set of options for the office in 1970 as opposed to 1969. The decision of the public defender's office to take an increasing number of cases to trial in response to the new unwillingness of superior court calendar deputies to negotiate cases presented the office with the consequences of its "plead and take your chances" policy that it had not anticipated, namely, the loss of an unusually high number of cases.[5] But the district attorney's environment not only is unstable, it is heterogeneous (the segments of the environment with which it must deal impose not only different but inconsistent demands upon the office almost simultaneously) and diverse (occupants of identical roles employ different decisional premises).

Proposition 6: The greater the degree to which the external information and cues on which production personnel depend are heterogeneous, the less management personnel will attempt to program decisions of production personnel and the more effectively will production personnel evade attempts to program decisions.

Proposition 7: The greater the degree to which the external information and cues on which production personnel depend are diverse, the less management personnel will attempt to program decisions of production personnel and the more effectively will production personnel evade attempts to program decisions.[6]

Since the prosecutor faces a diverse, heterogeneous, and unpredictable environment, those prosecutors who deal with that environment most frequently can best predict and adjust to environmental information and cues.

Proposition 8: The greater the ability of production personnel to predict and adjust to external information and cues relative to the ability of management to do so, the less likely is management to attempt to program the decisions of production personnel and the more effectively will production personnel evade attempts to program decisions.

Thompson puts the consequences of heterogeneous and shifting environments on organizational structure this way:

Here we would expect boundary-spanning units to be differentiated functionally to correspond to segments of the task environment, and each to operate on a decentralized basis to monitor and plan responses to fluctuations in its sector of the task environment.[7]

Thompson in this passage suggests that organizations dealing with changing and uncertain environments must decentralize units to cope with different segments of the environment. In Vario County, however, several factors limited the office's capacity to do more than create geographical and judicial divisions of labor. The office did not have enough deputies to place some exclusively in charge of dealing with police while others would work exclusively with judges or defense attorneys. Work flowed too irregularly to keep most men busy most of the time in highly specialized positions. (The Los Angeles district attorney's office, with several hundred deputies, is considerably more specialized.) Besides, the deputies' desire for trial experience made them wary of specialization that would remove some of them from the trial process altogether.

Other factors created by its legal setting limited the capacity of the Vario County office to adjust to environmental diversity and uncertainty. For example, Thompson proposes, "Organizations under norms of rationality seek to place their boundaries around those activities which if left to the task environment would be crucial contingencies,"[8] and more specifically regarding intensive technologies he proposes, "Organizations employing intensive technologies, and subject to rationality norms seek to expand their domains by incorporating the object worked on."[9] While a private business, for example, may seek by vertical merger to increase its control over a supplier on which its production heavily depends, a district attorney's office (and many other "public" offices whose function is defined and regulated by law) is effectively barred by the legal separation of functions from formally incorporating unpredictable elements of its environment.[10]

In summary, a great variety of factors in addition to policies and expectations of supervising deputies affect the behavior of prosecutors and, indeed, led some supervisors to provide no more than "advice" and to presume the educational system had instilled the requisite norms for action. The values and preferences of those with whom they worked outside the office—police, judges, defense attorneys, and citizens—when filtered through the deputies' own diverse preferences led different deputies in different directions. The differences in perceptions at different levels within the organization, such as the disagreement among prosecutors about the extent to which public criticism threatened the office, further fragmented prosecutorial behavior.

These propositions, then, suggest that a bureacratic, rule-oriented administrative model of management does not fit the nature of the job of criminal prosecution. Both theoretical literature and case studies of specific kinds of organizations with characteristics similar to those prosecutors in Vario County faced support this position. Writing theoretically, Eugene Litwak has argued

Weber's model is most efficient when the organization deals primarily with uniform events and with occupations stressing traditional areas of knowledge rather than social skills. The human-relations model will be most efficient for dealing with events which are not uniform (research, medical treatment, graduate training, designing) and with occupations emphasizing social skills as technical aspects of the job (as that of psychiatric social worker, salesman . . . , and politician).[11]

Examining mental hospitals specifically, Charles Perrow and William R. Rosengren have argued that technological ambiguity blocks administrative programming of outputs. Perrow, indeed, states flatly, "The reasons for the depressing conditions [in state mental hospitals] do not lie in the structure, processes, and goal commitments, but in the limitations of the available technology."[12]Charles E. Bidwell has described the incompatibility between bureaucratic authority and the job of teaching, and Arthur Stinchcombe has pointed out that the variety and unpredictability of problems in building construction have preserved what he calls a "craft" rather than bureaucratic administrative practices in that industry.[13]James Thompson summarizes that where an organization's technology and environment diffuse administrative power within it, "no inner circle emerges with sufficient stability to give direction to the organization. Although this situation is more visible at the level of national governments in various parts of the world, we believe it is approached in universities, voluntary hospitals, and local governments with some frequency."[14]

But identifying the shortcomings of bureaucratic management in such settings does not end our analysis, for two reasons. First, management strategies do exist that can, even in such uncertain settings, increase organizational uniformity. Herbert Kaufman has nicely described how the Forest Service implemented these strategies in the face of many "challenges to unity," and the next section will review these strategies briefly. Second, and more important, administrators may persist in seeking to impose order by following these strategies, even when their efforts consistently fail. When this happens (when, as Rosengren puts it, organizations "persist in an adherence to a plausible kind of bureaucratic structure" where they lack a clear technology and stable environment), "a rich and volatile informal organization is likely to emerge with both a form and content of communication which frequently contradicts the formal bureaucratic system."[15]In the remainder of this chapter we shall see how senior personnel in the Vario County office attempted unsuccessfully in 1970 to adopt these control strategies, and we shall review the consequences of these attempts on the organization and its members.

Techniques of Organizational Control

Specifying Rules and Procedures

Theoretically, organizational managers may adopt three techniques for specifying rules for performance. They can create an organizational rule book or manual; they can require employees to clear all decisions with supervisors; and they can require employees to keep detailed records of how they spend their time and money. To control behavior, a manual should cover in explicit detail the conditions in which an employee *may* take a specified action ("authorization"), *must* take a specified action ("direction"), and *shall not* take a specified action ("prohibition")[16] The effective manual will provide, in addition to these instructions, the procedures, such as those for keeping a personal budget, that will allow superiors to detect deviation.

Detecting and Discouraging Deviation

Superiors may require employees to file, in addition to budget reports, reports on the progress and outcome of specific projects and logs of time spent. An employee inclined to deviate from organizational rules would face an almost impossible task of falsifying two or three different records covering his activity so they would all agree. And even if he could, he risks detection if his records do not dovetail with those of a colleague. If, in addition to obtaining written records, superiors regularly inspect employees "on the job," if they shift to a new location employees who become excessively committed to co-workers and clients rather than superiors, and if they threaten and enforce the usual sanctions of reprimands, demotions, suspensions, and discharges, they will discourage deviation.[17]

Developing the Ability and Desire to Conform

An organization may invest considerable resources determining what men are well suited to the job and establishing recruitment and selection procedures to insure that it eliminates the unsuited. It may build both ability to do the job and loyalty to the organization by providing them with intensive postentry training and in some cases by adopting organizational symbols (mottoes, badges, insignias) and putting their employees in distinctive uniforms.[18]

In theory, the Vario County office could have adopted nearly all of these techniques. Indeed, it did formally adopt many of them, but they did not have a substantial impact on most decisions.

Rules and Policies in Vario County

Managing deputies in Vario County did attempt to control *some* decisions that their subordinates made. The approximately 150-page *Criminal Policy and Procedure Manual*, a sheaf of instructions fastened at the top in a heavy brown binder, would, judging from its table of contents, govern most decisions in the office. The *Manual* broke down into thirty-six separate chapters the subjects of issuing complaints, search warrants, the procedures for routing and filing paperwork, the procedures for preliminary examinations, the preparation of informations, pretrial preparations, the procedures to be followed for gathering accurate statistics, and so forth. The *Manual* contained explicit instructions concerning a considerable variety of activities. It instructed a deputy to send a written report to the law enforcement agency involved every time they refused to issue a complaint on a request of that agency, giving the reasons for the refusal. It instructed deputies explicitly to fill out "Interview Sheets" reporting the essential information they learned from police officers or complaining witnesses when they filed a case. It prohibited deputies from signing a complaint as a complaining witness when they had witnessed the commission of the crime themselves, without first checking with the district attorney or with the chief deputy. The *Manual* summarized various legal requirements. It reminded deputies, for example, that they must take a misdemeanor to trial within thirty days of arrest and a felony to trial within sixty days of arraignment unless the defendant intelligently waived his right to a speedy trial. Another section summarized the holding of the California Supreme Court concerning the inadmissability of confessions obtained without advising the suspect of his constitutional right to remain silent and to have the assistance of counsel.

But there were at least three reasons why the *Manual* did not in 1970 provide a clear-cut guide for most prosecutorial decisions. First, the *Manual* rarely directed or authorized or prohibited any one course of action where the deputy had to choose among competing considerations. At many points, the *Manual* amounted to no more than a restatement of the choices available and instruction to the deputy to use his own best judgment. Where the deputy must choose between civil hospitalization and jail for an intoxicated subject, the *Manual* reminds the deputy that on the one hand, "hospital beds are scarce and drunks ought to sober up in jail rather than in a hospital," and on the other hand that "a bad drunk can get extensive treatment in a hospital but not in a jail. The handling of these cases," the *Manual* states, "will be left to sound discretion of the individual deputy." Similarly, regarding the filing of charges, the *Manual* states only:

On occasions an irate citizen who "pays his taxes and your salary" will demand a complaint in a petty matter that would more properly be handled by citation or as a civil suit. A demand may be made for a felony complaint when a misdemeanor would more properly serve the ends of justice. All persons are to be treated equally and fairly. The proper charge, if any, is to be determined by the soundness of requests by peace officers for complaints. If there is any problem after your decision, take the matter up with your supervisor.

The second reason, very closely related to the first, is that on difficult substantive questions, the *Manual* was often altogether silent. The more a decision required sensitive competing criteria and the greater the possible categories of information potentially affecting the decision, the less the *Manual* had to say about the substance of the decision. For example, the *Manual* treated the most significant area of prosecutorial action, the dismissal and reduction of charges in exchange for pleas, in exactly two pages. These pages, which are quoted below in their entirety, are devoted exclusively to procedure and say nothing about the criteria that should influence the decision to dismiss or reduce:

PART III

DISMISSALS, REDUCTION REPORTING
PROCEDURES ON A COMPLAINT
REQUIRING DISMISSALS OR REDUCTION

Chapter 1.

Approval of Action
(Section 3100-3199)

3101.   *Procedure.*
In order to establish uniformity, reductions or dismissals in *all* cases are to be referred to the District Attorney or in the absence of the District Attorney, and only when immediate action is necessary, the Chief Criminal Deputy for prior approval. This administrative rule is not intended to limit exercise of discretion by deputies but is intended to guarantee uniformity in disposition of cases. Written report of dismissal or reduction will be made in all cases, including those approved by phone because of time limitations.

3102.   *Contacting Police Agency.*
In all cases of dismissal or reduction of a complaint previously filed at the request of a law enforcement agency, an advice of proposed disposition will be sent to the head of the agency on Form 2. A suspense notice will be initiated and followed up until a reply is received. The file will not be closed or action of dismissal or reduction taken until reply is received unless such action is approved by the District Attorney.

Chapter 2.

Reporting Procedures on Complaint
Refusals, Dismissals and Reductions
(Sections 3200-3299)

3202.   In order to clarify procedural requirements as to deputy decisions not to file complaints or to dismiss complaints, please be advised as follows: It is presently required that a report on *any* decision not to file a complaint be given immediately to the District Attorney, regardless of the source from which the request may come. Such report must be written and, in addition, if the matter appears important, a telephone call should be made to the District Attorney. The purpose of this report lies in the fact that law enforcement agencies and others complain directly to the District Attorney who is otherwise uninformed as to the circumstances of a case and must make an investigation, often requiring the return of the complainant at some later time and further criticism. This directive applies to all decisions not to file a complaint and has no exceptions.

It is not the intention to limit the discretion of deputies in this field, but to inform the District Attorney of decisions, so that policies may be formulated and response given immediately when questions are raised as to such decisions. The report will be made in writing on the form attached, and use of secretarial staff is to be avoided whenever possible. A carbon copy of the report is to be included in an appropriate file.

Secondly, and for the same reasons, and on the second form attached, a report is to be made in the same procedures for dismissals of *all* cases or reductions. "All" means precisely that and includes, without being limited to, cases in which a felony complaint is requested and a misdemeanor filed, dismissals of one or more counts of a multi-count complaint, either felony or misdemeanor, and all cases in which disposition other than by the court or jury results in trial or disposition of a case in any way lesser than the original form of the complaint.

The Vario County manual did not provide deputies with clear criteria for substantive action. And we shall see that its content and the selective manner in which it was "enforced" tended to alienate deputies.

The third and most important reason for the insignificance of the *Manual* is that in 1970 no one attempted to enforce or even refer to those sections of the *Manual* that were explicit. Prosecutors rarely followed the directives of Sections 3101 or 3102, and the forms specified in 3202, although usually filled out, were never routed to the district attorney and never used for any other purpose than to enable secretaries to code dispositions for their statistical summaries.[9] Art Pollack's statement concerning the *Manual* was typical. "I started to read the thing one rainy afternoon, but I fell asleep after ten minutes and have never bothered to look at it again."

The reasons for the *Manual*'s ineffectiveness lie in part in the office's history, which we shall explore below. But the superiors' reluctance to use the *Manual* as a control device arose basically from the consensus among the prosecutors that "when it comes right down to it, it isn't possible to make clear-cut rules for handling most cases that come through this office." (Twenty-nine percent of responding prosecutors strongly agreed, and 46 percent mildly agreed with this statement.)

Apart from the *Manual*, however, superiors in some instances did attempt to establish standards for the behavior of less experienced deputies. In some instances superiors made rules and policies that purported to specify the actions that should be taken when given circumstances existed. But policies that purported to specify behavior did not always succeed. Whether what superiors designated as policy in fact was translated into regularized behavior depended on the success with which the policy was communicated to all members so that they knew *when* to invoke it, and it depended on the extent to which deputies believed they *ought* to invoke it when they knew the designated circumstances existed.

Successful Policies

The best example of a policy that deputies regularly followed involved their willingness to dismiss a case when polygraph examination indicated the suspect's innocence. Dan Moore stated that the office would abide by the result of a polygraph test and dismiss a case against a suspect *if* a suspect claimed his innocence from the outset, *if* there was no conclusive evidence at the scene indicating his guilt (e.g., his fingerprints), *if* he requested the test "early in the game," and *if* the defense would stipulate that, in the event he failed the test, the results of the test would be admitted as evidence at trial. Prosecutors and defense attorneys in most circumstances implicitly agreed that if the suspect failed the test he would plead guilty rather than take the case to trial.

Some deputies doubted the substantive wisdom of this policy. One felt, and my conversations with defense attorneys substantiated his feeling, that the preconditions Moore set would discourage defendants from taking the polygraph in all but the most desperate cases, and that this could operate to the office's disadvantage, because encouraging them to take the test would induce more pleas of guilty when the suspects failed; an attorney who knows his client is lying or has lied will be less confident of his chances of winning at trial. Another deputy felt that it was precisely in those rare situations where positive evidence such as fingerprints points falsely to the suspect's guilt that the polygraph would be his only means of defense. Regardless of the wisdom of the policy, however, deputies did abide by it. The conditions for its application were clear. The decision to give the polygraph test was a simple yes/no decision that did not require continuous management or adjustment as new facts appeared. Finally, because prosecutors only rarely used the polygraph, they did not develop enough experience to know how to get one administered without asking Dan Moore, so that he effectively controlled these decisions.

A second policy to which most deputies conformed concerned the prohibition against the reduction of drunk driving charges (which in California can result in a suspended driver's license) to reckless driving (which need not lead to a loss of license). Again, the circumstances in which the policy could be applied were clear, and the decision did not require constant readjustment. Drunk driving (Calif. Vehicle Code Sec. 23102) differs from most crimes in that an objective measurement of the percentage of alcohol in the suspect's blood determines whether he violated the law. The office created and maintained this policy by and large successfully at the same time it made no comparably firm rules for most other criminal categories, because prosecutors sensed the damage done by drunk driving more acutely than the damage done by most other criminal offenses. They were aware of statistics indicating the dramatic correlation between the amount of alcohol consumed and the likelihood of having an accident. Prosecutors, like most middle- and upper-middle-class Americans, spent much time on the road and sensed as an objective matter that they were more likely to suffer personal injury by a drunk driver than by any other category of criminal. Finally, although they were probably not conscious of it, they may have appreciated the danger of drunk driving because that was the only serious crime any of them committed with any frequency.

Unsuccessful Policies

In contrast to the clarity and specificity of the polygraph and drunk driving policies, consider the example of a "policy" designed to insure that when deputies file cases they exercise considerable care. Several supervising deputies told me that their policy was: "If you issue the dog, you try the dog," meaning that anybody who issues a weak case on which the suspect will not plead must suffer the consequences of trying and very possibly losing the case. Peter Hoff stressed the policy's importance to me several times and mentioned it to younger deputies in at least one staff meeting. But most deputies learned that enforcement was unlikely. The policy was unenforcable in part because it is very difficult to identify a "dog." At the time of filing, many cases look strong but become weak only when further information comes to light. (Jennings's case exemplifies this possibility.) Furthermore, the policy was administratively too rigid: the man who filed a case need not belong to the area where the case arose, so that he would not necessarily participate in or observe the preparation of the case, which would enable him to try it intelligently. Besides, the trial schedules of deputies were uncertain enough that even if the supervising deputies could place the blame, they had no assurance that the issuing deputy would be free to try his "dog." Finally, if the case was "serious," perhaps because it received newspaper coverage, a supervisor like Moore would prefer to avoid the embarrassment of losing. An experienced and skilled trial deputy would most likely get the assignment regardless of who issued the questionable case. When I asked George Baker, a deputy working with Len Lewis at the beginning of the year, about the "dog" policy, Baker replied, "That's bullshit! The rule is, 'If you issue the dog, George tries the dog.' " One deputy described the feeling of most of his colleagues with respect to trying one's "dogs" when he commented, "They talk about it, but it's not a real threat."

To mold behavior effectively, policies must speak in terms that clearly specify the circumstances in which certain actions should take place, and those actions themselves must be clearly stated.[20] In the world of the prosecutor the uncertain consequences of events narrow the range of sensible policy. Here are three more examples:

1. In the Roger Savich regime, subordinate deputies were encouraged to ride regularly with patrolmen in their areas to get to know them and their problems better and to communicate some feeling of office concern for their problems. Shortly before he left, Savich distributed forms on which the deputies could record their impressions and suggestions for improvement of both police and office practices resulting from their observations. Only a third of the deputies interviewed said that they had ridden with their police departments more than a time or two, and the forms quickly fell into disuse. Some deputies reported simply that they had never had time to do so, but others reported that they had been discouraged from doing so by their superiors' nervousness about the prosecutors' becoming involved in incidents that might prove embarrassing, particularly if the prosecutor were called by the defense as a witness to establish police misconduct. Thus, one deputy complained, "They want you to ride patrol, but if you ride too much, that's bad." The policy fell into disuse as a policy not only because riding with police could produce both positive and negative results, but also because it was impossible for senior deputies to assess which consequence was more likely to occur. The inability to calculate risks, therefore, discouraged the enforcement of policy.

2. Having worked under Roger Savich, and thus having witnessed the destruction of morale and work quality that flowed from Savich's attempts to program office decisions strictly, Nolan hoped as D.A. to increase the deputies' sense of independent professional competence. In conversations with me, Nolan argued that the office ought to resemble the private law firm in which he worked briefly in San Francisco, where

we came in at nine in the morning and went straight to our offices and closed our doors. And we worked out our own problems. We didn't go crying to somebody whenever we got into a bind, and we went into the library and did our own research. We learned how to be real lawyers. Here, Jesus, it seems every time I go out in the hall, there's a group of people standing around somebody's door and half the time they're just shooting the shit.

The Hillside police chief reinforced Nolan's concern when, in June, he complained to Nolan that his officers seemed to be spending too much time "shooting the shit" in the prosecutor's office. In response to this criticism, Nolan distributed a memorandum instructing deputies to minimize conversations with each other and with police officers not required by the problems

posed by specific cases. Not surprisingly, the memo had no effect other than
to mildly irritate a number of deputies. John Hunt reacted: "If the police
would stop bringing in bum cases, then maybe we could cut this out, but if
Nolan's going to try to figure out who's bullshitting more, us or them, he's
going to have a hell of a time." Miss Denton said:

The memo just made everybody mad. Dick [Schwartz] and I talked about it for an
hour after it came out [*laughs*]. It probably caused everybody to talk more! A little
casual talk doesn't hurt—it probably does some good. Everybody gets their work
done. Dick and I will be talking about various officers, and I'll say, you know, "Dick,
I had some trouble with Officer X. What could you do about it so it doesn't come up
again?" That's very helpful sometimes.

The example illustrates how effective policy must often be negotiated with
those whose compliance is sought. Nolan, having little contact with the daily
operations of his staff, had learned neither the payoffs from informal conversation nor the alternatives he might have introduced to reduce the dependence
on informal exchange of information.

3. One of the more interesting illustrations of the absence of effective
office policy concerns the treatment of those, like Jennings, arrested for
possession of moderate quantities of marijuana. Although prosecuting and
defense attorneys agreed that in this area they had become increasingly
lenient over the past four years, the office made no formal policies concerning
marijuana treatment. As B.J. Chastain put it, "We really don't have a hard
and fast posture. If [the suspect] is really just experimenting, we treat him
that way. But if the kid is a horse's ass, say he's kept on experimenting or has
tried everything else besides, he may just get wiped." Superiors disagreed
among themselves concerning marijuana policy. Peter Hoff, for example,
repeatedly announced his feeling that marijuana cases should be issued as
felonies rather than misdemeanors. Hoff consciously cultivated the friendship
of police officers, and he encouraged the image, as he put it, of "a friend of
law enforcement." He felt police desired felony prosecutions for marijuana-
users, and Hoff preferred to let the judge "take the heat" where equity
dictated sentence reductions. But deputies under Hoff's direction made such
reductions anyway. Chastain analyzed marijuana "policy" this way:

We had an express policy not to reduce possession of marijuana to presence where
marijuana is being used. Hoff announced officially that we wouldn't do it. Well,
everybody was doing it, but we didn't tell Hoff. It was the silliest goddamn thing I ever
saw. The Condenado office did it and said it. We did it and didn't say it. . . . It's not a
science; it's an art. It's like a doctor: when so much of what you're doing is a matter of
judgment, no two people would do it alike anyway.[21]

The inevitable necessity for exercising judgment continually reasserts
itself in the prosecutor's world. Judge Thomas recalled a typical example

from his days as a private attorney, in an incident where his client had been accused of indecent exposure:

> [My client] came up with the story that he works at a machine shop and he gets very dirty, so he keeps a clean pair of pants around and then slips them on over his dirty pair before he goes home. He says he knew one of these girls, so he stopped the car. He thought he had zipped up the first pair, so he hadn't bothered to zip up the second pair, when in fact he had forgotten to zip up the first pair too, exposing himself. Well, that's not a bad story, so the prosecution put on its first witness, one of the girls, and she told her story, and then the D.A. asked her, "Do you see that man in this courtroom?" And she said, "No." So he went over and stood behind the defendant and asked, "Is this the man?" and she said, "No, that's not the man." Then the second girl got on the stand and positively identified him. So there I was, stuck in a quandary. If I put him on with his story, we'll lose whatever we've gained by the first victim's failure to identify him. So I asked the D.A., "Why don't you let me plead him to disturbing the peace?", and he said, "You're a gentleman," and that was that.

Prosecutors who seek to guide the behavior of subordinates are caught in the bind of maintaining some sense of obligation to stated policy while at the same time encouraging the skill of intelligent and sensitive response to unexpected events that Judge Thomas illustrates. Tom Gubser argued that senior deputies rarely reprimanded those who disobeyed a formal policy:

> I think around here the quality and judgment and wisdom of the deputy are going to be measured by the orders he disobeys, when he should have disobeyed. Drunk driving cases have always been important in this office—we have a reputation for being very rigid on the subject. (We really haven't changed much from Savich to Nolan, except that perhaps we're a little less moralistic about it.) But there are many times when deputies have reduced cases after being told specifically *in this case* not to, and they've probably done the right thing, because they've been closer to it than the superior. You don't find supervisors openly approving that, but sometimes they'll agree later *maybe* he was right.

Control Through Clearance

Routing felonies through Dan Moore and the superior court calendar division for pretrial preparation proved the most effective device for imposing a common set of standards on case dispositions. But this device regularly led to the prosecuting of some cases, like Jennings's, that not only contained weaknesses but were in most respects identical to cases that were processed as misdemeanors. Most deputies in interviews indicated they believed the office regularly became "locked-in" by the clearance procedure to trying cases that ought to be dismissed or reduced. In part, as Jennings's case indicated, Moore's own preferences created this tendency. But the process of clearance itself also increased the tendency to become locked-in, and the clearance process provides the best example of the danger of applying hierarchical administrative procedures to criminal prosecution.

Dan Moore believed, "Once we file a case in superior court, we better be able to prove it's a felony." As a result, the calendar division was very reluctant to authorize at pre-pretrial conferences reduction of felonies to misdemeanors or outright dismissal. In their dealings with defense attorneys in Judge Jensen's chambers, Lewis (or more likely the deputy assigned to Lewis—George Baker first, then B.J. Chastain, then John Hunt) had little chance to deviate from the decision reached at the pre-pretrial conference. That decision, as we have seen, boiled down to a choice between an insistence on state prison sentence or a willingness to abide by the probation report. Moore and Lewis instructed the deputy orally in each case on the position they expected him to take in pretrial negotiations, which he was then to enter in the file. The negotiating deputy returned the file to them with the report of results of the conference, so he knew that his superiors expected him to obey their instructions and would discover any deviation.

The calendar division could not similarly control the action of the deputy assigned to try cases that did not plead out, and at that stage the division deputies frequently enough subverted the division's position that Nolan called the only meeting for the entire office staff that year to attempt to correct the problem.

Most deputies felt that Moore particularly concerned himself with developing good office statistics, that is, statistics that cast a favorable light on the office. Moore had kept the office statistics for over five years, and he learned, when the issue of the office's conviction rate came up during one of Savich's reelection campaigns, that statistics might become a political issue. In 1970, as we have seen, the haphazard evidence of public concern seemed to indicate criticism not of a low conviction rate but of leniency in dealing, and Moore, with his new boss up for election, hoped that the statistics would not reflect the office's malfeasance in this respect.

But the inflexibility at this stage provoked considerable resentment. B.J. Chastain, who worked under Lewis during the middle part of 1970, complained:

People worry about keeping the goddamn statistics looking good. I think far too much importance is being placed on the goddamn stats. You go in and say, "We can't dismiss this case because of such and such, but we'll take a misdemeanor," and then you fight for hours and hours and phones are stuck in everybody's ear. I don't think we're doing anybody any service. We ought to have the guts to say so if we don't have the facts. Things blow up, and then you ought to dump it.

John Hunt described the point of view of the superior court calendar division:

The information is looked at statistically as "Now it's a felony." At this point there are problems in the case, but they ask, "Are the problems so great as to necessitate the showing of a reduction of the felony after it is filed?" At that point, the discretion that everybody has is a lot less, except for the people at the top [i.e., Moore], and they *are* concerned about statistics.

Deputies criticized the division's restrictions on negotiation because they saw little justification for them. Superiors made no attempt to persuade subordinates that the office benefitted from "good statistics," and it did seem, in fact, that the superiors themselves benefitted most. Deputies regularly witnessed instances where the clearance procedures prevented them from adapting sensibly to shifting information, but they had little occasion to feel public criticism directed at office statistics, as did their superiors. It is not surprising, then, in the light of the lack of understanding of each other's priorities, that superiors could win little enthusiasm for control through clearance.

When Dan Moore assumed that once a case had been filed in superior court the office ought to be able to prove it a felony, he ignored both the considerable diversity in the practices of the deputies that had handled the case at an earlier stage and the extent to which the segmented handling of a case prevented thorough investigation of its weaknesses. The filing decision itself could be superficial. Some superiors who approved issuing felonies tried to anticipate all possible weaknesses, while others did not. Stewart Douglas said:

I think there are some supervisors in the office who don't really look at felonies closely when they authorize. I took one to B.J. Chastain, and I started to read it, and he said, "What's the guy's name?" and I told him, and he said, "Oh, he's a baddie. Here, give me that," and he initialed it. I think the people who are going to have to go down and put the case on should make the review.

Because dispositions were handled by the division, most deputies who made initial decisions about the case could fairly assume that they would not bear the ultimate responsibility for its disposition. Moore, who participated in the filing decision only on very serious cases, did not realize the degree to which segmentation of work on a case prevented the discovery of weaknesses. Office records indicate that in only about 19 percent of cases does the issuing deputy also put that case on at the preliminary examination, so that at the preliminary examination the deputy may not be equipped to probe for weaknesses that may have crossed the mind of the issuing deputy. The deputies who filed and put on the prelim had little contact with the superior court calendar division deputies, and they often overestimated the probability that others would correct errors at subsequent stages.

Moore also did not fully appreciate how the segmented handling of cases, a segmentation designed to move the cases in an orderly fashion through the courts, discouraged the deputies from learning about the mistakes they made. In most cases, with both misdemeanors and felonies, the deputy who filed the case or put on the prelim would not learn its disposition. Deputies did not learn regularly what mistakes they made at this stage, because they did not regularly observe pretrial negotiations or the trial itself. Those who handled the case at later stages did not observe the initial decisions and, because they rarely knew how a mistake was made, were reluctant to criticize other deputies and pass on to them suggestions for improvements. But when a deputy never learned of the failure of a case, he assumed that the office had disposed of the case satisfactorily, and this assumption buttressed his satisfaction with his own performance. Dan Moore seemed to anticipate some screening of questionable cases by the courts. But in reality the tendency of the courts was to weed out only the blatantly defective cases, assuming that all others had been carefully scrutinized at an earlier stage. Don Smith, a highly successful trial attorney, complained bitterly about this buck-passing:

If the officer testifies that the defendant was within a hundred yards of the crime, the judge will hold him to answer. He may ask the D.A. to throw it out, but the D.A. may say, "You do it on your own." Maybe the D.A. will say he's got more evidence. So I'll make my argument but the judge will say, "Your recourse is a 995." So you take your 995 to superior court, and they say, "Well, I didn't hear the witnesses at the prelim. If the municipal court judge held him to answer that's good enough for me." And it's difficult to appeal the rejection of a 995, because the appellate court will just say, "What the hell. Go ahead and have a trial, and then we'll have a look at it if it's necessary."

In summary, the felony clearance procedures in Vario County not only failed to uncover case weaknesses, by passing the file to less informed deputies they actively discouraged accomplishing what organizations with intensive technologies must accomplish: learning new information from the production process itself.

The Absence of Measures

Prosecutors do not account for their time or their decisions in monetary terms. It is difficult to imagine how any prosecutor's office could specify the number of complaints to be issued or the number of cases to be dismissed or reduced, because the office has no control over the kinds of cases brought or the rate at which they are brought. A decision not to prosecute a case that the police or public might believe to be serious, because the budget did not permit, would surely arouse vociferous criticism from police and public, just as a decision to overfile a case or press it to trial because the budget permitted would anger defense attorneys and judges.

An office could conceivably resort to other currencies to judge decisions. It might, for example, attempt to measure the seriousness of offenses and offenders by requiring a certain specified disposition of all cases involving, for example, the hospitalization of the victim, or a suspect with more than five separate entries on his rap sheet. But the Vario County office made no such rules, and wisely so, because no single measure of comparison can capture more than a small slice of information about any one case. Lacking a simple device for communicating priorities to subordinates, superiors therefore possessed no efficient shorthand for detecting deviance, the subject to which we next turn.[22]

Detecting and Discouraging Deviation

We have seen that the Vario County office created relatively few firm policies and that subtle cues on which decisions so often depend made superiors reluctant to reprimand those who violated the few policies that did exist. Since it is difficult to specify just what is expected of a prosecutor, it is not surprising to find that the sanctions for discouraging deviation—salary increases, job promotions, and review of the work of subordinates—did not in practice influence significantly their behavior. Deputies were in fact only very rarely discharged outright. (Lewis could recall only one instance in his ten years in the office.) Instead of discharging men, the office had in the past signaled dissatisfaction with performance by denying the regularly scheduled salary increase specified by the Civil Service Commission. But the office denied increases only to those few deputies (Brian Savio and one other in 1970) who had repeatedly demonstrated both a difficulty working with others and a tendency to lose significantly more trials than they won over an extended period of time. Most deputies could safely assume they would win the regular salary increases.

Although deputies could win promotion, after taking an oral examination, promotion to area deputy or deputy in charge of a branch or to any other office position did not depend on the deputy's grade, and the few deputies eager for promotions did not need to worry about placing high on the Civil Service Commission's oral exam. In fact, a deputy who sought a career in the office could safely assume that, owing to the high rate of turnover, his advancement depended primarily on his accumulated seniority and experience, at least as long as he did not lose "too often," related effectively with others, and succeeded in articulating defensible reasons for the positions he took. Most deputies, then, felt that assessment was a very casual and not terribly important "vague balance of personality and performance," as one deputy put it. Few deputies felt they were assessed on their ability to win trials consistently, and most did not bother to keep track of their own records. The office did require superiors to fill out a rather long evaluation form on each of their immediate subordinates (the form requested "excellent", "satisfactory" or "unsatisfactory" rankings of each deputy on such items as "General Appearance," "Willingness to Work," "Understanding of

Office Procedures," "Ability to Work with Law Enforcement Officers," and so forth), but most deputies felt the forms were irrelevant. Steinway, for example, commented, when I asked him how the evaluation procedure worked, "God only knows. I fill out those forms on Hunt and Green every two months, but that's a crock of shit. Really, if they don't hear too much about you, and you're not losing too many, then you're safe." Ed Lee reported, "People are satisfied with me, but my record is mediocre. I've had some tough cases. I think they ask, 'Is he cheerful?' If not, they figure he can't be putting his heart into it." One deputy who began in mid-1970 but who had already received several difficult assignments because, as Moore put it, "He's the kind of guy that can relate to people instantly," indicated, "I think you could be doing a poor job and nobody would know it. If you're really obnoxious—and that's almost a personality thing—the word gets out."

Since most deputies had no sense of permanent commitment to the office and since standards of performance themselves were ambiguous, it is hardly surprising to find such modest efforts to evaluate performance. In fact, attempts to do so in such circumstances could (and in Roger Savich's case did) only appear arbitrary to deputies, arbitrary particularly because the prosecutor has been encouraged by his legal training to think independently and to question the validity of rules without reasons.

Encouraging Conformity

The Vario County office could not expect a career commitment from its deputies. But the office in theory could have recruited, selected, and trained deputies to conform to some consistent and definable pattern of behavior. They might have hired men with promise as effective trial attorneys, or men who believed in the efficacy of stern punishment, or men with evident interpersonal skills. Both the absence of an organizational identity and the absence of clear recruitment and training standards thwarted the development of organizational loyalty and conformity.

The Absence of Organizational Identity

Like Vario County itself, the district attorney's office there does not really have a continuous tradition. Rapid growth and turnover of personnel in the office have paralleled the rapid growth of the county, and while both office and county have a past, few traditions from that past have survived to influence the choices of the men who live and work there. In the 1940s and 1950s, when the county was smaller, the district attorney and his staff of no more than ten had firm ties with the local bar that often translated into a willingness to do a favor for a friend.

But that style came to an end when Roger Savich took office as district attorney in 1958. In that year the office consisted of ten attorneys, most of them young men with private practices on the side who worked as prosecutors to prevent insolvency. To Savich, an independently wealthy man from a family with substantial real estate holdings in the county, his predecessor's practices seemed too heavily laced with favoritism. Savich was particularly incensed that a man arrested for drunken driving could get the charge reduced to reckless driving, thus perhaps saving his license, only when represented by counsel. Superior Court Judge Thomas recalled Savich's successful campaign platform:

There were two things, actually. He campaigned on the reform that he and his deputies wouldn't engage in private practice, but he also promised, although he didn't make a big issue of it in the campaign, that he would eliminate plea bargaining—there would be no reduction in charges of offenses. He'd either plead guilty or stand trial. He was only able to make that stick in the case of drunk driving. The facts of life with respect to other offenses were that his office wasn't big enough to handle all the trials that would follow. He decided to run for this office because when he was a deputy district attorney he was very upset about the fact that a man with a lawyer could plead out to reckless in a drunk driving, whereas the man without a lawyer couldn't. So to cure the problem, he decided that nobody would be allowed to.

Attorneys and judges who had known him all agreed that Savich possessed three qualities: intelligence, incorruptibility, and a pronounced lack of interpersonal skills. He had had little practical experience with administration of any kind, and he cared less about shaping the substance of the daily dispositions of criminal cases than he cared about attempting to insure uniformity in the administration of the office's affairs. His obligations as county counsel, a post split off from that of district attorney only when Nolan was appointed, diverted Savich's attentions from the daily disposition of criminal cases, but to impose uniformity he created the *Manual* of policies and procedures, which he apparently enforced by browbeating those deputies whose deviations he discovered. The provisions of the *Manual* quoted above reveal several features of the Savich regime that tended to alienate deputies. Deputies who worked under Savich were frustrated by what they felt were stifling, confusing, and inconsistent attempts at strict, hierarchical direction; approximately seventy men left the office under Savich. The provisions quoted suggest first a blunt, insistent, and rationalistic tone that reflected Savich's direct relations with people. Deputies, like Gubser, who appreciated Savich's commitment to legal correctness, believed that, as Gubser put it, Savich suffered "from an inability to relate to people." Less sympathetic deputies, like B.J. Chastain, called him a "paranoid"; several interviewees used the phrase "crisis oriented" to describe his manner of governing the office. Chastain told me, "The only time I came in contact with Savich was when I picked up the phone and had him screaming in my goddamn ear about something or other that he knew nothing about. He was a sick man."

Second, most deputies found that the actual implementation of the *Manual* was selective and often arbitrary. Formal decisional authority was centered at the top in the name of uniformity and consistent policy application, but deputies soon learned that no synoptic review of decisions actually took place. As Richard Henderson, who left disgruntled to become the public defender in 1966 put it, "It was stifling. But the difficulty was not only policies that were stifling, but in addition a total inconsistency in the application of them. You never really knew whether you were doing the right thing or not." Rather than encouraging uniformity, the *Manual* became somewhat of a joke. Deputies filled out its required forms perfunctorily, often giving reasons they felt Savich would approve rather than the real ones for their decisions. Deputies tended to hide the necessary deviations from Savich, and younger deputies learned to appreciate the capacity of their immediate superiors to disguise deviations or otherwise keep Savich off their backs.

Third, despite his concern for achieving uniformity and his denunciation of favoritism, Savich seemed to his deputies to be extremely sensitive to criticism from the general public.[23] To some deputies, Savich seemed to panic when outsiders criticized a policy decision or suggested that undesirable things were happening in his office that Savich did not know about. Judge Thomas recalled:

Savich was ... extremely sensitive to criticism, even where it wasn't valid. For example, when he first took office, he dreamed up several ideas in order to evaluate his deputies. One of them was that if there was a not-guilty verdict, the deputy in charge of the case had to write a report explaining why there was a not-guilty verdict, from his point of view. Then, they were sending out questionnaires to the jurors on the conduct of the deputy. One department of the state college became very interested in these questionnaires, because it appeared we were going to get some kind of an idea of the ways jurors thought. And the Bar Association found out about it in a kind of back-handed way. The deputies started to ask questions of the prospective jurors on *voir dire* that sounded very strange. Chuck Wagner would ask, "Will the fact that I'm overweight affect you in any way?" I asked him, "Jees, Chuck, where did you get that question?" He said some juror wrote it in on a questionnaire. So some people started thinking maybe Savich was building up a file on jurors so he'd know good jurors from bad jurors. So the Bar Association appointed a committee to find out about it, and as soon as Savich found out about that, he stopped the whole thing. He didn't even wait to talk to them, didn't try to justify it to them, and I asked him afterwards, I said, "We didn't know what you were doing. If you had a good reason, we weren't prepared to criticize it." But he just said "Well ..." and that was that.

I'll give you another example. We had a very embarrassing case involving one of the judges where the defendant in the case and his two sisters in the courtroom kind of went wild and started throwing things at the judge. It was embarrassing and nobody wanted to try the thing. So we worked out a deal where the defendant in the case would go to prison and the sisters would get whatever the probation report gave them. Well, the case was scheduled to go to trial the following Monday. On the Thursday night, a newspaper printed a story very critical of the incident, and Savich called saying the deal was off. Dick Henderson ... was handling the case for the D.A.'s office then, and that's when he finally decided to quit the office.

The civil-service procedures that Savich initiated, together with his supervision of the dispositions of cases, did succeed in eliminating the favoritism that bothered him. In 1970 most prosecutors did not make concessions to defense attorneys simply on the basis of their professional standing or on the basis of personal friendship. But beyond this, Savich discouraged the growth of common practices, preferences, and loyalties. His attempts to control by direction frustrated deputies by forcing them to ignore repeatedly facts that they felt their decisions should reflect. The resulting increase in turnover and the necessity for hiding decisions from "the boss" prevented the emergence of any consistent set of preferences that new deputies could identify or adopt.

Recruitment, Selection, and Training

The office recruits new attorneys through the county's civil-service department, which periodically circulates announcements for positions to be filled for county counsel, district attorney, and public defender all in one circular. The most recent of these, after stating that beginning salary would range from $959 to $1110 per month, proceeds:

Vario County is seeking attorneys interested in public service. Current members of the California Bar and those awaiting results of the March, 1971 Bar examination should apply. The employment lists established by the examination will be used to fill any vacancies which may occur during the six months following promulgation of these lists....

Deputy District Attorneys are involved in criminal legal work offering an opportunity for trial practice. They are exposed to a complete cross-section of criminal cases and have direct participation in the investigation of crimes with police agencies.

Deputy Public Defenders typically advise and represent clients in criminal proceedings, analyze case materials, conduct research and cause investigations to be made where appropriate. They may also receive experience representing minors in juvenile court and persons facing civil commitment proceedings, and in arguing cases in appellate courts....

Requirements: Valid California Motor Vehicle Operator's license. Active membership in the California State Bar at the time of appointment.

Note: Candidates may file for Deputy County Counsel I, Deputy District Attorney I, Deputy Public Defender I, or for any combination of the three positions. *A separate application must be filed for each position....*

The competitive examination will consist of an oral interview in Centerville by a qualifications appraisal board which will review with the candidate his training experience and personal fitness for the job. Candidates must receive a rating of at least 70 from a majority of the board members to be ranked on the employment list. (Weighted 100%).... Employment lists are established by ranking candidates according to their overall scores in the examination. The candidates must be successful in each part of the examination. To fill each vacancy, the hiring department will make a selection from among the top three names on the employment list.

The civil service department circulates this notice to various county offices, universities, and law school placement offices. Those responding to the announcement submit applications to civil service, which then notifies the applicant of the date of the oral exam. Dan Moore had represented the district attorney's office at the oral examination, and he was joined by an employee of the civil service department and by a third person, perhaps a private attorney, perhaps a police officer. The oral examination board, which normally must review anywhere from fifty to eighty applicants in the space of two to three days, did not ask those who indicated an interest in a prosecutorial position a specific list of questions. They did not probe deeply into the applicant's views toward criminal justice, nor did they probe for evidence of the candidate's performance in law school. The board scored and ranked the deputies, and the office selected men from the top three men on the list.

Most deputies were selected through this process. Only Miss Denton had any relationship to someone active in the county's political or legal affairs. (Her uncle headed the Condenado school board.) Only four applied for the job because they knew someone in the office. Dan Moore indicated that he selected deputies from his impressions in the oral examination according to the following criteria:

Maturity, aggressiveness, appearance, the unknown quantity you can't really define. I've done so many of these I can pretty well tell. I prefer the guy who's had a lot of jobs, who's worked through school. Like I had been a truck driver and a choker setter and had done just about every damned thing. But the guy who's been skiing in Europe during vacations and has had a spoon in his mouth, he doesn't know people. So one of the things we look for—some of the deputies seem to have a holier than thou attitude, which is just a bad scene, especially with some of the secretaries. There is an image you want. It's a political office, and you have to go out and project an image. You have to understand that there is a D.A. and you're a deputy and not running your own office. Physically he can't be unattractive. How a person dresses or cuts his hair are part of him. As you can tell from my sideburns [they reached to mid-ear], I'm not a hung-up conservative on this—my kids have long hair. Not long in the back, but long on the sides. But beards, long sideburns, can lose a case. Dammit, this is how cases are decided. You have to eliminate all these things and get a sterile atmosphere. Then maybe the jury will look at the facts. Now we have the philosophy that we won't pass anybody on the civil-service test that we wouldn't be willing to hire. In the past, there were people on the list that frankly shouldn't have been there. Once you get 'em now, it's a tough row to hoe to get rid of 'em.

Moore succeeded in screening out some "extreme" types. There were no beards (although there were several mustaches), and although David Snow came close, no prosecutors attempted to challenge directly the premise that most forms of legally proscribed misconduct should receive some social sanction. And no prosecutor was physically repulsive. But, as we have seen, inside these limits there was considerable diversity, in part because vacancies occurred at irregular intervals so that the office must at times select months after the oral exam men from the lower portion of the list after those ranked higher had found jobs elsewhere. More important, Moore's criteria themselves, assuming that Moore could in fact correctly identify those traits in a fifteen-to-thirty-minute interview, carry no guarantee of internal consistency. The "aggressive" prosecutor Moore sought might well not play the bureaucratically docile role he preferred. In short, the selection process did not in Vario County screen into the office prosecutors with common motives or personality types.

The office had no formal training program. Superiors may have assumed that "learning by doing" was the best training, but in 1970 most superiors interviewed felt the office would benefit from a formal training program. Lewis, for example, felt that a training program might "help create some pride around here." But no superiors seemed particularly interested in assuming the burden of organizing a training program. Sarah Levy analyzed the problem this way:

We ... have lousy training. The men who know what they're doing are too busy to do any real training, and they don't know the techniques for training people, even if they wanted to. Normally an organization is related to what it is trying to do, but in changing circumstances like these, it's not so simple in this office.

While they are not formally trained, deputies worked into the job slowly enough that they picked up basic procedural information on their own. Most young deputies began working on contested traffic violations. The deputy received no area assignment at the outset, but moved where the minor traffic cases existed, as different jurisdictions hold traffic court on different days. In a month or so, if the work load in the office did not push him faster, the deputy began to handle minor penal code violations: disturbing the peace, simple battery, drunk in public, and so forth. He could in this period try his first jury trial, usually in a case where the defendant represented himself without assistance of counsel. After two or more months, depending on his progress, he received a specific area assignment, after which time he entered the regular routine of putting on preliminary examinations, preparing for misdemeanor trials (settling most of them without trial), and developing closer ties with the police, judges, and defense attorneys in his area.

While more experienced deputies may pass on hints to the new deputy, the office established no pattern for doing so. Supervising deputies only rarely observed the prosecutor's work in court, and most of the deputies with a year of experience or less indicated that no supervisor had ever sat through one of his trials in order to suggest possible improvements. A few area deputies, like John Lane, did take an active interest in the work of their subordinates, but most were too busy or felt the deputy should use his own judgment in building job skills. Jim Coe, a deputy Baum assigned to the San Pedro area (the assignment was probably dictated by a vacancy in the area rather than any attempt to match personalities to the judge or type of case in the area) and who worked under John Okamoto, a pleasant but noncommunicative Japanese-American, complained:

> I have never really been criticized for anything I've done around this office. And I haven't gotten many suggestions, either. That's my one big criticism of the office. Nobody wants to hurt anyone else's feelings, and nobody goes up and says, "Hey, you blew this one. What the hell is this?" The most that happens is that somebody comes by and says, here's a loser you filed, and then goes ahead and tries it. But he never tells me why it was a loser.

What Coe described was not simply a product of Okamoto's passive philosophy. Other deputies in other areas similarly complained about the absence of effective feedback and correction. Dick Schwartz felt that Bill Brown, a Mormon and a "crime fighter," made unfortunate decisions, but that superiors did not seek to correct his behavior:

> It's common knowledge that Brown was one of the worst deputies in the office. He'd file on some of the worst cases, even family beefs, because of his religious convictions. I didn't usually talk to Henry about personalities, but I told him I didn't want Brown issuing any more goddamn cases in my jurisdiction. But he went on doing it. A deputy can do pretty much what he wants until he asks for help; until then there's not too much we can do about it. Brown was the office patsy, and officers knew it and tried to take advantage of it.

The professional status of prosecuting attorneys cuts against rigorous selection and training procedures. A deputy is presumed competent by virtue of his education the day he begins work. Both rigorous training on the job and blunt attempts to change the way he does his job after he has begun imply not simply that the deputy needs to improve his skills as a prosecutor but that the deputy may be inadequate professionally. The weight of such an implication discourages prosecutors from attempting to correct the practices of other prosecutors.

Summary

Early in this chapter we noted that the job of prosecutor resembled other jobs—teaching, psychiatric social work, medicine, perhaps politics itself—where organizational ordering and control devices are likely to fail. The following five points summarize this argument.

1. Skilled employees in many work settings, by virtue of their training on the job, come to identify their occupational "selves" in terms of their organization's routines and values. The prosecuting attorney, on the other hand, not only owes his professional identity to a process of training in which his

employer played no part, he knows that his professional skills are marketable. Indeed, becoming a prosecutor may be, as we have seen, essentially a marketing strategy.

2. The lawyer's training not only lacks organizational referents, it consciously encourages independent thought. Law school training does not teach rules; it teaches the capacity to exploit complexity and ambiguity where there are few right answers and where one learns that better answers depend on more imaginative analysis, not on following a rule. The lawyer's training thus actively discourages him from accepting any cause/effect belief unless and until he independently verifies its worth.

3. Many employees see tangible, physical, measurable effects of their decisions and actions. For example, the forest ranger "knows" forest fires are undesirable and "knows," because his immediate experience confirms it, that if a fire is a hazard, closing a forest to recreational use will reduce the likelihood of a fire. The prosecutor cannot so confidently predict whether lenience or severity will reduce the incidence of future offenses. The prosecutor does not normally see the results of his decisions in terms that he can relate directly to the reasons why he prosecutes in the first place. He does not see the impact on the family of incarcerating the accused; he rarely sees or hears of the accused himself again after he has paid his penalty. The prosecutor can only adjust crudely to the facts of the cases as they reveal themselves. Substantive rules make little sense in the prosecutorial situation, because the information the prosecutor gets changes the weights he gives inconsistent objectives.

4. The prosecutor is very much a middleman, and his responsibilities thereby become amorphous. The police assume the primary responsibility for coping with the incidence of crime; the judge assumes the responsibility for insuring that dispositions meet legal standards. The prosecutor may assist police and judges in these respects, but he need not choose between them.

5. Prosecutors, at least in Vario County, saw their superiors requesting them to act in ways that carried little or no promise of benefitting either themselves or the office in order to respond to what most prosecutors believed were uninformed and irrelevant public demands.[24] In these circumstances, "playing the cases by ear," as Henry Baum put it, proved wiser than Moore's rules. Robert Nolan's inability to resolve these two points of view, to which we now turn, left deputies free to follow their own inclinations.

Uncertainty, Diversity, and the Reluctance to Govern: Robert Nolan

Not only did Roger Savich leave for Robert Nolan a staff that was for the most part young and inexperienced, his "treating of his deputies like stock clerks," as one defense attorney put it, had discouraged deputies from consulting Savich concerning the problems they faced, and Nolan (and Moore) therefore had some difficulty discovering what deputies were doing. Also, Nolan faced when he took office considerable disagreement among senior deputies concerning the direction they felt the office should be taking. Disagreement had evolved into evident hostilities between Moore and Levy and at best cool indifference between Moore and Hoff and Levy and Hoff. No doubt the fact that Moore, Levy, and Hoff all had hoped for the appointment to Nolan's position exacerbated their disagreements.

Nolan knew some of the problems that existed when he took office. He had worked under Savich himself. And his experience as a public defender, as a private attorney, and as president of the North County Bar Association taught him that defense attorneys had been critical of the prosecutor's inability to make commitments on cases without being overruled later by a superior.

When Nolan assumed office he hoped to increase both the quality of legal work of the deputies (he listed that as his first personal choice among office goals) and the degree to which defense attorneys could expect quick, careful, and realistic consideration of their cases. But Nolan did not anticipate five complications. First, he had not counted on the degree of differences among senior deputies. Second, he did not fully anticipate or understand the paradox that to implement his goals in the context of an intensive technology handled by independently trained professionals, he had to avoid the appearance of implementation or control. Nolan assumed that because he was the district attorney and ultimately responsible for office practices, he was obliged to "somehow grab hold," as he put it. Third, he did not anticipate that the grand jury's report and Judge Jensen's reaction to the report and critical newspaper articles would cut against his own initial objectives. Fourth, he did not anticipate the extent to which his campaign duties and, apart from the campaign, the continuing demands from outsiders to speak at a luncheon here, to moderate a police-community relations panel there, and to handle the frequent phone calls from outsiders would prevent him from closely following office operations. Fifth, he did not anticipate the extent to which the visibility of his decisions and the suspicion that he, like all elected politicians, acted for personal gain would cut from under him the referents of friendships and associations in the legal community that he assumed would support him. In summary, he did not fully understand the degree to which the inherent uncertainties in legal technology itself, the ultimate moral ambiguity of criminal administration, and the additional diversity and unpredictability that characterized his unique organization and political surroundings would complicate the task of leadership. Like Savich, he did not intuitively sense the truth of Chester Barnard's statement:

The limitations imposed by the physical environment and the biological constitution of human beings, the uncertainties of the outcome of cooperation, the difficulties of common understanding of purpose, the delicacy of the systems of communication essential to organization, the dispersive tendencies of individuals, the necessity of individual assent to establish the authority for coordination, the great role of persuasion in securing adherence to organization, and submission to its requirements, the complexity and instability of motives, the never-ending burden of decision—all these elements of organization, in which the moral factor finds its concrete expression, spell the necessity of leadership, the power of individuals to inspire cooperative personal decision by creating faith: faith in common understanding, faith in the probability of success, faith in the ultimate satisfaction of personal motives, faith in the integrity of objective authority, faith in the superiority of common purpose as a personal aim of those who partake in it.[25]

Nolan's posture as an organizational leader went through three stages. He began in 1969 by attempting to govern informally by calling meetings both for the senior staff and on one occasion for the entire office. When these meetings only generated additional debate and disagreement rather than increased mutual understanding, Nolan turned in June to the strategy of issuing formal directives and moving deputies to different positions in the office. By fall, when these impersonal directives had stimulated considerable personal criticism of Nolan both from inside and outside the office, Nolan began to doubt, as we shall see, his capacity to shape office practices at all.

Attempts at Informal Direction

Shortly after he took office, Nolan began to hold informal meetings in his office each Monday afternoon, which Moore, Levy, Baum, Hoff, and Lewis as well as Peter Kay, the office's chief investigator, attended. Lewis described these meetings as "disasters," and he continued:

Nobody got along with Levy, except me, and that was back when Dan and Hoff weren't seeing eye to eye, and Kay and Moore weren't seeing eye to eye, and Kay and Hoff weren't seeing eye to eye. Henry [Baum] was fine, but those meetings got to be pretty brutal. The boss didn't know how to run 'em, and when they just became fiascos, he gave up on them.

The grand jury report and Judge Jensen's reaction to it had led Nolan to instruct Moore and Lewis to make no sentence commitment in pretrial negotiations, but by April several weaknesses in this position had surfaced. The public defenders were insisting on taking more cases to trial, and most deputies felt they were overworked. Some deputies, furthermore, ignored the instructions by committing themselves to a sentence position after the pretrial conference but before the trial. To iron out the confusion and resentment of some deputies over these policies, and to attempt to reinforce the policies, Nolan called a staff meeting for the entire office (the only meeting for all staff during the year of which I was aware) to clarify his position. The abbreviated

transcript from that meeting, however, reveals that the meeting, like earlier
staff meetings with senior deputies, turned into an inconclusive general
debate:

Robert Nolan: I want to say a few things about superior court. First we shouldn't be
making any sentence guarantees during pretrials. I've had a number of chats with
Judge Jensen, and he approves this. Now I know the calendar is increasing rapidly, and I know that no guarantees will mean fewer pleas, but the public defender's
office is playing it that way. Some of the private lawyers are blaming me for it,
but the source is the public defender. Second, it's my understanding that the
grand jury would have come out much stronger against the pretrial system. The
report was watered down, and Jensen agrees that last year wasn't the ideal system
of pretrials. I talked to him last week, and he says he won't go along with any
sentencing deals because he reserves the right to look at the probation report.
Third, he told me, and I agree, that the worst thing to happen would be if we take
a pretrial position and then at trial the deputy makes his own deal and guarantee.
He thinks, obviously the system won't operate if we change after pretrial. If we've
gotta prepare trials on a Monday morning, it's a big burden, but if you've done
your work, you should be prepared to go to trial. Fourth, if there's something
wrong with the pretrial procedure, we have three alternatives. We can discard it,
we can live with it, or we can make some dramatic changes. I'm not wedded to
any particular system, except no guarantee, and Jensen doesn't go along with
that anyway, so I want to hear your suggestions. Fifth, Jensen's mail shows that a
lot of people are upset. You probably saw what the *Tribune* published in the
paper [referring to an article in one of the county's major newspapers that showed
some lenient felony dispositions in a box with a black border around it]. I saw
that on Jensen's desk. He's smart enough not to get that type of criticism. He's
going to be giving more jail time. So, if we have a mess, we have to make some
changes, so take a good look at the case and develop a realistic position at the
outset for pretrial. As a policy, the time to get rid of the dogs is at the preliminary. Once we get into the pretrial, we're stuck somewhere in the system. So with
doggy cases, get rid of them before superior court. If you've got a strong case,
deal from strength and let the chips fall. I know you have comments on the
system. Any suggestions on the office or the problem?

George Welsh: What about the border cases, where you know he's not going to get
CYA [California Youth Authority] or the joint [state prison]?

Nolan: I'll throw that right back at you.

Welsh: I think we should be honest about it. There've been cases recently where we
could have gotten a plea, where a guy went to trial on just a matchbox. [He is
referring to Jennings.] Often you just can't take a realistic look until you prepare
for trial.

Nolan: Why not before then?

Welsh: Nobody has time to prepare for trial before you're ready for trial. When you
start thinking about arguing before a jury, then you start thinking of the
problems.

Carl Steinway: When I go into pre-pretrial I haven't interviewed witnesses. I don't
know if our key witness will turn out to be a night fighter.

Nolan: That's extreme.

Henry Baum: Realistically, that's the way it is. We've got fifteen cases for next week, and I haven't looked at one of them. If these cases fall apart at the last minute, we're getting rid of them.

Nolan: Let me say this. I'd like to see the deputy taken off the hook. It's not his fault. It belongs to me and the way we say it's going to go at pretrial. If it won't go [plead] take it to trial and don't worry about it.

Baum: That Jennings case was a year old. We filed on a matchbox a year ago, today we don't [Condenado—Centerville under Hoff often did], and there's gotta be a way to get rid of these stinking rotten cases.

Tom Gubser: I can't believe we didn't know at pretrial there was a matchbox, but I can believe we didn't look at it realistically. We are boxing the area deputy into an unrealistic position by a few comments at the pre-pretrial. He's busy, and when we get a clean case on a clean search, we get excited and say, "Let's go." If we could say no state prison, we could get out of them.

Nolan: Beyond saying no state prison, what else?

Gubser: The defense attorneys want some assurance from us about how much time he's going to get. No promises, but I don't see why we can't just say, "My experience indicates . . . ."

B.J. Chastain: The judge used to say he'd get no more than sixty days, that's a commitment, but not now. There's been a real change. Now he says, "If all you say is true, it's not a state prison case, but sometimes I'm surprised at what the probation report digs up." He's really laying it on them so we can't be sure. We can't bind this judge by saying we'll ask for county jail. And sometimes the probation report on the matchbox *does* turn up a state prison case.

Steinway: Suppose we agree to no state prison, and the judge says, "The D.A. says no state prison" and puts it on our shoulders? As I see it, the defense attorney is usually more worried about disposition than whether it's a felony or a misdemeanor. We're worried about what to do at pre-pretrials, but once we've set that at pre-pretrial, we've got nothing to talk about, and we won't have much either.

John Okamoto: I see nothing wrong with being honest about it. Would you say we can say 99 percent of the time that this is not a joint case?

Dan Moore: Ninety percent, anyway.

Okamoto: We could be honest to the point of saying, this doesn't look like state prison to us.

Moore: Carl is saying that the defense attorney wants more than a recommendation, he wants a commitment. They want the assurance that we won't push for state prison on the facts. And I think we can be honest about this. It's part of our job.

Nolan: But it's not our job to cut out the probation department, and our probation department is bitchy about it.

Welsh: But Bob, you talk about uniformity. There isn't uniformity there in the probation department. If one officer says county jail and another says state prison and we don't correct this, we're not doing our job. I know probation bitches that they're just writing reports when the judge already makes a prior deal, but why doesn't the probation department talk to us! They never do. Give the area deputies lenience from these hard and fast positions.

John Hunt: Why not get an indication from the probation department? Well, I guess we'd have to do it before the plea, but that's no good, because the defendant won't be candid with the probation officer before the plea, so I guess that's not such a good idea.

Peter Hoff: You know, it's hard to stand up before five hundred people and explain plea bargaining. And the Marino County and the Limon County grand juries have been hitting plea bargaining too. The public can't understand sitting in a back room and deciding the cases. They're concerned not only about catching them, but convicting them. The question is how can we vary from the extreme and still live with the public.

Baum: We've got too many goddamn cases, and I'd say that communications between Centerville and Condenado have been pretty damn poor.

Welsh: Getting back to Ed's case [Jennings], if just before or just after the preliminary, if we reduce something like that on our own, are we going to get support from higher up?

Nolan: Frankly, I don't want to see every deputy deciding how to handle it, because what we're striving for is some continuity, and people are different.

Steinway: But there's no uniformity on disposition in this office now, that's for sure.

No deputies with whom I spoke after this meeting indicated that Nolan had succeeded in changing anyone's practices, and one felt that, by putting all the weaknesses of the inflexible policies on the table, Nolan had unintentionally encouraged deputies to break from them further. But the more common reaction was to describe it as Miss Denton did: "just another bull session." That meetings such as this failed to change practices confirms Thompson's proposition that the "more sources of uncertainty or contingency for the organization, the more bases there are for power and the larger the number of political positions in the organization" (p. 129).

How could Nolan have succeeded in persuading deputies to follow his direction? If, as Barnard suggests, effective leadership requires "individuals to inspire cooperative personal decisions by creating faith," then what faith could Nolan have inspired? He might have endorsed the substance of what he believed the public demanded, or he might have adopted the position that, regardless of the wisdom of the public position, the office was bound to follow it. But his own contacts with the public only demonstrated the frustrating ignorance of most members of the general public about legal matters. He recalled one particularly frustrating experience:

I had a press conference, actually it was a lunch where the reporters came and asked questions. Christ, I would have thought that these guys, men with college degrees most of them, would at least ask intelligent and informed questions. But it's just like the rest, questions about law and order and the crime wave and why are we so lenient and all that. When I first began making speeches I always used to say something about how it was our job to protect everybody equally—that we had an obligation not only to the public and to the victims, but to see that the defendant was treated fairly— but I don't do that anymore. People would start throwing questions at me like, "What do you mean, protect the criminal? We've had enough protection of the defendant.

Look at the crime rate! What about the rights of the people?" Well, how do you answer that? You can maybe sit down with the guy and talk awhile and begin to make some sense to him. But when you've got half an hour to stand up and say some things in front of an uninitiated audience, you can box yourself into a corner just like that. "He's just another goddamned social worker," they'll say. So what can you do?

If Nolan had held a strong personal belief, or a consistent model of desired criminal administration, he might have succeeded in generating a common commitment in the office by urging his perceptions upon deputies and ignoring the public consequences altogether. But in fact Nolan held a penal philosophy only tentatively:

I guess I basically believe in the old Catholic way of doing it. You commit the crime, you get caught, and you do your penance. It's not fun if you don't do your penance. When I was in the public defender's office, I'd go over to the jail first thing to see the client, and they'd have just been brought in, and they'd be hang-dog and want to get it off their chests. Christ, everybody feels bad when they first get caught, before they started building up their egos by talking with the other inmates. So often a guy just wants to get if off his chest and do his punishment and get it over with, that I think we may be flying in the face of human nature by erecting all these "safeguards" in the system.

Even if Nolan took this position more seriously than he did, he would not have pressed it upon others, for he understood that it was not consistent with current legal or penal theory. Additionally, he respected many of the younger deputies who, although Nolan perceived them as more liberal than himself, appeared to him to do their job conscientiously:

There's been a change in the last five years concerning what the law schools are turning out. The average graduate is liberal. I don't mean that they are radicals, but they are concerned with the rights of the individual. I sit back and marvel at these guys with, say, just a few years of experience who can see both sides and who are enthusiastic, who go home and catch up on the police reports and the advance sheets over the weekend. Some of the older men in here look at it like any other civil-service job, you know, they'll put in forty hours a week and that's it.

Lacking a well-defined philosophy of the nature of the prosecutor's responsibilities to which he might tie the specific requests he did make, e.g., that cases not be bargained at the last minute, and frustrated that he had not "grabbed hold" as he believed any head of an office should, Nolan decided that he could increase his authority over the office only by reducing the power of those below him.

Impersonal Management

When Nolan requested from the Board of Supervisors the creation of the position of assistant district attorney outside the civil-service ladder, he intended to bring his "own man" into the office to perform the daily tasks of management, for which Nolan had no time. Moore nevertheless believed that Nolan would likely appoint him to the position. Whether Nolan wanted to avoid hurting Moore's feelings, whether he sought to avoid personal embarrassment, or whether it was simply a matter of timing never became clear, but Nolan appointed Robert Johnson to fill the new position without informing Moore while Moore was away on his July vacation. Moore learned of the appointment from his son, who had read it in the newspaper, and both the decision and the way he heard it hurt him deeply: "He's putting himself aloof, like Savich. I never expected that Bob Nolan would ever be anything but a close friend to everyone in the office. But now he just won't sit down and talk things out with people. This is not good for the morale of the office." Most deputies, including those who disagreed with Moore's policies, sympathized with him and felt that Nolan had acted out of cowardice. Hoff and Lewis began speculating in front of other deputies that the Johnson appointment had been some sort of political payoff, since Johnson's father, a former coach at the local Catholic college and now a successful real estate developer, was a close friend of several of the Catholic supervisors who had sponsored Nolan's appointment.

Deputies who were inclined to give Nolan the benefit of the doubt regarding the Moore affair had second thoughts when Nolan announced in August that Baum and Hoff would exchange positions as office heads immediately. When Hoff resigned six weeks later, Nolan appointed Gubser to head the Condenado office. Gubser had had three years' experience in Centerville, while Welsh had had six in Condenado, but Nolan made these moves without consulting Welsh or any of the other deputies who might have expected the Condenado appointment by virtue of their seniority to Gubser. Both moves tended to confirm the impression that Nolan simply did not have the courage to bear the consequences of his own actions, for, if he wished to force Hoff and Baum to resign, why not make the request directly? When a local newspaper editorial printed similar criticisms of his handling of personnel that compounded the unsettling impact of Nolan's decisions (for a period of several weeks a secretary made all trial assignments because no supervising deputy would assume the responsibility), Nolan began to doubt the value of attempting to govern at all.

The Growing Reluctance to Govern

In our conversation in November, Nolan indicated that the events of the past fifteen months had left him perplexed and somewhat bitter and increasingly reluctant to become involved in office operations:

I've made some mistakes, and I think that my reputation has been tarnished somewhat, that people are beginning to be suspicious of my motives because of the way I made personnel changes. Obviously I should have handled personnel a bit differently, but Jesus Christ, you can't spend all your time in this business worrying about hurting everybody's feelings. You'd never get anything done.

So that's one thing. Number two, I have the feeling that things keep going out. For example, when I appointed Johnson, I said a few things off the top of my head to some people in the office, and the following week I started getting calls from the goddamn-est sources, guys, maybe old friends of mine, with wild ideas, saying, Hey, Bob. Did you really do this or are you really thinking about that? Believe me, I have absolutely no idea how these stories got out. I guess a guy goes down to the Village Inn for a few belts on Friday night and talks to a public defender and says a few things. Well, be that as it may, I just wish sometimes I had half the Machiavellian instincts people are beginning to say I have. Maybe I'm getting a little paranoid. I guess it sounds that way, but when these things keep happening, you start saying to yourself, "You know, what the hell is going on here? What the hell am I doing wrong?"

Number three, I think the fellas in the office are getting a lot of confidence in Johnson, so they open up their problems to him. I'm really a politician, I guess, and I'm not one of the boys. . . . It's tough for me to be an executive or an administrator. I've never really had any experience like this, not getting my nose into every file. It's difficult. . . . But as I was saying, you begin to think some people don't trust you. Well, not exactly that they don't trust you, but that maybe they think you're paying somebody off, which is absolutely false. It's a strange position to be in. Eighteen months ago I was everybody's buddy. [Eighteen months earlier Nolan was completing his term as the president of the North County Bar Association.] Of course we would get into fights all the time, but everybody understood what was going on. And now suddenly it's all different, and you wonder why people seem suspicious of your motives. I guess it's just difficult to learn to thicken your skin, to be a goddamn politician.

By being a politician Nolan meant that he would need to concentrate more on image and less on trying to make policy changes:

One thing I've learned in the last year is that an image is important. I just read *The Selling of the President* two weeks ago, and you get to realize that there are people out there who are goddamn phonies. Guys riding around on horses that never did a thing about the problems they talk about all the time. Frankly, Savich was like that in certain respects. He went on and on about welfare fraud, and the public thought he was just wonderful, but he never did half the things he said. Some of the things he said were out and out lies. So you start thinking about just what the hell is going on here, and you begin to realize that the first thing is survival, keeping your job. Second comes doing your job, and third comes crusading. Of course it's not really those fixed categories, there's really a mixture there, but, well, just for example, frankly it wouldn't bother me a bit to see marijuana legalized and treated like alcohol for adults. And a couple of times, in small groups of friends, I've just hinted at that a tiny bit, and you know, it's no big deal. But just try to say that at a lunch, and you would blow the roof off. I've done some reading about the need for leadership, but, well, I have a clipping that I keep around here somewhere where Stanley Mosk [former California attorney general] said that you should always do the best you can, but if you don't have the confidence of the people, you're just not worth much as a leader. . . . A lot of people talk about unifying all the forces and charging ahead, but so often you run into a stone wall.

I'll give you a personal example that I lay awake nights thinking about. When I first took this job, I took a position on the Drug Abuse Council. That wasn't just politics, I really felt that there was a great need for something to be done. But looking back on it so far, I think that has been one of the most frustrating things I've done since I became district attorney. In the first place, where you can't control the money, when you don't have a staff, really, just what the hell can you do? Second, it was all petty jealousies. Every time you'd take a position, somebody is always saying, "It's just a political move on Nolan's part." The harder you try to push for something concrete, the more suspicious people get. . . . The point I wanted to make is that after you beat your brains out a few times, like on the Drug Council . . . you begin to ask yourself, "You big jerk. Why didn't you leave well enough alone." It wasn't really my responsibility in the first place. Why should I give a shit? But no, I played the hero, and went in and tried to grab hold, and now I begin to regret it. I'm learning the bitter facts of political reality. You've got to pad budgets if you're going to get ahead. The frontal attack where you lay all your cards on the table may not be the best way to get at a problem. . . .

Take Chief Murphy [Condenado police chief]. I think Murph is a hell of a great guy, progressive, his heart is in the right place. But the same things have happened to him. He and I were talking the other day about the problem of blacks in Condenado, and I'll tell you, the police have been burned so often, they're gun-shy. Murphy is hiring community aides and firing cops who rough-up suspects unnecessarily and then some people start implying that he's a nigger-lover. And then he sent out a questionnaire just to find out what the hell is going on in the community, what people think, and the black groups and the civil rights groups start calling him a racist. So he's gotten shy and he's questioning just how much he can really do.

Machiavelli wrote in chapter 6 of *The Prince*:

It must be considered that there is nothing more difficult to carry out, nor more doubtful of success, nor more dangerous to handle, than to initiate a new order of things. For the reformer has enemies in all those who profit by the old order, and only lukewarm defenders in all those who would profit by the new order, this lukewarmness arising partly from fear of their adversaries, who have the laws in their favor; and partly from the incredulity of mankind, who do not truly believe in anything new until they have had actual experience of it.[26]

Robert Nolan was not a reformer. Lacking a specific program that he could defend in terms of a plausible relationship between program and desired ends, Nolan lacked means by which to defend himself against the unexpected rebuffs and criticisms that political action elicits. But even if he were a reformer, the task of reform of criminal administration presents special complications to any politician.

Public sentiments about a political issue do not normally assume the clear-cut character they have assumed in the area of crime and criminal administration, at least in Vario County. Where an elected official can, as he can on most issues, ascribe the views and requests and, occasionally, demands that individual citizens place upon him to the views of an identifiable interest group or minority, rather than to an undifferentiated public, he may buffer himself from such demands by seeking support from other groups, or perhaps simply by rationalizing that the position, because it is a minority position, need not place any legitimate claim upon him. But the issue of crime and its control is one of those relatively few areas in which an elected official cannot so buffer or rationalize away the need for response.

Clear-cut and unidirectional public sentiments rarely if ever capture the detailed complexity of a problem, rarely represent in themselves an adequate policy response to a problem. But the oversimplicity of public opinion need not frustrate an elected official who possesses a more detailed set of goals and beliefs. Where his beliefs appear or can be made to appear plausible to groups on whom the leader depends, an elected leader of an organization can reconcile action with his sense of the legitimacy of the democratic norm of responsiveness.

In the area of criminal administration—and we might expect to observe similar consequences in the Departments of Justice and Health, Education and Welfare concerning busing to achieve school integration—men subject to both organizational and public responsibilities must frequently contend with public sentiments that contradict norms and values of organization members. In such circumstances, what options are open to the man torn by role conflict? First, he may, as Savich did and as did Moore (who inherited much of Savich's point of view by working as his chief deputy for seven years) attempt to direct or program an office to conform to public expectations. While in theory nothing prevents a leader from seeking to persuade and convince organizational members of the importance of molding behavior to public expectations, in the professionalized context we have studied, where men have learned both to respect values at odds with public sentiments and to respect their own judgment, attempts at persuasion and indoctrination will very likely frustrate employees and fracture communication in the office.

A second route, if an elected official believes his posture must appear to correspond to public sentiments, is for the official to abandon the responsibility of office management, perhaps rationalizing the abandonment of whatever hopes he had for changes in office practices in terms of his maintenance of public confidence. But men, like Nolan, who elect this route may have difficulty in defining and measuring their success, and thus become cynical because they cannot escape the realization that they act toward the public under false pretenses: they misrepresent their capacity to translate public statements into policy.

A public official may, of course, ignore public sentiments that cut against his own sense of his office's capacities and objectives, but if we accept the premise that public peace depends ultimately upon maintaining the sense of public influence over decisions of public interest, we may doubt the wisdom of such a route, especially where issues like the control of crime actively worry so many people.

The official has two more options. The first, the route of pragmatism, again threatens to encourage cynicism, for here the leader attempts to shape his office consistently with office expectations, but shares with his office the secret that he must "keep the public happy" and that what he says publicly does not necessarily express his expectation for the office. Last, the official may attempt in fact "to initiate a new order of things," to seek to reconcile his public position with the directions in which he can move his office. To do so he must find, or create, a common ground between organizational facts and public sentiments. The last chapter suggests how a district attorney might do so, and why he should.

6

Justice in Vario County: The Direction of Reform

The introductory section of this book presented two arguments: first, we *should* not demand order and uniformity from those who do justice; second, we cannot realistically expect to achieve these goals. These arguments intertwine, since both derive from a body of organization theory dealing with consequences for organizations of uncertain technologies and environments. But the preceding three chapters have examined the second argument more thoroughly than the first, and in this final chapter we must return to the first argument.

You will recall that in chapter 1 we did not dismiss the importance or desirability of the values of order and uniformity. Instead, chapter 1 suggested that uncertainty presents us with a practical and difficult tradeoff: the administrative procedures necessary to increase uniformity may impose high costs in the form of reduced learning and adaptation. Where technologies and environments are uncertain, learning and adaptation are themselves vital to the achievement of policy objectives.

But this argument must satisfy a heavy burden of proof, for when we assess how prosecutors perform, we deal with men and organizations that possess considerable power to harm others arbitrarily. Not only do prosecutors possess this power, we know they have used it, in the prosecution of Clay Shaw in New Orleans, in the presumed complicity in the police killings of Black Panthers in Chicago (and in the prosecution of the survivors of that police attack), and in the protection or cover-up of police abuses documented in Paul Chevigny's book *Police Power*.[1]

This final chapter seeks to make more explicit an argument implicit in preceding chapters, that the soundest approach to minimizing these very real dangers does not necessarily require a trial of all cases (or at least of all felonies), nor does it necessarily require conversion of prosecutors' offices to rule-ordered organizations. Rather, reform should seek out and experiment with methods that hold some promise for improving the prosecutor's ability to identify and tentatively resolve the inherent tradeoffs and ambiguities of his job. Men in organizations that succeed in doing so may in turn successfully generate uniformity where it is feasible.

The reform directions suggested here build from the elements of organizational "revitalization" prescribed in Warren Bennis's and Philip Slater's *The Temporary Society.*[2] These elements are:

an ability to learn from experience and to codify, store, and retrieve the relevant knowledge;

an ability to learn how to learn, that is, to develop methods for improving
the learning process;

an ability to acquire and use feedback mechanisms on performance, in
short, to be self-analytical; and

an ability to direct one's own destiny.[3]

Three points about these elements: First, they embody learning and change values that, as we have seen, belong among the mix of values incorporated into the idea of justice. Second, these elements in no way suggest strategies for incorporating them into organizational activity; they are starting points only.[4] Third, the human relations management approach, of which Bennis is a major advocate, has critics as well.[5] The reform discussion here hardly reflects "settled" questions in the field of administrative theory. Given both the state of the academic art and the great variety of legal, social, and political contexts in which prosecutors operate, it would be foolish to claim universal validity or applicability for what follows.

The problems of prosecutorial reform are so closely related to the full range of criminal justice reform that no one chapter can adequately deal with them. Instead, this chapter seeks only to propose—and tentatively at that— some arguments generated by the Vario County experience that ought to enter reform discussions. One caveat, however: this discussion presumes that short-run economic and political conditions will not permit increased tax rates to support major changes in the operation of courts and prosecutors' offices. These reforms do not claim to produce an "ideal" system of justice.

Defects in the Process of Criminal Prosecution

Reform discussions in any substantive area of administration should identify at the outset those deficiencies that pose the most serious obstacles to achieving policy goals. Let us begin the assessment of deficiencies by reviewing an alleged deficiency that, on the basis of the observations in Vario County, may impose lower costs than is generally believed: the problem of dispositions without trial.

In theory trials avoid several evils. They minimize the degree to which those who decide the issue of guilt—jurors in most cases—decide on the basis of simple stereotypes and personal prejudices rather than on fact. The tendency toward "global," "undifferentiated," and "dichotomous" thinking, the tendency to pigeonhole people on the basis of inadequate information— all distort judgment and decision, and the trial in theory minimizes the chances that those accused of crime will be punished erroneously.[6] Second, the trial permits the accused to observe that his conviction does not result from a compromise of his own rights or interests. His presence at the trial may enhance his acceptance of punishment and the chances for eventual reconciliation with society. But dispositions without trial may also benefit defendants.

Tangible Benefits to the Defendant from
Settlement Without Trial

The bulk of misdemeanor convictions impose fines or jail sentences that for many defendants amount to significantly less than the cost of an attorney. Most attorneys in Vario County charge an additional fee if the case goes to trial, and a fee for a two-day trial runs from $500 to $1000. Unless the standards for indigency are substantially increased, for a paying client a trial may work a greater hardship than a plea, and it is difficult to imagine a better measure, short of providing public counsel in all cases, than the suspect's judgment on this matter. Other tangible benefits do not depend on financial considerations. Especially for the first offender, the negotiation process works toward leniency in a way that mandatory trials cannot. If prosecutors must try all cases, the first offender arrested for marijuana possession when caught smoking marijuana in a park, or the first offender caught in a night-time burglary, can be tried only on those charges. The former cannot be tried on the lesser charge of possessing paraphernalia, and the latter cannot be charged with receiving stolen property, unless they also committed these offenses. Yet these lenient dispositions were common for first offenders in these circumstances. Furthermore, the suspect who avoids trial may benefit from the privatization of his offense. A trial may, for example, expose him to the risk of losing his job. Furthermore, by avoiding public trial he may avoid a process that tends to confirm his definition of himself as a "deviant."

The Intangible Benefit of Certainty

Most people are uncomfortable when forces with a potentially major impact on their lives seem uncertain. Indeed, penal legislation itself derives less from a rational assessment of the damage crimes cause than from the attempt to exorcise our uncertainties about events that might damage us.[7] When confronted by uncertainty concerning vital events and interests, men frequently prefer a low-risk solution to minimize uncertainty. Nolan chose a low-risk, noninnovative posture in regard to political uncertainty. Most, if not all, lawyers know the difference between the suspect who possesses a possible legal defense, a triable issue, and the suspect with a "strong case." They know that they cannot predict the outcome of trial for their client, and they know that trials can at times reveal new information that will increase the length of sentence upon conviction. Since in most instances it is not possible to predict either the outcome of trial or the sentence upon conviction, when a defendant receives an offer with a firm sentence commitment he may voluntarily choose the sentence over the added uncertainty of a trial. Of course, whether the defendant ultimately benefits from such a decision depends on the adequacy of the initial investigating and filing decisions by police and prosecutors and the extent to which the defense has had an opportunity to learn fully about the prosecution's case in advance of settlement. The Vario County office did routinely release all reports and documents concerning a case (with the exception of their own work sheets) upon the request of the defense attorney, and defense attorneys in Vario County felt in the interviews that prosecutors did not hide the facts of cases from them. We must, however, ask how likely it is that the prosecutor proceeds on cases where there is substantial doubt about the suspect's culpability, and we must ask whether the dynamics of plea negotiations lead defense attorneys regularly to sacrifice strong defenses.

Charging the Culpable

All available evidence in Vario County indicates that prosecutors rarely charged those who factually did not commit the act that formed the basis for the complaint, and that conviction of the "wrong man" was even rarer. Most Vario County prosecutors consciously assumed responsibility for separating the innocent from the guilty. (Prosecutors rated that goal highest among the nine in terms of personal preference, and all but six rated "very successful" the achievement of the goal. "Separating the innocent from the guilty" was rated on achievement "very successful" four times more frequently than any other of the nine goals.) Defense attorneys, particularly young public defenders who took that job from a concern for the inadequacies of criminal justice, and who were presumably therefore motivated to criticize where their experience supported it, indicated repeatedly in interviews that the police and prosecution almost never "get the wrong man."[8] Defense attorneys indicated, and my observations confirmed, that a defense attorney who offered the prosecution any trustworthy evidence suggesting that the suspect did not do the alleged act gained an immediate review of the matter. It is likely that prosecutors listen in such circumstances in part because they have no strong ties to the office or to the role of prosecution and because they are not themselves case-hardened by long experience as a prosecutor. We have seen, of course, that deputies disagreed concerning the degree to which they should actively screen out cases with evidentiary weaknesses and the degree to which they should file on all charges sustained by police reports or only on those that they feel correspond to the ultimate "worth" of the case, but there was little disagreement that they charged defendants for acts they had in all probability committed.

Pretrial Negotiations as Persuasive Interactions

Does a defense attorney need to abandon legal or evidentiary defenses in order to convince the prosecutor, on the basis of exonerating or mitigating information, that charges should be reduced? Need a defense attorney sacrifice his client's interests to maintain "credibility" in the district attorneys' office? Professor Alschuler's study, for example, concluded that a spirit of reasonableness and cooperation dominated successful negotiations, that attorneys were reluctant to press ambiguous defenses, and that both sides tended to presume not the innocence of the suspect but that he had committed an act for which he ought legitimately to receive some sanction.[9] Thus, the literature supports the proposition that bargained settlement of cases does increase the extent to which the adjudicator fails to hear or consider plausible defenses. In Vario County, defense attorneys regularly disposed of cases without forcefully advocating plausible legal issues, but it was by no means clear that they did so in ways that systematically sacrificed their clients' interests. We have already seen that the inherent uncertainty and unpredictability of the results of trial make it difficult in most cases for a defense attorney to feel confident that a defense, even an apparently strong one, will prevail. More important, results from experiments in persuasion, Wildavsky's analysis of effective administrative strategies in appearances before Congressional appropriations committees, and my own observations indicate that the abandonment of the adversary setting need not diminish and may increase the degree to which case dispositions incorporate accurate information about the suspect and the crime. Let us review each of these areas in turn.

William J. McGuire's extensive review of the findings concerning persuasion and attitude change indicates that while the sender's ability to induce attitude or belief changes in a receiver depends heavily on the receiver's perception of the sender's credibility, the sender's credibility does not depend on the degree to which he avoids the appearance of attempting to persuade.[10] Credibility depends upon the receiver's perceptions of the sender as competent and trustworthy, that is, honest and objective in his representations. Wildavsky's findings confirm this framework nicely. The administrator who wins budget requests in Congress does so by playing the role expected of him.[11] He is expected to defend the integrity of his programs and to seek to improve them, and his candor and frankness in this respect are rewarded, not discouraged.

How do these findings translate into pretrial relationships? First, it is true that successful attorneys do not attempt to misrepresent the character of their client. If the client has had repeated contacts with the law, the defense must not hide from that fact and its implications. However, candor and honesty do not require the defense attorney to depart from his role as representative of his client's interests or to tell the prosecutor what he wants to hear. Prosecutors perceive defense attorneys as legitimately representing their clients in what may become a genuine adversary contest. The defense attorney who, by repeatedly making no case for his client, appears to the prosecutor to be acting consciously against his client's interest decreases his credibility. To return to McGuire's analysis, the defense attorney may become both less competent and less trustworthy in the eyes of the prosecutor if he does so. It is therefore not surprising that most prosecutors indicated that the success of a defense attorney depended less on his ability to "be a good guy" than on his basic competence as an attorney, both in trial and in his informal presentation of arguments. Defense attorneys who challenge the conscientiousness of the prosecutor, or who challenge the veracity of the arresting officer without backing up such positions with credible information, and attorneys who assume belligerent postures, will not elicit the prosecutor's cooperation. However, the persuasive presentation of either legal arguments or mitigating but legally irrelevant information about the client is not in any way reduced by the requirement for frankness and honesty. In Vario County the only attorneys with whom prosecutors consistently refused to deal were those whom prosecutors suspected of slighting their client's interests. Several prosecutors refused to deal with one defense attorney who had reportedly been asked to represent a suspect in a drunk driving case that had produced injuries. The suspect told him his story, making several admissions of possible fault, and only after he was done did the attorney tell him that he represented the victim of the suspect's accident and could not therefore represent the suspect.

In contrast to this attorney, Walt Tyler, an older attorney who rarely tried cases but who earned a reputation both for trial ability and for unusual honesty, repeatedly appeared to win dispositions favorable to his client. He explained his approach this way:

If you go up there in a threatening manner, what the hell, you're talking to a fellow human being. He's got the aces or you wouldn't be there in the first place. I've often felt a case was lightweight from the D.A.'s standpoint, and why put it through a five- or seven-day jury trial. But I never use that as a threat. I say, "Here's my file. Have a look at it. Is this worth a jury?" I've had deputies say, "Let me take this back to the office and have another look at it." But it's always as two reasonable human beings, never as a threat. I don't believe in threats.

Walt Tyler, and those attorneys who did not approach the prosecutor in a manner that questioned the prosecutor's motives or competence and who appeared willing to acknowledge uncontroverted facts, repeatedly convinced prosecutors that they could and should revise their initial assumptions about the seriousness of the case and the punishment appropriate for the suspect. A mandatory trial requirement would cut against introduction of mitigating information. Consider these examples:

1. The wife of a man accused of child abuse indicated to the prosecutor

that her husband had consented to see a psychiatrist and that trial on the felony could interfere with his improvement. The prosecutor reduced the case to simple battery, a misdemeanor.

2. A police report showed that defendants A, B, and C severely beat up D and E with a tire iron after D and E had thrown a beer can at the three suspects' passing car on a back road. When in pretrial conference the defense attorney established that the tire iron had come from the car of D and E, not from the suspects' car, and that D and E had been drinking heavily and had presumably initiated an attack on the suspects with the tire iron, the prosecutor reduced the charge from the felony of assault with a deadly weapon to the misdemeanor of malicious mischief.

3. A felony charge of drunk driving arising from an accident involving an injury was reduced to a misdemeanor when the victim's injuries, which looked serious from the amount of blood at the scene, proved to be minor.

4. A physical assault on a police officer was reduced to a misdemeanor when the defense attorney explained that the suspect, a woman, had at the time just witnessed the arrest of her son. The police officer had not been injured.

5. A felony burglary charge was reduced to a misdemeanor theft charge. The deputy explained on the reduction sheet: "Codefendant a burglar and the heavy in this case. This defendant has no record and just returned from Vietnam. Gave him a break." Any decision to require the trial of all cases must weigh the value of informal devices to introduce mitigating information that the rules of evidence at formal trials exclude.

It is not at all clear that attorneys could make these adjustments in a formal trial setting, given the present rules of evidentiary relevance. Indeed, any attempt to monitor officially the discretion exercised in such exchanges may inhibit adjustments. Any public visibility of this process may, unless public attitudes about crime change or we stop electing district attorneys, prevent candid exchanges of information. Trustful exchanges, where neither side expects to use the fact of exchange in future exchanges—where neither side "keeps score"—will increase the greater the privacy of the exchange. Learning and adaptation may proceed best where the parties needn't fear how "the boss" or "the judge" or "the press" will react.

The critical issue concerning the guilty plea system is whether such procedures arbitrarily disadvantage suspects, particularly in ways that may encourage future criminal behavior. We have no clear empirical picture of the relationship between mode of conviction and recidivism. The preceding section does suggest that by allowing the disposition process to adjust to changing information about the nature of the crime and the suspect, some of which is legally inadmissible, dispositions without trial may work to the suspects' advantage. The Vario County experience did not, in any event, indicate that defense attorneys regularly abandoned the possibility of acquittal at trial in order to maintain "friendly" or accomodating images in the eyes of prosecutors. From the defense attorney's viewpoint, nearly all prosecutions contain (or may be amended or refiled to contain) some charges that a trial will in all likelihood sustain. Compromise in such circumstances is neither systematically irrational nor systematically unfair. But this conclusion hardly exhausts the problem of deficiency. Previous pages have described undesirable practices and consequences that should be and can be eliminated or mitigated by enhancing the learning capacity of prosecutors' offices. Six serious deficiencies follow.

First, we have seen that Vario County prosecutors became "locked-in" to the prosecution of cases not only where evidentiary weaknesses had revealed themselves near the time of trial, but where prosecutors had learned that the trial and possible punishment upon conviction might impose hardships on the suspect inappropriate to his circumstances.

Segmentation of work and responsibility for case dispositions inhibited learning fully about a case. The assumption that because a case was filed as a felony, it must *be* a felony not only ignored the segmentation of the learning process, it ignored the fact that what Don Smith called "judicial buck-passing" provided no independent check of case quality.

The combination of loyalty toward police and concern for police criticism at times led to filing questionable cases to lever information from a suspect or more severe prosecution of cases than the events or the character of the suspect warranted. Howard Wright, for example, recalled filing a case against a suspect for scuffling briefly with an officer in the presence of the officer's police chief. The scuffle occurred during an arrest of a friend of the suspect, who tried to "rescue" his friend from the officer's custody and even temporarily succeeded. It was not clear that the chief actually became involved in the scuffle, but he insisted on having the associate charged with lynching, which is defined as "the taking by means of a riot of any person from the lawful custody of any peace officer" and carries a maximum sentence of twenty years in prison.[12] Howard Wright explained:

I suppose technically it was a lynching, but if it had just been a couple of officers, it would probably have gone as a 148, like the case I had a month ago where there was a hassle, and the officers just let the suspects go because they had their names. They picked them up later on 148s. If the sheriff or undersheriff had been there, I'm sure we would have charged a felony assault on a police officer and so forth. Since they are who they are, you can't very well reduce it and tell them it's just a 148. In these kinds of cases you have conflicting interest.

Finally, the fear of public criticism inhibited changing positions when prosecutors discovered such information.[13]

Second, particularly where "competitors" were concerned, the manner in which prosecutors learned information depended too heavily on the defense attorney's mastery of the techniques of persuasion. Clients of attorneys lacking such skills could, depending on the prosecutor, receive arbitrary treatment.

Third, overfiling, even though the prosecutor charges only crimes that the crime reports sustain, does in some circumstances constitute what Tom Gubser called "legal blackmail." Where, for example, a suspect on a misdemeanor charge has previously been convicted for a comparable offense, the prosecutor may gain a state prison conviction for the misdemeanor by establishing in court the prior conviction. Where on a minor crime like petty theft the prosecutor says he will charge the "prior" if the suspect does not plead, the suspect is very likely to abandon even a very promising legal defense, where he may choose between the certainty of five days in jail or the possibility of a year or more in prison.

Fourth, helping to explain the belief of nearly all public and private defense attorneys that blacks were treated as leniently, if not more, than whites in Vario County was the fact that prosecutors neither understood nor cared much about the quality of life in poor black neighborhoods. Prosecutors often assumed that a crime in a black neighborhood would be more difficult to prove because witnesses might not appear or be credible on the witness stand. Prosecutors' work experiences validated this assumption. The deficiency arises because, rather than assuming responsibility for seeking to correct the problem, some prosecutors tended instead to ignore criminal activity that imposed harsh costs on black victims and confirmed suspicions about the unresponsiveness of local government.

Fifth, prosecutors were not in fact trained or motivated to assess the consequences of punishment. What bothered defense attorneys was not that prosecutors insisted on taking positions they could not legally support but that prosecutors often recommended sentences that did not adapt enough to the needs or prospects of the defendant. As one public defender put it:

You have people there like B.J. Chastain making terribly important decisions about people's lives, and, given the way Jensen functions, the prosecutor has as much authority as Jensen does over sentencing, if not more. Yet none, or very few, prosecutors have any training or education other than what we all got in criminal law in law school. . . . I think Len Lewis is an exception, but Chastain will flame away about state prison from a position of total ignorance, as far as I can see.

Often the prosecutor's position, if not totally ignorant, is at least chosen without a thorough exploration of its hidden assumptions. The premise that the seriousness of injuries suffered in an unintentional accident should determine the degree of punishment the suspect deserves lacks any *a priori* validation other than to serve the suspect goal of retribution. More important, the inferences that prosecutors draw from rap sheets, often, as we have seen, because the rap sheet is the only seemingly neutral or certain measure of appropriate punishment available to the prosecutor, often bear little or no relationship to the nature of the crime or the degree to which incarceration will help or harm the suspect, his family, or the community (Appendix C).

These deficiencies each remind us of Bennis's elements of revitalization. Becoming locked-in to a case, the reliance on interpersonal skills, the unverified and varied assumptions on which prosecutors based filing and disposition decisions—all reflect the inability to codify, store, and retrieve relevant knowledge, the failure to "develop methods for improving the learning process," the misuse or nonuse of feedback mechanisms, and the absence of self-analysis.

Together these deficiencies produced a final deficiency. Dick Schwartz and Tom Gubser correctly believed that many prosecutors in Vario County did not place high importance on legal craftsmanship, except in preparation for trial itself. While this may have been an efficient practice, since most judges did not emphasize legal craftsmanship themselves, the deemphasis of what is the intellectual core of the profession tended to breed in many Vario County prosecutors a kind of nonchalance or low interest in the creative aspects of the job. They did not regularly seek out ways of improving either the office's or their own performance. Most prosecutors expressed satisfaction with their job because they believed the personal contacts and occasional trial experiences contributed to their eventual careers as private attorneys. In this sense they felt comfortable about their ability to direct their destiny, as Bennis's fourth element puts it. If, however, we assume that professionalized organizations will change only when employees find the new behavior rewarding, then the private career motive may block prosecutorial change, at least in jurisdictions offering few lucrative careers in criminal defense.

These six deficiencies remind us that prosecutors in Vario County did not decide like cases alike under publicly stated rules of general applicability. There has been considerable recent discussion of requiring prosecutors to articulate general rules and prosecutorial policies, to write specific findings of fact into decisions not to charge or to drop or reduce charges, and to publicize both. Kenneth Culp Davis has strongly supported such reforms.[14]

Norman Abrams has carefully reviewed the circumstances in which such rules are feasible, and he has suggested some of the difficulties that must be overcome.[15] Clearly, proponents of these procedures to formalize policy are correct, in the sense that some prosecutorial questions may be handled uniformly by policy directives. Abrams's analysis is worth reading and need not be repeated here, other than to note that he provides examples of instances in which the United States Department of Justice has promulgated formal prosecution policy successfully.

There are, however, at least four difficulties with the proposal. While some formal policies do prove feasible, there is no way of formulating a rule that specifies the circumstances in which prosecutors must proceed by formal policy. Hence, prosecutors increase uniformity of case dispositions by announcing formal policy only if they choose to do so. The legal system cannot compel such policies unless it compels policies in all cases, and in most cases policy cannot be formulated or enforced concretely enough to influence daily prosecutorial decisions. Furthermore the proposal to support decisions with published opinions containing findings of fact ignores the reality of the prosecutor's fact-finding process. Given the nature of communications with defense attorneys and the need for rapid decisions and commitments, the written opinion will in most cases be a post hoc set of rationalizations. Also, the bulk of criminal defendants being indigent, it is difficult to imagine how they would litigate a potential weakness revealed in published explanations of decisions.

Finally, the Vario County experience suggests that prosecutors' offices today do not necessarily generate the incentives and rewards that would motivate prosecutors either to discover circumstances where formal policy is appropriate, to formulate it wisely, or to abide by it when made. The remainder of the chapter therefore outlines the kind of prosecutors' office that might best avoid the defects that recurred in Vario County and that could effectively determine where to advance uniformity through formal policy. These suggestions assume that prosecutors will find these practices rewarding, that given the opportunity to engage in them, they will do so willingly. Here are a few reasons to suppose that lawyers may willingly engage in these reforms. Today we widely perceive crime as a most serious social problem. Both government and the academic community now support and legitimate creative thinking and experimentation with respect to the management of crime. More important, in 1974 federal funds seem abundantly available to support experimentation. Lawyers emerge from law school with well-developed analytical skills, a respect for collective attempts to solve social problems, and a professional tradition of participation in policy innovation, in the development of the industrial corporation and, more recently, in the development of the regulatory process. Whether these possibilities are widely enough perceived and strongly enough believed to make prosecutors want to understand and minimize organizational shortcomings and seek improved knowledge about criminal administration remains, for the moment, problematic.

Recommendations

Accept the Requirements of Intensive Technologies

Where actors cannot predict with reasonable certainty the consequences of their actions, and where their actions can rebound on them in unpredictable ways, those in supervising positions must accept the fact that actors handling the problem are in the best position to deal with it sensibly. Rules that dictate case dispositions, like Vario County's short-lived seven-day rule, and procedures, like the separation of superior court calendar division, that segment the handling of cases and prevent actors from learning the consequences their actions have are inappropriate for intensive technologies. At least for felony prosecutions, cases should be assigned as frequently as possible to one man, who is then left to deal with the case in any sensible way he can. Such a strategy does, of course, increase the degree of idiosyncratic behavior—people in similar organizational positions will operate differently— but in conditions of technological and informational ambiguity and uncertainty, diverse behavior is rational, not only because it avoids wasteful segmentation and duplication of effort but because diverse behavior is a wise strategy for seeking ways of improving the technology itself.[16]

Reinforce the Capacity to Adapt

Law school trains lawyers less to advocate than to research and analyze. Since, unless all cases are tried, the prosecutor cannot escape the fact that he is an adjudicator as much as an advocate, a district attorney's office may feasibly reinforce the skills of legal research, of argumentation, of fact finding and of model building. A district attorney should define the function of his office as the search for whatever information will improve the ability of those agencies responsible for dealing with the crime problem to reduce the harm of crime and the costs of correction to the community. Implementation should include the following steps:

1. The office need not abandon a civil-service format for announcing new positions, for interviewing applicants, and determining salaries, but it should use this format only as part of seeking and recruiting men with an active concern for the quality of criminal justice. The process of recruitment should make clear to applicants the following points: that knowledge of the causes and remedies of crime and the criteria for punishment are inadequate; that the organization perceives itself as having been assigned by its client, the community, the task of seeking out and translating into practice the best information available regarding the problem of crime and its correction; that attorneys will be expected to spend no more than four years of their professional career in the office, during which time they will seek to research and practice any strategy that shows some promise of reducing the cost of crime; that in taking the job, prosecutors assume the obligations of articulating to each other any information they believe can assist each other and of listening to the recommendations of others.

2. While recruitment and selection procedures should incorporate references from professors and should weight positively any optional work the applicant has done in law school, the office should rely on the self-selection screen of its own expectations and should not attempt to eliminate any attitude toward crime or its control. Prosecutors will presumably benefit

from the diversity of viewpoints, and from lessons of those who fail.

3. As a basic part of their introduction to the work of prosecution, deputies should spend as much time as possible learning about the physical contexts in which their assumptions operate. Each prosecutor should spend several nights in jail and in prison, and he should observe whatever diagnostic testing takes place. Deputies should become thoroughly familiar with the sentencing alternatives available, both their physical nature and their theoretical premises and shortcomings.

4. The prosecutor should receive near the beginning of his employment, and perhaps periodically thereafter, explicit exposure to the nature of the interaction between personal relations, perceptions of facts, and decisions. Prosecutors should receive informal group training that emphasizes the dangers of becoming psychologically overcommitted to the police and of "scapegoating," as one prosecutor put it, the client of the undiplomatic defense attorney. These sessions should focus on why prosecutors may become locked-in to cases, why prosecutors may disadvantage a suspect through overfiling, and how interpersonal loyalties can mislead a judgment.

5. These sessions should also explore the moral ambiguities of the prosecutor's job. Prosecutors so inclined should be encouraged to work closely with police departments, with the objective of increasing the accuracy and legality of police investigations, and these sessions should seek to help prosecutors understand and accept the nature of the persuasion and compromise required in such situations.[17]

6. The office should permit each deputy to devote perhaps one week in six or eight to the research of any problem of interest to him in the area of criminal law, penology, office administration, or public opinion that relates to problems the office must handle. One prosecutor might explore ways to decrease the frequency with which black victims and witnesses fail to show up to support the prosecution's case at trial, or ways to gauge the expectations of blacks toward law enforcement. Another might prepare a working paper contrasting American and Scandinavian criminal administration. Another might attempt some cost comparisons of incarceration, recidivism, and the return for expenditures on incarceration. Prosecutors would be expected to circulate reports of project expectations and findings and discuss them. Making this expectation clear in the recruitment and selection process may screen out those uninterested in research activities.

Respond to Public Expectations

We have seen that in Vario County, the fear of public criticism, the uncertainty concerning the actions that might elicit public criticism, and the uncertainty concerning the consequences that might follow from public criticism cut against flexibility and ultimately contributed as much as any factor to lock the office in to cases and to reduce communication and individual learning. But how can an elected official without a political machine or other source of stable support to buffer him from the electorate succeed in adopting policies that he perceives run counter to public expectations?

The recommendations offered here, recommendations that seek to enable prosecutors to deal directly with uncertainty and to move at times against public expectations, paradoxically give the district attorney a more concrete and certain model or platform from which he may publicly defend his actions. He can, under such a plan, credibly say with California's Republican attorney general Younger that a "prosecutor worthy of the position must use the mantle which has been placed on his shoulder to assume a role of leadership in the entire community and help bring what has been character-ized as a 'sick society' back to a condition where decent people can live peacefully in the enjoyment of their rights and property without the fear of molestation or attack from the criminal element."[18] The district attorney benefits primarily from such a program because he can, with appropriate rhetorical simplification, claim legitimately in public that his sole objective will be to minimize the harm of crime to the community, and because he can defend his organizational practices in terms of publicly acceptable values: innovation, the potential for budget cutting, and common sense. If, in addition, the district attorney recognizes that public memories are short and that he can build a personal constituency through police cooperation and in the bar, and if he accepts the necessity for making compromises that protect his organizational core, he can survive, and perhaps even succeed in improv-ing public understanding of the nature of crime and its control.

An organization whose members develop the capacity to "learn from experience" and to store and share relevant knowledge with each other will fill the major prerequisite for generating sensible policies for increasing the uniformity and orderliness of justice.

Some Final Thoughts

Paul Freund introduces his discussion of "Social Justice and the Law" by reminding us of the quotation from Justinian's *Institutes* inscribed on the walls of Harvard Law School's library: "The precepts of the law are these: to live honorably, not to injure another, to render to each his due."[19] In a curiously repetitive way these three principles, of keeping one's promises, of due care, and of good faith, underlie this analysis. Police, prosecutors, de-fense attorneys, and judges expect each other to represent honestly and accu-rately what they are and what they believe. It is, I suspect, the expectation of men that life's affairs ought to conform to these principles, and their dissatisfaction with men and affairs when they do not, that often paradoxically appear to suppress legality. These principles are the source of prosecutor empathy for police and for the downplaying of the legitimacy of speculative argument outside the courtroom. Finally, a politician must, to retain the sort of confidence of which Nolan was aware, treat public expectations honorably and in good faith, and it was Nolan's attempts to do so that deflected him from his organizational responsibilities.

In the context of criminal administration (as in most political affairs), where conflicting values create conflicting expectations about good faith, the politician is tempted to resolve the conflict by creating an image and by adjusting without plan to the expectations of the moment. If there is any alternative to this route, however, it would seem to lie in the "good faith" of accepting ambiguity and ignorance. If the ultimate task of law is a profoundly political one, a task requiring compromises among the eternally conflicting values of "personal security and moral responsibility, knowledge and privacy, triumph and fraternity,"[20] it may be well to assume that lawyers as well as social scientists possess competence in policy innovation. The prosecutor, by virtue of his intermediary position in criminal administration, is well situated to gather information, assess its significance, and teach it to others. And an astute politician can reconcile this approach with public expectations.

Appendix A
Misdemeanor Procedures
in Vario County

In 1970 the office processed 12,442 misdemeanor complaints. Of these, a police officer initiated the prosecution by filing a complaint in the municipal or justice court directly on 1859 cases, mostly routine traffic cases, while a deputy district attorney initiated the remainder of the complaints. Most likely the complaint, if a deputy filed it, was filed in the following manner: The police make a misdemeanor arrest and present a deputy with copies of the arrest and crime reports the following day.[1] The deputy who discusses the case with the officer—in all likelihood, not the arresting street officer but a desk officer assigned the job of taking the previous day's cases to the D.A. for complaints—in theory will be one of the less experienced trial deputies, assigned to sit on the complaint desk on a rotating basis. The complaint desk deputy, besides handling the daily intake of police cases, handles the complaints of citizens who feel a crime has been committed and who wish to see someone prosecuted but either called no police officer to the scene or failed to convince one who did appear that a crime occurred and an arrest should be made. (Misdemeanor arrests are authorized by law by a peace officer only when "he has reasonable cause to believe that the person to be arrested has committed a public offense in his presence.")[2]

If the complaint deputy is not busy, the arriving officer may review the cases he has brought with him briefly with the deputy. If the deputy is busy, the officer may simply leave the reports with him or with a secretary who will later give them to the deputy, or he may take the reports to another deputy. The officer may avoid the complaint deputy if that deputy does not regularly work in his area and if the officer believes that the rapport he has built up with a deputy with whom he regularly works in his area will be more sympathetic to his case. But it should be borne in mind that most misdemeanor arrests are thoroughly routine, and in a majority of situations the officer neither knows much nor cares much what happens to the cases he brings over. He knows that the D.A. will file complaints on most of them, and unless the particular suspect is a known troublemaker whom the police feel must be prosecuted in whatever manner possible, the officer will not care which prosecutor handles them.

When the deputy receives the arrest reports, he probably will file a complaint. He may, however, refuse to do so, in which case he may or may not decide to call the suspect in for a citation hearing (a lecture and warning to the suspect that if the behavior is continued, the D.A. will have to prosecute the next time), or the deputy may decide to file a complaint on charges that appear to be substantiated in the report but for which the arrest was not made. For example, a man may be arrested for a violation of Penal Code 148, which states, "Every person who willfully resists, delays, or obstructs any public officer, in the discharge or attempt to discharge any duty of his office" is punishable for a misdemeanor. If the 148 arose out of another crime, say marijuana possession, the deputy may, if he feels the 148 is weak, issue only the marijuana charge. Where police officers are "victims," most deputies usually make their decisions after consultation with the victimized officer.

Once the deputy decides what complaint to issue, he will fill in the issuing form (designed for both felony and misdemeanor complaints in the municipal court) and give it to a secretary, who will type the complaint and send it to the court clerk. In Vario County a young deputy with less than a year of experience in the office usually made the misdemeanor filing decision. If he chose, he could consult either his area deputy or another deputy who happened to be free at the time, perhaps one of his peers, but he could issue on his own if he wished. If he decided not to issue, he would complete a form explaining why he refused; this form was then routed, together with the arrest reports, to either the area deputy or the deputy in charge of the office.

If the deputy who issued the complaint worked in the area in which the crime took place, the case-folder was occasionally routed back to him after filing the complaint, more often routed back through the area deputy, who briefly assessed its merits and then assigned the case to a "pretrial" deputy. The pretrial deputy took the case to a pretrial conference before the municipal court judge, usually about a month after the arrest and a month or so before the trial, which, unless the defendant "waived time," must by law be held within sixty days of the filing of the complaint. Often enough the deputy taking the case to pretrial conferences examined the case carefully just before the conference. He knew that the defense attorney would probably not look seriously at the case until the conference, so it was not worth spending a lot of time in preparation until the defense had a chance to assess its position.

Somewhere between the pretrial conference and the trial itself, most misdemeanor suspects pled guilty. Although sometimes on the morning of the weekly pretrial conference the public defender and the prosecutor privately resolved the obvious cases, in order to save themselves time later in chambers, a private attorney would more likely plead his client "on the courthouse steps" the day before or the day of trial when both sides had finally done the detailed preparation for trial. By this time, of course, another deputy could be handling the case for the D.A., since the man who regularly attends the pretrial conferences cannot expect to prepare all those cases for trial himself.

In 1970, office records indicated that of the 12,442 misdemeanor complaints filed, 239 actually went to trial before a jury, and 2630 more went to trial before a judge sitting as a trier of fact. The D.A. won roughly 60 percent of the jury trials and roughly 75 percent of the court trials, over half of which were minor traffic offenses. Of the remainder, roughly 10 percent were dismissed. Ninety percent either pled guilty or forfeited a fine or were still pending at the end of the year.

Appendix B
Felony Dispositions in 1970

The felony statistics for the year 1970 give a fair picture of the kind of screening that takes place at each stage through which cases proceed. Of 1808 felony complaints filed in the municipal court, 162 defendants pleaded guilty to a felony charge at the time scheduled for the preliminary examination in municipal court. Fifty-one defendants waived the preliminary hearing, 743 were held to answer, and 32 were not held to answer at the preliminary hearing. 129 more felony complaints were transferred to juvenile court. Some 474 defendants pleaded guilty to misdemeanors, either before the preliminary hearing or between the preliminary hearing and the time, within fifteen days of the hearing, when the prosecutor must file the information of the preliminary hearing in superior court. The prosecutor dismissed 217 more cases prior to filing them in superior court, but a dismissal is as likely to indicate that the suspect has agreed to plead guilty to an entirely separate charge as it is to indicate the charge was unsustainable.

In 38 cases prosecutors avoided the preliminary examination process altogether by submitting the case to the Vario County grand jury, which issued 38 indictments. 763 informations were actually submitted in superior court, 20 having been transferred to Vario County from other jurisdictions at that stage. In addition to the 38 indictments and 763 informations, 164 cases were transferred to the Vario County superior court from other jurisdictions where informations and indictments had first been filed, so that a total of 965 felonies were prosecuted in that court in 1970.

In 191 of these cases the defense filed a motion in superior court claiming that the evidence submitted at the preliminary hearing was insufficient to sustain the information under Penal Code Sec. 995. In 147 cases the defense filed a motion under Penal Code Sec. 1538.5 to suppress the introduction of evidence on the ground that it was illegally seized, that is, seized in violation of constitutional standards. The superior court granted 27 of the Sec. 995 motions and 15 of the Sec. 1538.5 motions.

Of the 923 cases remaining after motions were granted, 680 pleaded guilty to felony charges, 67 pleaded guilty to misdemeanor charges, 30 went to trial before a judge without jury (half of which the prosecutor's office lost), and 97 went to trial before a jury (28 of which the office lost). The remaining cases were either dismissed or were still pending at the end of the year.

To summarize, misdemeanor complaints pass through three stages: the decision whether to file, the pretrial negotiations, and, if necessary, the trial. A felony goes through five stages: the decision whether to file, the preliminary hearing and negotiations (or indictment), the filing of the case in superior court, the pretrial negotiations in superior court, and, if necessary, the trial.

Appendix C
Setting Personal Priorities
According to Suspects'
Criminal Record

The rap sheet lists by name and birthdate of suspects the charge for which a given suspect has been arrested, the date of the arrest, the arresting police agency, and the disposition of the case. No doubt its utility stems from the fact that there are few other cumulative standards of the defendant's character that are equally reliable. The rap sheet appears to be neutral and empirical, whereas both the police officer and the defense attorney may prove either ignorant or prone to puffing their case. Because of its appearance of neutrality, prosecutors may rely on a record too heavily. The rap sheet says nothing about the facts of the present offense, of which the defendant is presumed innocent until convicted, and the rap sheet itself may be inaccurate. There are dangers in the use of the rap sheet. The number of entries on the rap sheet provides a crude measure of the suspect's dangerousness, yet in some instances many entries may refer to only one offense and conviction. Many entries, furthermore, result from contacts with law enforcement agencies that did not result in convictions.

A man's prior record can prevent consideration of mitigating criteria, and nearly all public defenders interviewed cited examples where they felt the record of their client led to ignoring mitigating factors. For example, one public defender described the imposition of a severe sentence on a man who wrote $200 worth of bad checks:

I had a guy yesterday. He wrote some checks because his ex-wife, a very neurotic woman, just got out of the hospital and didn't have any clothes and begged him. So he wrote $200 worth of bad checks on a single day at Macy's and bought some stuff for her. This guy's a master carpenter; a radio dispatcher who works for the Hillside police department says this man has baby-sat for his kids. He told me, "He's going to build an addition to my house, and I can keep him busy for a couple of months doing that. He's a good man." A lot of people were worried for him. Problem: he went to prison for armed robbery and got out eight years ago. No entries on his rap sheet since. He had been to the Youth Authority before that. So it comes down to, should he go to prison for $200 worth of checks? Well, he avoided prison, but he got state prison suspended and a year in the county jail. A year in the county jail for $200 worth of checks on one day. I went back and told him and he said, "Jesus. Five years for an armed robbery; you never stop paying for it, do you?" That was a very profound statement. Even if you do your time, they're going to sock it to you again. All the time the D.A. or the judge says, "Whoops, prior felony," and off he goes.

Despite such cases, the prosecutor sees the rap sheet in a context that tends to reinforce its validity. He sees many cases involving many pages of entries for prior crimes in which the rap sheet is in fact an accurate prediction

173

of the likelihood of further criminal behavior. Since, as a factual matter, virtually all the cases they see support the thesis that, as one deputy put it, "You don't have police contacts without some kind of trouble floating around," prosecutors tend to assume that a rap sheet entry without conviction is significant. Besides, they know from their own experience that offenders are not caught most of the time. One deputy argued, "Say a defendant has got three moving violations. Hell, think how many times you've broken the law and never been caught. Now, what about a guy with ten moving violations on his rap sheet."

Prosecutors also find little fault in reliance on the rap sheet because it can cut both ways. If a defendant has no rap sheet, they know it works to the defendant's advantage. Finally, most prosecutors do not believe that an isolated error in the rap sheet will hurt the defendant. The prosecutor knows that this disposition does not require a detailed analysis of the rap sheet. Because his options are limited and often dichotomized (Should I file a felony or misdemeanor? Should I insist on state prison or agree to county jail?), he often need do no more than determine whether the rap sheet is "minor" or serious, a judgment that a single error on the rap sheet will not affect. One ex-deputy recalled his generalized approach to the rap sheet:

That rap sheet is so important. I know when I was a D.A., if the guy had a long enough rap sheet, I'd just say, "Screw it. He's had his chance. He just wanted to come back one more time." It really works on the rap sheet basis. And it should, too. Good guys should get breaks, and bad guys shouldn't.

Thus, all but five prosecutors agreed (eight strongly and seventeen mildly) with the statement "Being realistic about it, in some cases we must consider the total number of contacts with the law indicated on the suspect's rap sheet, even where the rap sheet shows few or no convictions." Deputies may, however, disagree with each other concerning the point at which contacts without convictions become significant. Bob Stern, a public defender, told me, "One prosecutor sees five police contacts and says it's serious, while another will say, 'This case is Mickey Mouse. The guy's got no convictions.' "

Few prosecutors worry that their reliance on a rap sheet without convictions contravenes the presumption of innocence. To the prosecutor, the presumption of innocence is an evidentiary rule designed to encourage jurors to be open-minded. It has no bearing on his factual determination of character. The prosecutor can easily draw on his own experience to imagine reasons why an arrest might not lead to a conviction that have nothing to do with a defendant's factual innocence. The suspect could have cooperated as an informer, the arrest or related search may have been improper, witnesses may have refused to testify, or the case may have been dropped in conjunction with a plea of guilty in a different matter. Besides, he knows that the accurate registration of dispositions ultimately depends on overworked girls like those in his own office filling out forms and sending them to Sacramento, and that administrative delay alone may account for the missing entry of a conviction.

In summary, the rap sheet does provide a measure that helps deputies determine their approach to cases, but it does not perform a major or control function because it leaves many contingencies untouched.

Appendix D
The Research Questionnaire

Memorandum

To: Vario County Prosecuting Attorneys

From: Lief H. Carter

Re: Questionnaire for Prosecuting Attorneys

As many of you know already, I am doing Ph.D. dissertation research in the organization and operation of prosecuting attorneys' offices. I have benefitted greatly from looking over your shoulders and from many informal conversations with you in the past few months. However, since I plan to compare the function of this office with the function of other offices in other counties, I must go one step further and apply a roughly standardized set of questions to all offices. (Unless he does this, the researcher never knows whether he is comparing apples to apples or apples to oranges.)

One typical way to standardize research is through questionnaires. However, I personally have reservations about how accurate questionnaires can be. Especially in your work, it is difficult to capture the complexity of any one concrete decision in an abstract sentence or two. Short questions and statements are always to some extent out of context, and very thoughtful answers to such questions can be misleading.

To minimize these shortcomings, I would like to couple the questionnaire with a chance to talk with you after you have completed it, in order to give you a chance to tell me more about the job than the questionnaire permits, and also to give you a chance to tell me how I could improve the questionnaire for future use.

One final point about the questions. Most of them ask you for generalizations about the job. In many cases, you may not really "know" the answer to the question, but I would appreciate your giving me your best guess or "hunch" for an answer. IF YOU FEEL YOU SIMPLY CANNOT ANSWER THE QUESTION THE WAY IT IS WORDED, PLEASE SKIP IT. I don't want to "force" you in any way to respond in ways that misrepresent your position.

NOTE: ALL YOUR ANSWERS WILL BE HELD IN STRICT CONFIDENCE, BOTH INSIDE AND OUTSIDE THE OFFICE. However, consistent with protecting individual confidences, I will be happy to discuss and distribute to all of you the statistical summaries of the materials when they are available.

177

Research in the Administration of Criminal Justice

Lief H. Carter
Doctoral Candidate
Department of Political Science
University of California
Berkeley, California

Item: Questionnaire for Prosecuting Attorneys (Tentative Draft)

SECTION I. The short answers in this section are self-explanatory.

1. Age_____. 2. Birthplace_____.

3. In what city(ies) or town(s) did you live most of your life before you went to college? _____.

4. College_____. Year graduated_____.

5. Law School _____. Year graduated_____.

6. How long have you worked in this office? _____.

7. Have you ever practiced privately?_____. If "yes," where and when?
_____

8. Have you ever practiced for any other governmental or public organization?_____. If "yes," where, what office, and when?_____.

9. Where do you expect to be practicing five years from now?

____In this office.

____Private practice in this county or area.

____Private practice elsewhere in the state.

____Private practice, can't say where.

____Other (please specify)_____.

10. In what city or town do you currently live? _____.

11. Why, briefly, did you become a prosecuting attorney? _____.

12. What is your father's occupation?_____.

13. Below are listed some goals that prosecuting attorneys say they try to achieve in their work. Please indicate your feelings about these goals by ranking them in two ways. IN THE LEFT COLUMN, please use the following four-point scale to indicate how strongly *your office as a whole* tries to achieve each of these goals:

4—Very important goal; we are all trying to achieve this constantly.
3—Generally important goal in most but not all cases.

2—Occasionally an important goal that varies from case to case and person to person.

1—Not an important goal; we are not generally concerned with achieving this goal.

IN THE RIGHT COLUMN, please use the following four-point scale to indicate how successful *your office as a whole* is in achieving these goals:

4—Office is very successful in achieving this goal.

3—Office is successful in achieving this goal most but not all the time.

2—Office succeeds in achieving this goal sometimes, but not very often.

1—Office generally not successful in achieving this goal.

	Importance of Goal	Goal Achievement	
1.	_____	_____	Reducing the crime rate.
2.	_____	_____	Maintaining a high level of professional legal performance.
3.	_____	_____	Separating the innocent from the guilty.
4.	_____	_____	Striking a fair balance between the conflicting interests and desires of victims, police, judges, defense counsel, the public, and so forth.
5.	_____	_____	Treating similar cases uniformly.
6.	_____	_____	Keeping the cases moving.
7.	_____	_____	Maximizing the sentences imposed on criminals.
8.	_____	_____	Convincing the public that the office is doing something about the crime problem.
9.	_____	_____	Minimizing the number of cases dismissed outright or acquitted.

NOTE: In the space below, please list if you wish any other goals that your office tries to achieve and then rank them as above.

10. _____   _____

11. _____   _____

12. _____   _____

14. Of those goals above, including the ones you may have added, which do you *personally* feel are the 3-4 most important goals this office *should be* trying to achieve? (Please list them by number.) _____.

15. Which of the following nonlegal occupations seem to you to be most similar to your work as a prosecuting attorney? (Please circle no more than three items).

a. a baseball umpire   d. a private detective   g. a union bargaining
b. a factory foreman   e. a patrolman   representative
c. a coach   f. a salesman   h. a physician

16. About how many attorneys in the office work under you, either directly or indirectly?_____.

17. (Optional) How would you describe your political point of view? _____

_____

18. (Optional) What is your religious preference?_____.

SECTION II. In this section, please indicate the degree of your agreement or disagreement with the following statements by circling "SA" if you strongly agree with it, "MA" if you mildly agree with it, "N" if you are neutral, i.e., could go either way on the statement, "MD" if you mildly disagree with it, and "SD" if you strongly disagree. If you have no opinion at all about the statement, please circle "O".

1. Generally speaking, subordinates in this office feel completely free to discuss all aspects of their work with their superiors.   SA MA N MD SD O

2. The formal manual of rules and policies in this office is the most important source of information on how to do our job.   SA MA N MD SD O

3. New men in this office receive fully adequate training on how to do their job.   SA MA N MD SD O

4. Superiors seem to understand the problems of subordinates very well.   SA MA N MD SD O

5. People in this office are generally very friendly with each other regardless of rank or experience.   SA MA N MD SD O

6. Superiors generally back up subordinates against outside criticism once they have made decisions.   SA MA N MD SD O

7. Superiors allow a good deal of discretion and personal judgment to subordinates.   SA MA N MD SD O

8. Policies in the office seem to change very frequently.   SA MA N MD SD O

9. Men have relatively complete and accurate information when they make most decisions in this office.   SA MA N MD SD O

10. When I get into a jam on my work, I can count on my co-workers in this office to help me out.   SA MA N MD SD O

11. If we didn't have so much work to do in this office, we would be inclined to take a tougher position than we do in many cases.   SA MA N MD SD O

12. In this county, the district attorney himself doesn't really have very much influence on the day-to-day operation of the office.   SA MA N MD SD O

13. The public is poorly informed about the nature of our system of criminal justice.   SA MA N MD SD O

14. In nearly all cases I handle, including those I refuse to issue on, all the required papers and forms have been completed.   SA MA N MD SD O

15. When I decide how to handle a case I usually don't think about how my decision will affect office statistics.   SA MA N MD SD O

16. Sometimes it seems that we don't learn from our mistakes as well as we ought to around here.   SA MA N MD SD O

17. Our jobs in this office are too specialized and compartmentalized.   SA MA N MD SD O

18. Due to differences in their personality and/or philosophy, different people assigned to the same task may do it quite differently in this office.   SA MA N MD SD O

19. I usually don't consider public opinion when I decide what position to take on a case.   SA MA N MD SD O

20. When it comes right down to it, it isn't possible to make clear-cut rules for handling most cases that come through this office.   SA MA N MD SD O

21. It is impossible to generalize about the job of prosecuting attorney, because each suspect and each crime are to some degree unique.   SA MA N MD SD O

SECTION III. For each of the following questions, PLEASE INDICATE YOUR BEST GUESS OR "HUNCH" concerning how often the event specified in the question seems to happen.

1. In what percent of cases you take to court do you and the defense attorney get into a serious disagreement or "hassle" over how to dispose of the case?_____%

2. What percent of cases you have lost at trial would you have had a good chance of winning if you had had more time to prepare for trial?_____%

3. What is your best guess as to the percent of names on the files that cross your desk that you recognize so that you can supply some facts from your own mind to flesh out the record?_____%

4. In roughly what percent of cases you handle does the victim or his relatives let you know personally that he cares strongly that the defendant be punished?_____%

5. What percent of your time do you spend doing things that any well-trained secretary or clerk could do just as well?_____%

6. For the office as a whole, in what percent of cases issued as felonies does a suspect plead to or get convicted of a misdemeanor, would you guess?_____%

7. Roughly what percent of arrests made and reported to the office as felonies are issued as misdemeanors?_____%

8. Based on your experience, what percent of cases that would otherwise be prosecuted aggressively do you find you have to refuse to issue or settle for a relatively minor punishment of the defendant *because* the investigation of the case was inadequate?_____%

SECTION IV. We all feel bothered occasionally by certain problems we face in our work. Listed below are some examples of things that sometimes bother people. Please indicate how frequently you feel bothered by each item in your job.

1. Being unclear on just what the scope and responsibilities of your job are.

   Never   Rarely   Sometimes   Rather often   Very often

2. Not knowing what opportunities for advancement the job offers.

   Never   Rarely   Sometimes   Rather often   Very often

3. Feeling that you have too heavy a work load—one that you can't finish to your satisfaction in a normal work day.

   Never   Rarely   Sometimes   Rather often   Very often

4. Feeling that you're not fully trained to handle your job.

   Never   Rarely   Sometimes   Rather often   Very often

5. Not knowing what the people you work for expect of you.

Never   Rarely   Sometimes   Rather often   Very often

6. Feeling that the job interferes with your family life.

Never   Rarely   Sometimes   Rather often   Very often

7. Feeling that the amount of work you have to do cuts down on the quality of your work.

Never   Rarely   Sometimes   Rather often   Very often

8. Feeling that you don't have all the necessary information at the time when you must make a decision.

Never   Rarely   Sometimes   Rather often   Very often

9. Feeling that the people you deal with may be hostile to you because of the decisions you must make.

Never   Rarely   Sometimes   Rather often   Very often

10. Feeling unable to influence the decisions of superiors that affect you personally.

Never   Rarely   Sometimes   Rather often   Very often

11. Feeling that you have to do some things on the job against your better judgment.

Never   Rarely   Sometimes   Rather often   Very often

SECTION V. Please answer the following questions the way you did those in Section II, above.

1. On the whole, the law, like water, finds its own level; the predominant standards of the community modify the strict language of statutes.   SA MA N MD SD O

2. In most cases that go to trial, the defense tells a good sounding story, but we know it departs materially from the truth.   SA MA N MD SD O

3. Being realistic about it, in some cases we must consider the total number of contacts with the law indicated on the suspect's rap sheet, even where the rap sheet shows few or no convictions.   SA MA N MD SD O

4. It should be a general rule in this office that we file a case "for all it's worth" in order to deal from a position of strength in pretrial negotiations.   SA MA N MD SD O

5. Ideally this office should be dealing on the weak cases and taking the good ones to trial.   SA MA N MD SD O

6. In practice, we often end up dealing the good cases and taking the dogs to trial.   SA MA N MD SD O

7. It's hard for outside pressures to influence the day-to-day operations of the office.   SA MA N MD SD O

8. I don't usually think about how my decisions in this office could affect the boss' chances for reelection.   SA MA N MD SD O

9. Swift and certain punishment is a key to solving the problem of crime in our society.   SA MA N MD SD O

10. Respect for law in a tough neighborhood depends primarily upon the willingness of patrolmen to use force frequently and effectively.   SA MA N MD SD O

11. Probation is not generally effective for rehabilitative purposes.   SA MA N MD SD O

12. The probation officer has more power over a defendant than any other person in the criminal justice system.   SA MA N MD SD O

13. I am less inclined to issue a complaint on a police report indicating we may have some evidence problems in the case if I am satisfied the suspect is not a real danger to society.   SA MA N MD SD O

14. In a county the size of ours, I personally don't need to worry about how the public will react to my handling of any one case.   SA MA N MD SD O

15. The most efficient way to dispose of cases in this office is to file charges realistically so that defense counsel knows where we stand at the outset.   SA MA N MD SD O

16. Judges should indicate a range of sentence in pretrial so that the defense counsel can make accurate calculations.   SA MA N MD SD O

17. Generally speaking, the police I work with take a flexible and humanistic approach to the problems of Negroes.   SA MA N MD SD O

18. On the whole, the recent "major" decisions from the California and federal appellate courts expanding the rights of the accused have improved rather than injured the quality of criminal justice in this country.   SA MA N MD SD O

19. I usually try to clear it with the police department involved before I dismiss a case altogether.   SA MA N MD SD O

20. I often have the feeling after we have completed a case that neither the prosecution nor the defense nor the judge ever learned the real facts and motives of the crime and the suspect.   SA MA N MD SD O

21. By and large, the defense attorney who is not familiar with the personalities and policies of this office usually does less for his client than the attorney who "knows the system."   SA MA N MD SD O

22. It is often better for the defendant that a case be settled fast than that it be settled purely according to legal procedures.   SA MA N MD SD O

23. Some people are so antisocial that the only solution is to isolate them.   SA MA N MD SD O

24. There are some crimes, such as sexual aggression against children, that must be prosecuted regardless of the state of the evidence.   SA MA N MD SD O

25. If a prosecuting attorney and a defense attorney don't get along with each other, it can affect a lot of little decisions (such as whether to grant a continuance) that together could make or break a case.   SA MA N MD SD O

26. Once we actually issue a complaint, we try not to dismiss it outright if weaknesses later turn up.   SA MA N MD SD O

27. There is really not much difference between the personality of the average felon we prosecute and the average man on the street.   SA MA N MD SD O

27a. The prosecutor should go ahead and issue on a police report that raises real evidentiary problems rather than substitute our judgment for judge and jury.   SA MA N MD SD O

28. Where there is no doubt about an individual's guilt, and he is merely fighting the case on its technicalities, this can indicate a lack of contrition on his part that will influence our feelings about the punishment he deserves.   SA MA N MD SD O

29. Sometimes I have the feeling that we are just too busy to stop and look at the long-range implications of what we do.   SA MA N MD SD O

30. This country should adopt laws providing for the compulsory sterilization of those convicted of felonies involving violence and threats of violence.   SA MA N MD SD O

31. I favor preventive detention of the hardened criminal who is awaiting trial.   SA MA N MD SD O

32. Although some describe the crime problem as a cancer eating away at society, the crime problem strikes me as being more like that of the common cold.   SA MA N MD SD O

33. Parents these days are too lenient with their kids.   SA MA N MD SD O

34. Books and movies that deal with the sordid and seamy side of life are partly responsible for increasing crime rates.   SA MA N MD SD O

35. The best way to maintain the judge's and defense counsel's trust in our evaluation of a case is to be candid about weak cases and to say so when we feel mild punishment would be appropriate.   SA MA N MD SD O

SECTION VI. Please circle the answer that seems most appropriate.

1. In general, how well satisfied are you with law as a profession?

| Well satisfied | Neutral | Very dissatisfied |
| Satisfied with qualifications | Somewhat dissatisfied | Don't know |

2. Do you believe your law school training adequately prepared you to work as a prosecuting attorney?

Fully adequately   Barely adequately   Inadequately

3. In general, how satisfied are you with your experience as a prosecuting attorney?

Very satisfied   Neutral   Very dissatisfied
Satisfied with qualifications   Somewhat dissatisfied   Don't know

4. Would you expect that the rest of the men in this office would answer the questions you have just answered in this questionnaire:

   1. just about the same way you have?
   2. very differently from the way you have?
   3. some same, some different, so that there won't be any patterns in the answers.
   4. other: _____
   _____

Notes

CHAPTER 1: Order, Learning, and Justice

1. All proper names throughout this study are fictitious.

2. See Edmund Cahn, *The Sense of Injustice* (Bloomington: Indiana University Press, 1964).

3. The analytical framework developed in Herbert Kaufman's *The Forest Ranger* (Baltimore: Johns Hopkins University Press, 1960) will prove particularly useful.

4. See Appendix D.

5. Herbert Kaufman, *The Forest Ranger*; Jerome Skolnick, *Justice Without Trial* (New York: John Wiley and Sons, 1966).

6. Crozier's summary of his own research posture applies here:
Hypotheses are tested throughout the course of [the book]; but these are descriptive hypotheses which permit only an understanding, and in part a measurement, of the diverse systems of relations constituting the phenomenon under analysis in the particular case studied. They are directly valid only for the case under investigation and the lessons they furnish do not constitute laws, but only *examples*—examples of models of systems of relations in action. These examples, however, can teach us more about the functioning of social systems of the same order and of even vaster systems than laws which a premature rigor has kept from being adequately comprehensive. Michael Crozier, *The Bureaucratic Phenomenon* (Chicago: University of Chicago Press, 1964), p. 5.

7. Benjamin Cardozo, *The Nature of the Judicial Process* (New Haven: Yale University Press, 1921), p. 112.

8. For an attack on discretionary justice and a defense of rule-conforming behavior, see Kenneth C. Davis, *Discretionary Justice* (Baton Rouge: L.S.U. Press, 1969).

9. Carl Freidrich, *The Philosophy of Law in Historical Perspective* (Chicago: University of Chicago Press, 1963), p. 25.

10. Friedrich, p. 25.

11. Aristotle, *Rhetoric* i. 13. 13, quoted in Friedrich, p. 25. In *The Guns of August* (New York: Macmillan, 1962), Barbara Tuchman, describing the German sack of Louvain following a few incidents of sniping, paraphrases Goethe's comment, "If there has to be a choice between injustice and disorder, . . . the German prefers injustice" (p. 355).

12. Quoted in Richard Field and Benjamin Kaplan, *Civil Procedure* (Brooklyn: The Foundation Press, 1953), p. 273, emphasis added.

13. Crozier, p. 52.

14. Daniel Katz and Robert L. Kahn, *The Social Psychology of Organizations* (New York: John Wiley and Sons, 1966), p. 340.

15. Warren Bennis, "Beyond Bureaucracy," Trans-action 2 (July-August, 1965): 32, quoted in Jerome Skolnick, *Justice Without Trial* (New York: Wiley, 1966), pp. 243-44. See also Warren Bennis and Philip Slater, *The Temporary Society* (New York: Harper & Row, 1968). Recent research also suggests that organizations that must adapt to unpredictably shifting environments do so less effectively the more hierarchical their structure. See Paul Lawrence and Jay Lorsch, *Organization and Environment* (Boston: Harvard Graduate School of Business, 1967); and F.E. Emery and E.L. Trist, "The Causal Texture of Organizational Environments," *Human Relations* 18 (February 1965): 21.

16. John Kaplan summarizes these limitations in *Criminal Justice* (Mineola: The Foundation Press, 1973), pp. 226-58.

17. See Herbert Packer, *The Limits of the Criminal Sanction* (Stanford: Stanford University Press, 1968). See also Morris Cohen, "Moral Aspects of the Criminal Law," *Yale Law Journal* 49 (April 1940): 987.

18. Lon Fuller discusses these and similar criteria more extensively in *The Morality of Law* (New Haven: Yale University Press, 1964), pp. 46-94.

19. John Griffiths, "The Limits of Criminal Law Scholarship," reprinted by permission of the Yale Law Journal Company and Fred. B. Rothman & Company from the *Yale Law Journal*, Vol. 79, p. 1390.

20. Jerome Frank, *Courts on Trial* (Princeton: Princeton University Press, 1949), p. 14.

21. Ibid., p. 410.

22. Karl Mannheim, *Man and Society in an Age of Reconstruction* (New York: Harcourt Brace & World, 1949), p. 53; Max Weber, *The Theory of Social and Economic Organization* (New York: Oxford University Press, 1947), pp. 184-86.

23. James D. Thompson, *Organizations in Action* (New York: McGraw Hill, 1967), p. 14.

24. Ibid.

25. Ibid., p. 17. Thompson describes two other types of organizational technologies. The first of these he calls a "long-linked" technology in which, like a production line, Z can perform a desired act only after Y has performed an act, and Y similarly depends on X. A long-linked technology producing a given product at a given rate permits the development of clear-cut criteria for assessing the efficiency of cause/effect operations. Repetition of the process provides the experience that weeds out the technology's imperfections. The second type Thompson calls a "mediating" technology, which links "clients or customers who are or wish to be interdependent. The commercial bank links depositors and borrowers. . . . The telephone company links those who would call and those who would be called." The mediating technology does

not so much face the problem of linking one operation with the next as it faces the problem of standardizing its treatment of a wide variety of clients. For example:

The commercial bank must find and aggregate deposits from diverse depositors; but however diverse the depositors, the transaction must conform to standard terms and to uniform bookkeeping and accounting procedures. It must also find borrowers; but no matter how varied their needs or desires, loans must be made according to standardized criteria and on terms uniformly applied to the category appropriate to the particular borrower. Poor risks who receive favored treatment jeopardize bank solvency (pp. 16-17).

For a district attorney's practical view of his technology and environment that corresponds to my own findings, see Harry A. Ackley, "The Awesome Responsibility," *California Trial Lawyers Association Journal*, Summer 1970, p. 17.

26. Thompson, pp. 72-73.

27. See Alvin W. Gouldner, "Cosmopolitans and Locals," *Administrative Science Quarterly* 2 (December 1957-March 1958): 281, 444; and see Blau and Scott, *Formal Organizations* (San Francisco: Chandler, 1962), p. 64.

28. Aaron Wildavsky, *The Politics of the Budgetary Process* (Boston: Little Brown & Co., 1964), pp. 63-64.

29. Ibid., pp. 75-76.

30. James Eisenstein, "The Federal Prosecutor and His Environment" (paper delivered at the 1968 annual meeting of the American Political Science Association, Washington, D.C., September 2-7), p. 18.

31. The United States Supreme Court approved the practice of plea bargaining in the case of Brady v. United States, 397 U.S. 742 (1969). Although the suspect must be questioned in open court as to the voluntariness of his plea before the court will accept it, these requirements do not prohibit prosecutors and judges from communicating to the defense the disposition they have in mind if a plea is entered; thus, they have had little impact on the process of case settlement.

32. Eisenstein, p. 4, and John Kaplan, "The Prosecutorial Discretion—A Comment," *Northwestern University Law Review* 60 (May-June 1965): 174.

33. Eisenstein and see also, "Comment: Prosecutorial Discretion in the Initiation of Criminal Complaints," *Southern California Law Review* 42 (Spring 1969): 519.

34. Frank Miller, *Prosecution: The Decision to Charge a Suspect with a Crime* (Boston: Little Brown, 1970), esp. pp. 173-280.

35. Eisenstein, and George Cole, "The Decision to Prosecute," *Law and Society Review* 4 (February 1970): 331.

36. Albert W. Alschuler, "The Prosecutor's Role in Plea Bargaining,"

36 U. Chi. L. Rev. 50, 54, 79-80 (1968). Donald J. Newman, "Pleading Guilty for Considerations: A Study of Bargain Justice," *Journal of Criminal Law, Criminology and Police Science* 46 (1956): 780; David Sudnow, "Normal Crimes: Sociological Features of the Penal Code in a Public Defender Office," *Social Problems* 22 (Winter 1965): 255; Jerome Skolnick, "Social Control in the Adversary System," *Journal of Conflict Resolution* 11 (March 1967): 52.

37. Anthony Castberg, *Prosecutorial Discretion: A Case Study* (unpublished Ph.D. dissertation, Northwestern University, 1968).

38. Kenneth Vines and Herbert Jacob, *Studies in Judicial Politics* (New Orleans: Tulane University, 1963), pp. 77-98. Martin Levin, "Urban Politics and Policy Outcomes: The Criminal Courts," in George Cole, ed., *Criminal Justice* (North Scituate: Duxbury Press, 1972), pp. 330-63.

39. Abraham Blumberg, *Criminal Justice* (Chicago: Quadrangle, 1967), p. xi.

40. James Q. Wilson, *Varieties of Police Behavior* (Cambridge: Harvard University Press, 1968).

41. See John Gardiner, *Traffic and the Police* (Cambridge: Harvard University Press, 1969), and Martin Levin, *op. cit.*

42. See, among many sources on this subject, Chester Barnard, *The Functions of the Executive* (Cambridge: Harvard University Press, 1938); Herbert Simon, *Administrative Behavior* (New York: The Free Press, 1957); Harry Eckstein, *The English Health Service* (Cambridge: Harvard University Press, 1958); Braybrooke and Lindblom, *A Strategy of Decision* (New York: The Free Press, 1963); Cyert and March, *A Behavioral Theory of the Firm* (Englewood Cliffs: Prentice-Hall, 1963); James Thompson, *Organizations in Action* (New York: McGraw Hill, 1967).

CHAPTER 2: The District Attorney's Office and Its Work

1. For a more detailed description of the office's misdemeanor procedures, see Appendix A.

2. Appendix B presents a statistical description of felony dispositions in the year 1970.

3. As a legal matter prosecutors unquestionably have "discretion" in the sense that they are immune (in the absence of a show of personal malice directed against the defendant by the prosecutor) from legal challenge to their decision not to prosecute clear violations of the law or to proceed with prosecution of those whose connections with an alleged crime prove extremely tenuous. In California *Wilson* v. *Sharp*, 42 Cal.2d 675 (1954) holds that in

the absence of a specific statutory command to act when certain circumstances exist, e.g., under California's "Red Light Abatement Act," a county counsel and a prosecutor may at their discretion refuse to investigate or prosecute a case on any grounds they choose.

The general language of many penal statutes allows the prosecutor to choose from among a number of alternate charges for a given act, charges that may carry widely different sentences upon conviction. No law prohibits prosecutors from altering these charges or recommending a sentence position in exchange for a plea of guilty.

4. *People* v. *Cahan*, 44 Cal.2d 434, 282 P.2d 905 (1955).

5. See Calif. Penal Code Secs. 859 and 860.

6. Calif. Penal Code Sec. 1382.

7. Chapter 4 reviews the criticism of negotiated settlements that various public groups and citizens had then directed at the office.

8. See chapter 4: note *1*.

CHAPTER 3: Prosecuting Attorneys in Vario County

1. Diversity is, of course, a relative term the significance of which depends on the level of analysis that the analyst deems most useful. For chapters 3 through 5 we shall focus on what Kaufman in *The Forest Ranger* calls the "challenge to unity."

2. I eliminated from the questionnaire during the pretest the "Likert Scale" question: "I don't consider the personality of the judge or the defense attorney when I handle a case," because the respondents strongly and unanimously agreed that personality was vital.

3. In the spring and summer of 1970, the median age of the prosecutors in Vario County was thirty, the mean age was thirty-three, and the single mode was twenty-eight. Moore's length of service—twelve years—exceeded that of all other prosecutors. Only three other prosecutors, one of whom entered private practice during 1970, had served more than seven years in the office. Thus, both age and experience separated Moore from most prosecutors in the office. In contrast to Moore's 144 months in the office, the mean length of service was thirty-one months, the median was eighteen months, and the mode was approximately twelve months.

4. Two of the prosecutors questioned were born and raised in the county and five more were raised there. Five more prosecutors were raised within a fifty-mile radius of Vario County; six were raised in other parts of California; the remaining eleven on whom I gathered data were raised in widely scattered parts of the country. None of the seven senior deputies and only two of the six

area deputies grew up in or near Vario County. The pattern of "immigration" of attorneys extends to private attorneys and public defenders as well. Of the forty-nine private attorneys (model age forty) and sixteen public defenders (model age thirty) who responded, only eleven grew up in the county. Seven of the fifteen judges did, however, report growing up in Vario County, and three more grew up in adjacent counties. While this evidence might suggest that roots and contacts in a community facilitate entry into political office in that community, judges may more likely be tied to the county simply because they are older (average age fifty-four) and became established in the county before the county's population began to "boom."

5. There is no substantial difference between the percentage of prosecutors and the percentage of private attorneys that came from laboring families. However, only one private attorney listed his father's occupation as clearly that of a large business executive. Given the small n and the difficulty of classifying many responses, this data carries little weight, although it does suggest that at least in Vario County the job of prosecutor does not attract men from any socioeconomic backgrounds that differ substantially from the profession as a whole.

6. Wilson, *Varieties of Police Behavior*, chapters 1-3.

7. Chapter 5 discusses how civil-service personnel procedures increased the diversity of preferences of Vario County prosecutors and how, by protecting the jobs of career prosecutors, these procedures encouraged them to adopt different and partially conflicting methods in their work.

8. A student of open-minded and close-minded personalities might find it significant that Moore answered 57 percent of the Likert scale questions on the questionnaire in either the strong agree or strong disagree column, while Lewis did so 40 percent of the time, and Nolan, the politician, responded 35 percent of the time in either of the two "strong" columns. See Milton Rokeach, *The Open and Closed Mind* (New York: Basic Books, 1960).

9. David Riesman, *Individualism Reconsidered* (Glencoe: Free Press, 1954), p. 450.

10. James David Barber, *The Lawmakers* (New Haven: Yale University Press, 1965), p. 261.

11. See Herbert Packer, *The Limits of the Criminal Sanction* (Stanford: Stanford University Press, 1968), pp. 158-73.

12. The first continuum actually collapses two continua into one. Some prosecutors expressed both high concern for the importance of crime control and high identification with the due process model, and some prosecutors expressed a low concern for both. I have limited the analysis to a four-cell table, because only a few men—Moore was one—fit in these additional categories.

13. Peter Blau, *Exchange and Power in Social Life* (New York: John Wiley, 1964), p. 17. John Griffiths has criticized the due process/crime control dichotomy because both categories presume that the relationship between prosecution and defense, either in an adversary trial or in plea negotiations, is a zero-sum game. He proposes an alternative "family model," in which the disposition of cases may reflect exchanges that seek to enhance the position of the state and the defendant. Griffiths correctly believes that radical changes in ideology must precede the institutionalization of a family model. John Griffiths, "Ideology in Criminal Procedure, or A Third 'Model' of the Criminal Process," *Yale Law Journal* 79 (January 1970): 359.

14. Regarding question V-28, another deputy who falls in the "analyst" category concurred:

Oh, everybody says that: "That son of a bitch is fighting a cold case. Let's sock it to him." But in reality, the fact that he exercises his constitutional rights doesn't affect his punishment, I don't think. It depends on how he's fighting it, I suppose. The mere fact that he wants to go to trial doesn't make me mad. We get mad when he puts us on the spot because of a defect in the case, and if that's true he *ought* to take it to trial.

CHAPTER 4: The Working Environment of the Prosecutor

1. Kaufman's definition of the process of "preforming decisions" applies equally well to the term "programming" here:

events and conditions in the field are anticipated as fully as possible, and courses of action to be taken for designated categories of such events and conditions are described. The field officer then need determine only into what category a particular circumstance falls; once this determination is made, he then simply follows the series of steps applicable to that category. Within each category, therefore, the decisions are "preformed" (*The Forest Ranger*, p. 91).

2. For a further refinement of "heterogeneity," see Thompson, *Organizations in Action*, p. 72 ff., and chapter 5.

3. Of the nine goals listed in question 1-13, prosecutors marked "striking a fair balance between the conflicting interests and desires of victims, police, judges, defense counsel, the public, etc." third in importance (behind "maintaining a high level of professional legal performance" and "separating the innocent from the guilty") and second in terms of success (behind "separating the innocent from the guilty").

4. See e.g., *People* v. *Watson*, 44 Cal. Rptr. 306, 234 C.A.2d 203 (1965) and *People* v. *Morse*, 76 Cal. Rptr. 391, 452 P.2d 607 (1969).

5. In the interviews I asked prosecutors how they would have ranked the goal of "controlling police discretion" if I had included it in the questionnaire. All deputies but one indicated they would have ranked it a "3" or a "4", but no deputy felt that the office was very successful in "controlling

police discretion." The response to questionnaire item I-23 distributed to defense attorneys and judges indicates most believed "undiscovered" illegal searches and seizures take place "all too often," 37 percent strongly agreed, 26 percent mildly agreed, 6 percent were neutral, 11 percent mildly disagreed, 10 percent strongly disagreed, and 10 percent had no opinion. (Seven of the fifteen responding judges expressed no opinion on this question.)

6. Twenty-six percent of the prosecutors questioned disagreed mildly or strongly with the statement "On the whole, the recent 'major' decisions from the California and Federal appellate courts expanding the rights of the accused have improved rather than injured the quality of criminal justice in this country."

7. Contrast this statement with Moore's defense of the polygraph in chapter 3.

8. One of the services that a defense attorney with prosecutorial experience can offer his client is to use his friendships in the police department to "clear" with the police reductions or dismissals of cases in advance of negotiations with the prosecution. Several defense attorneys with prosecutorial experience in the county reported their success in this regard. One reported, "I find if I can square something with the police department, the D.A.'s office suddenly becomes much easier to deal with." Prosecutors' questionnaire responses also confirmed this point. Seven strongly agreed "I usually try to clear it with the police department before I dismiss a case altogether," while twelve more mildly agreed, four mildly disagreed, one strongly disagreed, and the rest were neutral or expressed no opinion on the item.

9. Defense attorneys indicated on the questionnaire no consensus concerning two questions. Thirteen attorneys strongly agreed that "prosecutors don't really bargain or 'haggle' on most cases. That is, most deals result from a 'take it or leave it' offer by the prosecuting attorney," and twenty mildly agreed, but fifteen mildly disagreed and six strongly disagreed. Eleven defense attorneys strongly agreed that "it is often better for the defendant that a case be settled fast than that it be settled purely according to legal procedures," while thirteen strongly disagreed. (Twenty-two mildly agreed, while sixteen mildly disagreed with that item.)

10. Municipal court judges serve six-year terms. The governor appoints men to fill vacancies that occur in midterm (California Government Code Sec. 71145).

11. While three judges strongly agreed and three more judges mildly agreed with the statement that "on the whole, the recent 'major' decisions from the California and Federal appellate courts expanding the rights of the accused have improved rather than injured the quality of criminal justice in

this country," two judges mildly disagreed with the statement and six strongly disagreed. Thus, eight of fifteen judges disagreed with the item, whereas only one of sixteen public defenders, seven of thirty prosecutors, and thirteen of forty-nine private attorneys disagreed with this statement.

12. Since it is difficult to predict precisely what sentence would be given if the case went to trial, it is difficult to identify just how much, if anything, the prosecutor gives up in exchange for a plea. Although state prison sentences are indeterminate, only roughly a third of felony convictions receive state institution sentences. If the felony is one that the Penal Code classifies as punishable either as a felony or as a misdemeanor, then the trial judge will make that choice. If it is punishable only as a felony, California law specifies an indeterminate sentence (one to ten years, for example) the exact length of which the Adult Authority determines for each case. See Penal Code Sec. 1168. While the sentencing judge cannot therefore specify the length of a state prison sentence he can, even for "straight felonies," send the defendant under Penal Code Sec. 1203.03 to one of the state's medical facilities, where medical officers may recommend one of the alternatives to state prison. Or he may make one of the alternate recommendations himself. In pretrial negotiations, the defense attorney normally seeks a commitment from the judge that will minimize the length of his client's incarceration. But attorneys further feel that even if the sentence is not particularly lenient, a client who knows precisely what sentence he will receive is more likely to plead guilty, since all but straight state prison sentences are usually considerably below the maximum possible sentence for the offense or offenses charged. The sentencing judge thus can choose among a number of options in most cases. His preferences therefore influence the choices of defense attorneys and prosecutors.

13. Ninety-seven felonies were tried before a jury in 1970 out of a total of 801 felonies prosecuted. In 1969, of 1063 felonies prosecuted, thirty-four went to jury trial.

14. Superior court judges are elected every six years, and the governor fills intervening vacancies. California Constitution, Art. VI, Sec. 5.

15. Shapiro in fact granted about 19½ percent of these motions in 1969, while Jensen granted about 12½ percent in 1970.

CHAPTER 5: Managing Diversity and Uncertainty

1. Thompson, *Organizations in Action*, pp. 84-87.
2. See also discussion of "segmentation" in chapter 4.
3. Thompson, *Organizations in Action*, p. 107, emphasis in original.

4. Ibid., pp. 105-8, and pp. 110-15.

5. See chapter 4.

6. William R. Dill, "Environment as an Influence on Managerial Autonomy," *Administrative Science Quarterly* 2 (March 1958): 409.

7. Thompson, p. 73.

8. Ibid., p. 39.

9. Ibid., p. 43.

10. It is not, however, entirely correct to say that the office does not seek to place its boundaries around environmental contingencies. Plea bargaining, by seeking to reduce one source of uncertainty—that which exists at the judicial and trial stage—at least partially incorporates "the object worked on."

11. Eugene Litwak, "Models of Bureaucracy Which Permit Conflict," *American Journal of Sociology* 67 (September 1961): 177-84 at 177. © 1961 by the University of Chicago. Reprinted with permission.

12. Charles Perrow, "Hospitals: Technology, Structure, and Goals," in James G. March (ed.), *Handbook of Organizations* (Chicago: Rand McNally, 1965) p. 925. William R. Rosengren, "Communication, Organization and Conduct in a 'Therapeutic Milieu,' " *Administrative Science Quarterly* 9 (June 1964): 70-90.

13. Charles E. Bidwell, "The School as a Formal Organization," in March, op. cit. and Arthur E. Stinchcombe, "Bureaucratic and Craft Administration of Production: A Comparative Study," *Administrative Science Quarterly* 4 (September 1959): 168-87.

14. Thompson, pp. 153-54.

15. Rosengren, p. 89.

16. Kaufman, chapter 4.

17. Ibid., pp. 157-58.

18. Ibid., p. 184.

19. Only one deputy agreed (mildly) with the statement "The formal manual of rules and policies in this office is the most important source of information on how to do our job," and all but six strongly disagreed.

20. There is an interesting legal parallel to this behavioral hypothesis: courts consistently strike down statutes that impose penalties on certain forms of behavior when the courts find that the language of such statutes is vague and ambiguous. To reach this conclusion the courts reason that it is unfair to expect a man to conform to a rule if he does not understand the circumstances in which the rule should apply.

21. Policy ambiguity was of course not confined to the D.A.'s office. At one time the Vario County probation department had in its north and south

county branches two diametrically opposed policies with respect to separating children from delinquent mothers. The north end rarely separated children from delinquent mothers except in unusual and hopeless cases because of the psychological damage to both mother and child. The south end preferred to separate child and mother because they felt they could then reward the mother for improving her condition by giving the child back to her. Neither branch had any social science data to support either position, so each continued its own practice. To give another example, deputies in the public defender's office were discouraged from pleading any client guilty prior to the preliminary hearing, in order for the attorney at least to get a look at the witnesses before assessing his case. But public defenders freely admitted that the deal available prior to the preliminary hearing was, given their client's admission of guilt in their private discussions, often too attractive to pass up, and they accepted.

22. Although the office has made no rules or policies concerning the significance of the rap sheet, and while deputies disagree concerning the implications of a given number and type of entries on any given rap sheet, the rap sheet does permit the deputy himself to develop his own crude scale of priorities. Appendix C describes the ways the rap sheet was used in Vario County.

23. The portions of the *Manual* quoted above depict Savich's concern that he be in a position to accomodate outside criticism from police, which he feared could be translated into public criticism.

24. Seventeen strongly agreed and eight mildly agreed "the public is poorly informed about the nature of our system of criminal justice."

25. Chester Barnard, *The Functions of the Executive*, p. 259.

26. Niccolò Machiavelli, *The Prince*, Trans. Luigi Ricci (New York: Modern Library, 1950), p. 21.

CHAPTER 6: Justice in Vario County: The Direction of Reform

1. Paul Chevigny, *Police Power* (New York: Pantheon, 1969).

2. Warren Bennis and Philip Slater, *The Temporary Society* (New York: Harper and Row, 1968).

3. Ibid., p. 71. Bennis and Slater base the bulk of their arguments on the assertion that technologies and environments of most purposive action are becoming increasingly uncertain and changeable.

4. Bennis might more accurately have labeled these the "consequences

of revitalization" rather than "elements," which connote process and strategy.

5. Charles Perrow, *Complex Organizations: A Critical Essay* (Glenview: Scott Foresman & Co., 1972).

6. Daniel Katz and Robert Kahn, *The Social Psychology of Organizations* (New York: Wiley and Sons, 1966), chapter 10.

7. We frequently label as undesirable that which is unknown or unpredictable. At the age of four, my older son, who was just then discovering the politics of nursery school, reported, "Some of the boys at school are bad." When I asked him what made a boy bad, he replied, "Some boys are bad boys because I don't know what they're going to do."

8. The high estimate in interviews with defense attorneys and judges was 2 percent, but most defense attorneys interviewed estimated the percentage of those prosecuted who did not in fact commit the act alleged at less than 1 percent and said they had never in their own experience witnessed the conviction of someone whom they believed did not commit the act.

9. Albert W. Alschuler, "The Prosecutor's Role in Plea Bargaining," *University of Chicago Law Review* 36 (Fall 1968): 50; Donald J. Newman, "Pleading Guilty for Considerations: A Study of Bargain Justice," *Journal of Criminal Law, Criminology and Police Science* 46 (1956): 780; David Sudnow, "Normal Crimes: Sociological Features of the Penal Code in a Public Defender Office," *Social Problems* 12 (Winter 1965): 255; Jerome Skolnick, "Social Control in the Adversary System," *Journal of Conflict Resolution* 11 (March 1967): 52.

10. William J. McGuire, "The Nature of Attitudes and Attitude Change," in *The Handbook of Social Psychology*, ed. by Gardner Lindzey and Elliot Aronson (Reading: Addison-Wesley, 1969), p. 136 at pp. 177-87.

11. Wildavsky, *The Politics of the Budgetary Process*, pp. 74-76.

12. Calif. Penal Code Section 405a.

13. George Baker, who had worked with the superior court calendar division for over a year before he resigned in 1970, described the difficulties he had to contend with in dealing realistically with a serious felony:

There's no question about the locking-in effect at all. The problem is a very human one and it's common in every large office where one deputy doesn't handle the case all the way through the mill. Let's take a homicide. If you go out to the scene before any arrests are made, it's not too hard to refuse to issue on the spot. The facts may be right in front of you; perhaps from the way a house is torn apart or from what the witnesses or even a suspect say, you can be pretty sure the killing was in self-defense. But let's assume there has been a homicide and an officer has made an arrest. Number one, you get a statistic of a murder arrest that goes to the state. Number two, the newspapers announce that Lief Carter has been arrested for first-degree murder. At this point it comes into the office for the first time, the officer has somebody in custody for murder, and the [police reports] are dropped on your desk. Well, you're busy, and you can look at the thing and you can see a lot of problems in it, but you figure, "Gee, we can probably get those straightened out." It may be a real tough case, but somebody's been arrested for murder. Besides, if you issue, there's less heat from someone up the line. If you don't issue, the officer goes to his lieutenant, who goes to his captain, who calls Peter Hoff complaining, "Hell, we're letting people get away with murder." So you go ahead and charge him with murder. (You won't charge him with manslaughter except in very rare cases.) You charge him with murder because as a practical matter California law doesn't differentiate between degrees of murder, and the newspapers will call it first-degree murder because that's what people usually associate with murder.

Then you may give a "write it don't say it" memo to the police officer to get him to do more investigation, which he may or may not do, depending on how busy he is. He may have two more homicides before you see him again.

So there it goes to the preliminary hearing. You've issued the complaint, and you know it's shaky, but you don't want to turn the officer down. You're already committed to the officer who made the arrest—look at the possibility of a false arrest suit—so you take it to the preliminary. At this point the case may be assigned to a young deputy, perhaps this is his first murder prelim. Deputies get upset when we lose prelims because we simply don't lose many prelims around here. So the deputy puts the case on, and undoubtedly there's sufficient evidence to hold to answer.

Next there may be motions in superior court. Now if that is assigned to me, I'm going to try to win it, because my job is to win motions, just like the job of the lower deputy is to win preliminaries, and just like the job of the detective who brings the arrest report over is to get a complaint from us. So I go out and win the motion, because if I lose the motion it's a big hassle to refile and talk to the head honcho.

Now you're going to trial, and it stinks. It's no better—in fact it's probably worse because memories have faded—than the day you issued it in the first place. We are committed. I talked to the police academy for a whole hour about not arresting people indiscriminately, but it's hard to get through to them because they keep asking, "What are we going to tell our lieutenant?"

At any rate, you take it to trial. And are you going to try to reduce it before the trial and earn a reputation of not having the guts to try a case in a pinch? Oh, no! I've tried a couple of cases like this over the last year. You go down in a blaze of glory. You're faced with a dilemma when you wash out any serious crime. I think you have to pass the heat on to his honor or the jury.

14. Kenneth C. Davis, *Administrative Law: Cases-Text-Problems* (St. Paul: West Publishing Co.), Fifth Edition, 1973, pp. 477-515, and see his *Discretionary Justice*, op. cit.

15. Norman Abrams, "Internal Policy: Guiding the Exercise of Prosecutorial Discretion," *U.C.L.A. Law Review* 19 (1971): 1.

16. This argument has, of course, always been a foundation of federalism, and it is also one of the benefits of incremental as opposed to intendedly synoptic decision-making. See Charles Lindblom, *The Intelligence of Democracy* (New York: The Free Press, 1965).

17. Dick Schwartz described one moral dilemma in which he could not directly intervene:

I think the most difficult part of my job is when I learn things I wouldn't like to know. There's one case in which a fairly prominent citizen is being pressured into giving information about a criminal in a major case, and the police are telling him they've got material they could use against him in court, when in fact, if he would get a lawyer, he would learn that both legally and from the point of view of publicity he would have nothing to worry about. But this is a big case, and what they say they've got to use against him is apparently putting a real psychological drain on this guy; it's the kind of stuff where he might take his own life. The police show no sympathy for informers in this position. They simply want to get the goods. You may know the dialogue between Erasmus and Sir Thomas More in which Erasmus says one shouldn't get involved in cases in which one bears no direct responsiblity, and More replies, in effect, life is too short not to get involved when you think your involvement can make a difference. The fact that I can remember the dilemma, as Erasmus and More faced it, probably makes me more able to accept the pressures of the work I do than most people, and there's an ego thing here: I'd rather have myself in this spot than some others I know. ... I never had the slightest hesitation to dismiss a case if I learned there's something hinky about it. But this crap, this business about getting information, is much more bothersome to me personally. Where other lawyers are involved I figure they can take care of themselves, but the pressuring, the lying, the threatening a man with infamy in order to get information from him really bother me. I have never been the moving party in that, but I know about it when it goes on.

18. Quoted in B. James George, Jr., and Ira Cohen, eds., *The Prosecutor's Sourcebook* (New York: Practicing Law Institute, 1969), Vol. I, pp. 5-6.

19. Richard B. Brandt, ed., *Social Justice* (Englewood Cliffs: Prentice-Hall, 1962), p .94.

20. Ibid., p. 117.

APPENDIX A: Misdemeanor Procedures in Vario County

1. In 1969, of the 11,622 misdemeanor arrests in the county, 620 were for assault and battery, 745 for petty theft, 2436 for drunk and disorderly conduct, 556 for disturbing the peace, 4868 for traffic violations, 109 for sex offenses, and 2288 fit other categories (California Bureau of Criminal Statistics). Of this total, 460 were released, 683 were turned over to other jurisdictions, and the remaining roughly 90 percent were prosecuted in the county.

2. Calif. Penal Code Sec. 836.

APPENDIX B: Felony Dispositions in 1970

1. A suspect may plead guilty not only to the charge in the complaint but to any "necessarily included offense." The California courts initially defined a necessarily included offense: "where an offense cannot be committed without necessarily committing another offense, the latter is a necessarily included offense" (*People* v. *Greer*, 30 Cal.2d 589, 596 [1947]). However, prosecutors frequently concede, in exchange for a plea, that an offense is a necessarily included offense when that offense was in no way

committed in the course of the actual offense. The California Supreme Court sanctioned this practice in *People* v. *West*, 91 Cal. Rep. 385, 477 P.2d 409 (1970) where defendant West, in whose car marijuana had been found, pleaded guilty not to the felony of marijuana possession but to the Misdemeanor of maintaining a place in which marijuana could be sold, Penal Code Sec. 11557, after the prosecutor conceded that Sec. 11557 was necessarily included in 11530. The *West* test, which replaced *Greer*, now holds simply that the defendant may plead guilty to any offense "reasonably related to the defendant's conduct" (477 P.2d at 420).

2. For a description of juvenile procedures, see California Welfare and Institutions Code, Secs. 500-914.

3. The figure of thirty-two cases held not to answer by the municipal court judges at preliminary hearings, when contrasted with 217 cases dismissed by the prosecutor at that stage, indicates the relative significance of these two roles at the early stages of criminal proceedings.

Index

About the Author

Lief H. Carter received the A.B. from Harvard College and the J.D. degree from Harvard Law School in 1965. Pressures from the military draft in late 1965 cut short his association with a Washington, D.C. law firm. Dr. Carter and his wife taught in Bolivia in the Peace Corps in 1966 and 1967, when he returned to the graduate program in political science at the University of California, Berkeley.

Dr. Carter received the Edward S. Corwin Award of the American Political Science Association for the best dissertation in public law (broadly defined). This volume is a revised version of that dissertation.

Dr. Carter has taught in the School of Business Administration, University of California, Berkeley, as a lecturer in law, and held the position of Assistant Professor of Political Science at the University of Tennessee, Chattanooga, from 1971 to 1973. He is now an Assistant Professor of Political Science at the University of Georgia, Athens.